NILE NOTES of A HOWADJI

HICKS DEL.

LOSSING-BARRITT SC.

NILE NOTES

OF A HOWADJI.

NEW YORK:
HARPER & BROTHERS, PUBLISHERS,
329 & 331 PEARL STREET
FRANKLIN SQUARE.
1852.

"A foutra for the world and worldlings base,
I sing of Africa and golden joys."

King Henry IV., Part ii.

"————or I described
Great Egypt's flaring sky, or Spain's cork groves."

Robert Browning's "Paracelsus."

"If it be asked why it is called the Nile, the answer is, because it has beautiful and good water."

Werne's "White Nile."

"What then is a Howadji?" said the Emperor of Ethiopia, draining a beaker of crocodile tears.

"Howadji," replied the astute Arabian, "is our name for merchants, and as only merchants travel, we so call travelers."

"Allah-'hu Ak-bar," said the Emperor of Ethiopia. "God is great."

Linkum Fidelius' "Calm Crocodile, or the Sphinx unriddled."

"——He saw all the rarities at Cairo, as also the pyramids, and sailing up the Nile, viewed the famous towns on each side of that river."

Story of Ali Cogia in the Arabian Nights.

"Canopus is afar off, Memnon resoundeth not to the sun, and Nilus heareth strange voices."

Sir Thomas Browne.

"——There can one chat with mummies in a pyramid, and breakfast on basilisk's eggs. Thither, then, Homunculus Mandrake, son of the great Paracelsus; languish no more in the ignorance of those climes, but abroad with alembic and crucible, and weigh anchor for Egypt."

Death's Jest Book, or the Fool's Tragedy.

Preface.

When the Persian Poet Hafiz was asked by the Philosopher Zenda what he was good for, he replied—

"Of what use is a flower?"

"A flower is good to smell," said the philosopher.

"And I am good to smell it," said the poet.

CONTENTS.

NILE NOTES.

I.

Going to Boulak.

In a gold and purple December sunset, the Pacha and I walked down to the boat at Boulak, the port of Cairo. The Pacha was my friend, and it does not concern you, gracious reader, to know if he were Sicilian, or Syrian; whether he wore coat or kaftan, had a hareem, or was a baleful bachelor. The air was warm, like a May evening in Italy. Behind us, the slim minarets of Cairo spired shiningly in the brilliance, like the towers of a fairy city, under the sunset sea.

These minarets make the Eastern cities so beautiful. The heavy mound-like domes and belfries of western Europe are of the earth, earthy. But the mingled mass of building, which a city is, soars lightly to the sky in the lofty minarets on whose gold crescent crowns the sun lingers and lingers, making them the earliest stars of evening.

To our new eyes every thing was picture. Vainly the broad road was crowded with Muslim artisans, home-returning from their work. To the mere Muslim observer, they were carpenters, masons, laborers and tradesmen of all kinds. We passed many a meditating Cairene, to whom there was nothing but the monotony of an old story in that evening and on that road. But we saw all the pageantry of oriental romance quietly donkeying into Cairo. Camels too, swaying and waving like huge phantoms of the twilight, horses with strange gay trappings curbed by tawny turbaned equestrians, the peaked toe of the red slipper resting in the shovel stirrup. It was a fair festal evening. The whole world was masquerading, and so well that it seemed reality.

I saw Fadladeen with a gorgeous turban and a gay sash. His chibouque, wound with colored silk and gold threads, was borne behind him by a black slave. Fat and funny was Fadladeen as of old; and though Fermorz was not by, it was clear to see in the languid droop of his eye, that choice Arabian verses were sung by the twilight in his mind.

Yet was Venus still the evening star; for behind him, closely veiled, came Lalla Rookh. She was wrapped in a vast black silken bag, that bulged like a balloon over her donkey. But a star-suffused evening cloud was that bulky blackness, as her twin eyes shone forth liquidly lustrous.

Abon Hassan sat at the city gate, and I saw Haroun Alrashid quietly coming up in that disguise of a Moussoul merchant. I could not but wink at Abon, for I knew him so long ago in the Arabian Nights. But he rather stared than saluted, as friends may, in a masquerade. There was Sinbad the porter, too, hurrying to Sinbad the sailor.

I turned and watched his form fade in the twilight, yet I doubt if he reached Bagdad in time for the eighth history.

Scarce had he passed when a long string of donkeys ambled by, bearing each, one of the inflated balloons. It was a hareem taking the evening air. A huge eunuch was the captain, and rode before. They are bloated, dead-eyed creatures, the eunuchs—but there be no eyes of greater importance to marital minds. The ladies came gayly after, in single file, chatting together, and although Araby's daughters are still born to blush unseen, they looked earnestly upon the staring strangers. Did those strangers long to behold that hidden beauty? Could they help it if all the softness and sweetness of hidden faces radiated from melting eyes?

Then came Sakkas—men with hog skins slung over their backs, full of water. I remembered the land and the time of putting wine into old bottles, and was shoved back beyond glass. Pedlers—swarthy fatalists in lovely lengths of robe and turban, cried their wares. To our Frank ears, it was mere Babel jargon. Yet had erudite Mr. Lane accompanied us, Mr. Lane, the eastern Englishman, who has given us so many golden glimpses into the silence and mystery of oriental life, like a good genius revealing to ardent lovers the very hallowed heart of the hareem, we should have understood those cries.

We should have heard "Sycamore figs—O Grapes"—meaning that said figs were offered, and the sweetness of sense and sound that "grape" hath was only bait for the attention; or "Odors of Paradise, O flowers of the henna," causing Muslim maidens to tingle to their very nails' ends; or, indeed, these Pedler Poets, vending watermelons, sang, "Consoler of the embarrassed, O Pips." Were they not poets, these pedlers, and full of all oriental extravagance? For the sweet association of poetic names shed silvery sheen over the actual article offered. The unwary philosopher might fancy that he was buying comfort in a green watermelon, and the pietist dream of mementoes of heaven, in the mere earthly vanity of henna.

But the philanthropic merchant of sour limes cries, "God make them light—limes"—meaning not the fruit nor the stomach of the purchaser, but his purse. And what would the prisoners of the passing black balloons say to the ambiguousness of "The work of the bull, O maidens!" innocently indicating a kind of cotton cloth made by bull-moved machinery? Will they never have done with hieroglyphics and sphinxes, these Egyptians? Here a man, rose-embowered, chants, "The rose is a thorn, from the sweat of the prophet it bloomed"—meaning simply, "Fresh roses."

These are masquerade manners, but they are pleasant. The maiden buys not henna only, but a thought of heaven. The poet not watermelons only, but a dream of consolation, which truly he will need. When shall we hear in Broadway, "Spring blush of the hillsides, O Strawberries," or "Breast buds of Venus, O milk." Never, never, until milkmen are turbaned, and berry-women ballooned.

A pair of Persians wound among these pedlers, clad in their strange costume. They wore high shaggy hats and undressed skins, and in their girdles shone silver-mounted pistols and daggers. They had come into the West, and were loitering along, amazed at what was extremest East to us. They had been famous in Gotham, no Muscat envoy more admired. But nobody stared at them here except us. We were the odd and observed. We had strayed into the universal revel, and had forgotten to don turbans at the gate. O Pyramids! thought I, to be where Persians are commonplace.

In this brilliant bewilderment we played only the part of Howadji, which is the universal name for traveler—the "Forestiero" of Italy. It signifies merchant or shopkeeper; and truly the Egyptians must agree with the bilious Frenchman that the English are a nation of shopkeepers, seeing them swarm forever through his land. For those who dwell at Karnak and in the shadow of Memnon, who build their mud huts upon the Edfoo Temple, and break up Colossi for lime, can not imagine any travel but that for direct golden gain. Belzoni was held in the wiser native mind to be a mere Dousterswivel of a treasure-hunter. Did not Hamed Aga come rushing two days' journey with two hundred men, and demand of him that large golden cock full of diamonds and pearls? Think how easily the Arabian Nights must have come to such men! Sublime stupidity! O Egyptians.

And so advancing, the massively foliaged acacias bowered us in golden gloom. They fringed and arched the long road. Between their trunks, like noble columns of the foreground, we saw the pyramids rosier in the western rosiness. Their forms were sculptured sharply in the sunset. We knew that they were on the edge of the desert; that their awful shadows darkened the sphinx. For so fair and festal is still the evening picture in that delicious climate, in that poetic land. We breathed the golden air, and it bathed our eyes with new vision. Peach-Blossom, who came with us from Malta, solemnly intent "to catch the spirit of the East," could not have resisted the infection of that enchanted evening.

I know you will ask me if an Eastern book can not be written without a dash of the Arabian Nights, if we can not get on without Haroun Alrashid. No, impatient reader, the East hath throughout that fine flavor. The history of Eastern life is embroidered to our youngest eyes in that airy arabesque. What to even many of us very wise ones is the history of Bagdad, more than the story of our revered caliph? Then the romance of travel is real. It is the man going to take possession of the boy's heritage, those dear dreams of stolen school-hours over wild romance; and in vain would he separate his poetry from his prose. Given a turban, a camel or a palm-tree, and Zobeide, the Princess Badoura and the youngest brother of the Barber step forward into the prose of experience.

For as we leave the main road and turn finally from the towers, whose gold is graying now, behold the parting picture and confess the East.

The moon has gathered the golden light in her shallow cup, and pours it paler over a bivouac of camels, by a sheik's white-domed tomb. They growl and blubber as they kneel with their packs of dates and almonds and grain, oriental freight mostly, while others are already down, still as Sphinxes. The rest sway their curved necks silently, and glance contemptuously at the world.

The drivers, in dark turbans and long white robes coax and command. The dome of the sheik's crumbling tomb is whiter in the moonlight. The brilliant bustle recedes behind those trees. A few Cairenes pass by unnoticing, but we are in desert depths. For us all the caravans of all Arabian romance are there encamping.

The Howadji reached at length the Nile, gleaming calm in the moonlight. A fleet of river boats lay moored to the steep stony bank. The Nile and the pyramids had bewitched the night, for it was full of marvelous pictures and told tales too fair. Yet do not listen too closely upon the shore, lest we hear the plash and plunge of a doomed wife or slave. These things have not passed away. This luxuriant beauty, this poetry of new impressions, has its balance. This tropical sun suckles serpents with the same light that adorns the gorgeous flowers. In the lush jungle, splendid tigers lurk,—ah! in our poetic Orient beauty is more beautiful, but deformity more deformed. The excellent Effendi or paternal Pacha has twenty or two hundred wives, and is, of necessity, unfaithful. But if the ballooned Georgian or Circassian slips up, it is into the remorseless river.

Yet with what solemn shadows do these musings endow the Egyptian moonlight. They move invisible over the face of the waters, and evoke another creation. Columbus sailed out of the Mediterranean to a new world. We have sailed into it, to a new one. The South seduces now, as the West of old. When we reach one end of the world, the other has receded into romantic dimness, and beckons us backward to explore. The Howadji seek Cathay. In the morning, with wide-winged sails, we shall fly beyond our history. Listen! How like a Pedler-Poet of Cairo chanting his wares, moans Time through the Eternity—" Cobwebs and fable, O history!"

II.

The Drag'-o-men.

As we stepped on board, we should have said, "In the name of God, the compassionate, the merciful." For so say all pious Muslim, undertaking an arduous task; and so let all pious Howadji exclaim when they set forth with any of those "guides, philosophers, and friends," the couriers of the Orient—the Dragomen.

These gentry figure well in the Eastern books. The young traveler, already enamored of Eothen's Dhemetri, or Warburton's Mahmoud, or Harriet Martineau's Alee, leaps ashore expecting to find a very Pythias to his Damon mood, and in his constant companion to embrace a concrete Orient. These are his Alexandrian emotions and hopes. Those poets, Harriet and Eliot, are guilty of much. Possibly as the youth descends the Lebanon to Beyrout, five months later, he will still confess that it was the concrete Orient; but own that he knew not the East, in those merely Mediterranean moods of hope and romantic reading.

The Howadji lands at Alexandria, and is immediately invested by long lines of men in bright turbans and baggy breeches. If you have a slight poetic tendency, it is usually too much for you. You succumb to the rainbow sash and red slippers. "Which is Alee?" cry you, in enthusiasm; and lo! all are Alee. No, but with Dhemetri might there not be rich Eastern material and a brighter Eothen? Yes, but all are Dhemetri. "Mahmoud, Mahmoud!" and the world of baggy breeches responds, "Yes, sir."

If you are heroic, you dismiss the confusing crowd, and then the individuals steal separately and secretly to your room and claim an audience. They have volumes of their own praise. Traveling Cockaigne has striven to express its satisfaction in the most graceful and epigrammatic manner. The "characters" in all the books have a sonnet-like air, each filling its page, and going to the same tune. There is no skepticism, and no dragoman has a fault. Records of such intelligence, such heroism, such perseverance, honesty, and good cooking, exist in no other literature. It is Eothen and the other poets in a more portable form.

Some Howadji can not resist the sonnets and the slippers, and take the fatal plunge even at Alexandria. Wines and the ecstatic Irish doctor did so under our eyes, and returned six weeks later to Cairo, from the upper Nile, with just vigor enough remaining to get rid of their man. For the Turkish costume and the fine testimonials are only the illuminated initials of the chapter. Very darkly monotonous is the reading that follows.

The Dragoman is of four species: the Maltese, or the able knave,—the Greek, or the cunning knave,—the

Syrian, or the active knave,—and the Egyptian, or the stupid knave. They wear generally the Eastern costume. But the Maltese and the Greeks often sport bad hats and coats, and call themselves Christians. They are the most ignorant, vain, incapable, and unsatisfactory class of men that the wandering Howadji meets. They travel constantly the same route, yet have no eyes to see nor ears to hear. If on the Nile, they smoke and sleep in the boat. If on the desert, they smoke and sleep on the camel. If in Syria, they smoke and sleep, if they can, on the horse. It is their own comfort—their own convenience and profit, which they constantly pursue. The Howadji is a bag of treasure thrown by a kind fate upon their shores, and they are the wreckers who squeeze, tear, and pull him, top, bottom, and sideways, to bleed him of his burden.

They should be able to give you every information about your boat, and what is necessary, and what useless. Much talk you do indeed get, and assurance that every thing will be accurately arranged; but you are fairly afloat upon the Nile before you discover how lost upon the dragoman have been all his previous voyages.

With miserable weakness they seek to smooth the moment, and perpetually baffle your plans, by telling you not the truth, but what they suppose you wish the truth to be. Nothing is ever more than an hour or two distant. They involve you in absurd arrangements because "it is the custom;" and he is a hardy Howadji who struggles against the vis inertiæ of ignorant incapacity and miserable cheating through the whole tour.

Active intelligence on the Howadji's part is very disgusting to them. If he scrutinize his expenses,—if he pretend to know his own will or way—much more to have it executed, the end of things clearly approaches to the dragomanic mind. The small knaveries of cheating in the price of every thing purchased, and in the amount of bucksheesh or gratuity on all occasions, are not to be seriously heeded, because they are universal. The real evils are the taking you out of your way for their own comfort,—the favoring a poor resting-place or hotel, because they are well paid there,—and the universally unreliable information that they afford. Were they good servants, it were some consolation. But a servile Eastern can not satisfy the Western idea of good service.

Perhaps it was a bad year for dragomen, as it was for potatoes. But such was the result of universal testimony.

Nero found a Greek at Alexandria, whose recommendations from men known to him were quite enthusiastic. He engaged him, and the dragoman was the sole plague of Nero's Egyptian experience, but one combining the misery of all the rest. There were Wind and Rain, too, whose man was a crack dragoman, and of all such, oh! enthusiastic reader, especially beware. They returned to Cairo chanting "miserere—miserere"—and in the spring, sought solace in the bosom of the scarlet Lady at Jerusalem. For which latter step, however, not even irate I, hold the dragoman responsible.

Mutton Suet's man furnished his Nile larder, at the rate of eight boxes of sweet biscuit, and twenty bottles of pickles to two towels—a lickerous larder, truly, but I am convinced Mutton Suet's man's palate required sharp stimulants.

The little Verde Giovane and Gunning changed their dragoman weekly while they remained at Cairo. The difficulty was not all on one side. The dragòman wanted to be master, and Verde knew not how to help it, and Gunning was ill of a fever. Those excellent Howadji did not recover from the East without a course of a half-dozen dragomen.

But most melancholy was the case of a Howadji, whom we met wandering in the remote regions of the Nile. He was a kind of flying Dutchman, always gliding about in a barque haunted by a dragoman, and a Reis or captain, who would not suffer him to arrive anywhere. The moons of three months had waxed and waned since they left Cairo. Winds never blew for that unhappy boat, currents were always adverse,—illness and inability seized the crew. Landing at lonely towns the dragoman sold him his own provisions, previously sent ashore for the purpose, at an admirable advance. Gradually he was becoming the Ancient Mariner of the Nile. He must have grown grisly,—I am sure that he was sad.

One day as the fated boat or Dahabieh came spectrally sliding over the calm, our dragoman told us the story with sardonic smiles, and we looked with awful interest at the haunted barque. I saw the demoniac dragoman smoking by the kitchen, and the crew, faintly rowing, sang the slowest of slow songs. The flag, wind-rent and sun-bleached, clung in motionless despair to the mast. The sails were furled away almost out of sight. It was a windless day, and the sun shone spectrally.

I looked for the mariner, but saw only a female figure in a London bonnet sitting motionless at the cabin window.

The dragoman-ridden was probably putting on his hat. Was it a game of their despair to play arriving, and getting ready to go—for the lady sat as ladies sit in steamers, when they near the wharf—or was this only a melancholy remembrance of days and places, when they could don hat and bonnet, and choose their own way—or simply a mood of madness?

They passed, and we saw them no more. I never heard of them again. They are still sailing on doubtless, and you will hear the slow song and see the unnecessary bonnet, and behold a Howadji buying his own provisions. Say "Pax vobiscum" as they pass, nor bless the dragomen.

I heard but one Howadji speak well of his dragoman, and he only comparatively and partially. At Jerusalem the Rev. Dr. Duck dismissed his Maltese, and took an Egyptian—which was the Rev. Dr. Duck's method of stepping from the pan into the fire. At the same time Eschylus,—not our Greek, but a modern man of affairs, and not easily appalled at circumstances, banished his brace of Maltese, and declared that he was wild with dragomen, and did not believe a decent one could exist.

Yet Eschylus, in sad seriousness of purpose to accomplish the East, took another dragoman at Jerusalem, a baleful mortal with one eye, and a more able bandit than the rest. For this man Eschylus paid twenty piasters a day, board, at the hotel in Jerusalem. Polyphemus requested him with a noble frankness not to give the money to him, but to pay it directly to the landlord in person—meanwhile he delayed him, and delayed, in Jerusalem, until at parting, the landlord with equal frankness told Eschylus, that he was obliged to refund to the dragomen every thing paid for them, as otherwise he would discover that some cat or dog had twitched his table cloths, and destroyed whole services of glass and china—and this best hotel in the East, was to be discontinued for that and similar reasons. For the landlord had sparks of human sympathy even with mere Howadji, and the dragomen had sworn his ruin. All Howadji were taken to another house, and it was only by positive insistance that we reached this.

Of all the knavery of Polyphemus, this book would not contain the history. At the end Eschylus, told him quietly, that he had robbed him repeatedly—that since engaging him he had heard that he was a noted scamp,—that he had been insolent to Madame Eschylus—that, in short—waxing warm as he perorated, that he was a damned rascal. Then he paid him,—for litigation is useless in the East, where the Christian word is valueless,—informed him that all English Howadji should be informed of his name and nature, after which, Polyphemus endeavored to kiss his hand!

Then consider Leisurelie's Domenico Chiesa, Sunday Church, "begging your pardon, sir, I am il primo dragomano del mondo,—the first dragoman in the world."

" Domenico," said Leisurelie one day in Jerusalem, " where is Mount Calvary ?" You know, my young friend of fourteen years, that it is in the church of the holy sepulcher—but il primo dragomano del mondo waved his hand vaguely around the horizon, with his eyes wandering about the far blue mountains of Moab, and " O, begging your pardon, sir, it's there, just there."

Such are our Arabic interpreters, such your concrete Orient. Yet if you believe all your dragoman says—if you will only believe that he does know something, and put your nose into his fingers, you will go very smoothly to Beyrout, dripping gold all the way, and then improvise a brief pean in the book of sonnets. But if the Howadji mean to be master, the romance will unroll like a cloud wreath, from that poetic tawny friend, and he will find all and more than the faults of an European courier, with none of his capacities.

O, golden-sleeved Commander of the Faithful, what a prelude to your praises. For Mohammad was the best we saw, and so agreed all who knew him. Dogberry was already his Laureate. Mohammad was truly " tolerable and not to be endured." He was ignorant, vain, and cowardly, but fairly honest,—extremely good-humored, and an abominable cook. He was a devout Muslim, and had a pious abhorrence of ham. His deportment was grave and pompous, blending the Turkish and Egyptian elements of his parentage. Like a child he shrunk and shriveled under the least pain or exposure. But he loved the high places and the sweet morsels; and to be called of men, Effendi, dilated his soul with delight. He was always well dressed in the Egyptian manner, and bent in awful reverence before "them old Turks" who, surrounded by a multitudinous hareem, and an army of slaves, were the august peerage of his imagination.

His great glory, however, was a golden-sleeved bournouse of goat's hair, presented to him at Damascus by some friendly Howadji. This he gathered about him on all convenient occasions to create an impression,—at the little towns on the Nile, and among the Arabs of the desert, how imposing was the golden-sleeved Commander! Occasionally he waited at dinner in this robe—and then was never Jove so superbly served. Yet the grandeur, as usual, was inconsonant with agility, and many a wrecked dish of pudding or potatoes paid the penalty of splendor.

So here our commander of the faithful steps into history, goldenly arrayed. Let him not speak for himself. For, although his English was intelligible and quite sufficient, yet he recognized no auxiliary but "*be*," and no tense but the present. Hence, when he wished to say that the tobacco would be milder when it had absorbed the water, he darkly suggested, "He be better when he be drink his water;" and a huge hulk of iron lying just outside Cairo, was "the steamer's saucepan;" being the boiler of a Suez steamer. Nor will the pacha forget that sunny Syrian morning, when the commander led us far and far out of our way for a "short cut." Wandering, lost, and tangled in flaunting flowers, through long valleys and up steep hillsides, we emerged at length upon the path which we ought never to have left, and the good commander lighting his chibouque with the air of a general lighting his cigar after victory, announced impressively, "I be found that way by my sense, by my head!" Too vain to ask or to learn, he subjected us to the same inconveniences day after day, for the Past disappears from the dragomanic mind as utterly as yesterday's landscape from his eye.

The moon brightened the golden sleeve that first Nile evening, as the commander descended the steep bank, superintending the embarking of the luggage; and while he spreads the cloth and the crew gather about the kitchen to sing, we will hang in our gallery the portrait of his coadjutor, Hadji Hamed, the cook.

III.

Hadji Hamed.

I WAS donkeying one morning through the bazaars of Cairo, looking up at the exquisitely elaborated overhanging lattices, wondering if the fences of Paradise were not so rarely enwrought, dreaming of the fair Persian slave, of the Princess Shemselnihar, the three ladies of Bagdad, and other mere star dust, my eye surfeiting itself the while with forms and costumes that had hitherto existed only in poems and pictures, when I heard suddenly, "Have you laid in any potatoes?" and beheld beaming elderly John Bull by my side.

"It occurred to me," said he, "that the long days upon the Nile might be a little monotonous, and I thought the dinner would be quite an event."

"Allah!" cried I, as the three ladies of Bagdad faded upon my fancy, "I thought we should live on sunsets on the Nile."

The beaming elderly Bull smiled quietly and glanced at his gentle rotundity, while I saw bottles, boxes, canisters, baskets, and packages of all sizes laid aside in the shop—little anti-monotonous arrangements for the Nile.

B*

"I hope you have a good cook," said John Bull, as he moved placidly away upon his donkey, and was lost in the dim depths of the bazaar.

Truly we were loved of the Prophet, for our cook was also a Mohammad, an Alexandrian, and doubtless especially favored, not for his name's sake only, but because he had been a pilgrim to Mecca, and hence a Hadji forever after. It is a Mohammadan title, equivalent to our "major" and "colonel" as a term of honor, with this difference, that with us it is not always necessary to have been a captain to be called such; but in Arabia is no man a Hadji who has not performed the Mecca pilgrimage. Whether a pilgrimage to Paris, and devotion to sundry shrines upon the Boulevards, had not been as advantageous to Hadji Hamed as kissing the holy Mecca-stone, was a speculation which we did not indulge; for his cuisine was admirable.

Yet I sometimes fancied the long lankness of the Hadji Hamed's figure, streaming in his far-flowing whiteness of garment up the Boulevards, and claiming kindred with the artistes of the "Café" or of the "Maison dorée." They would needs have *sacrè bleu'd.* Yet might the Hadji have well challenged them to the "Kara Kooseh," or "Warah Mahshee," or the "Yakhnee," nor feared the result. Those are the cabalistic names of stuffed gourds, of a kind of mince-pie in a pastry of cabbage leaves, and of a stewed meat seasoned with chopped onions. Nor is the Christian palate so hopelessly heretic that it can not enjoy those genuine Muslim morsels. For we are nothing on the Nile if not Eastern. The Egyptians like sweet dishes; even fowls they stuff with raisins, and the rich conclude their repasts with draughts of khushaf—a water boiled with raisins and sugar, and flavored with rose. Mr. Lane says it is the "sweet water" of the Persians.

And who has dreamed through the Arabian Nights that could eat without a thrill, lamb stuffed with pistachio nuts, or quaff sherbet of roses, haply of violet, without a vision of Haroun's pavilion and his lovely ladies? Is a pastry cook's shop, a mere pastry cook's shop when you eat cheesecakes there? Shines not the Syrian sun suddenly over it, making all the world Damascus, and all people Agib, and Benreddin Hassan, and the lady of beauty? Even in these slightest details no region is so purely the property of the imagination as the East. We know it only in poetry, and although there is dirt and direful deformity, the traveler sees it no more than the fast-flying swallow, to whom the dreadful mountain abysses and dumb deserts are but soft shadows and shining lights in his air-seen picture of the world.

The materials for this poetic Eastern larder are very few upon the Nile; chickens and mutton are the staple, and chance pigeons shot on the shore, during a morning's stroll. The genius of the artiste is shown in his adroit arrangement and concealment of this monotonous material. Hadji Hamed's genius was Italian, and every dinner was a success. He made every dinner the event which Bull was convinced it would be, or ought to be; and, perhaps, after all, the Hadji's soft custard was much the same as the sunset diet of which, in those Cairo days, I dreamed.

Our own larder was very limited; for as we sailed slowly along those shores of sleep, we observed too intense an intimacy of the goats with the sheep.

The white bearded goats wandered too much at their own sweet will with the unsuspecting lambs, or the not all unwilling elderly sheep. The natives are not fastidious, and do not mind a mellow goat flavor. They drink a favorite broth made of the head, feet, skin, wool, and hoofs, thrust into a pot and half boiled. Then they eat with unction, the unctuous remains. We began bravely with roast and boiled; but orders were issued at length, that no more sheep should be bought, so sadly convinced were the Howadji that evil communications corrupt good mutton.

Yet in Herodotean days, the goats were sacred to one part of Egypt and sheep to another. The Thebans abstained from sheep, and sacrificed goats only. For they said, that Hercules was very desirous of seeing Jupiter, but Jupiter was unwilling to be seen. As Hercules persisted, however, Jupiter flayed a ram, cut off the head and held it before his face, and having donned the fleece, so showed himself to Hercules—hence, our familiar Jupiter Ammon.

But those of the Mendesian district, still says Herodotus, abstained from goats and sacrificed sheep. For they said that Pan was one of the original eight gods, and their sculptors and painters represented him with the face and legs of a goat. Why they did so, Herodotus prefers not to mention; as, indeed, our good father of history was so careful of his children's morals, that he usually preferred not to mention precisely what they most wish to know.

It is curious to find that the elder Egyptians had the Jewish and Mohammadan horror of swine. The swine-herds were a separate race, like the headsmen of some modern lands, and married among themselves. Herodotus knows, as usual, why swine were abhorred, except on the festivals of the moon and of Bacchus, but as usual considers it more becoming not to mention the reason.

Is it not strange, as we sweep up the broad river, to see the figure of that genial, garrulous, old gossip, stalking vaguely through the dim morning twilight of history, plainly seeing what we can never know, audibly conversing with us of what he will, but ignoring what we wish, and answering no questions forever? One of the profoundest mysteries of the Egyptian belief, and in lesser degrees of all antique faiths, constantly and especially symbolized throughout Egypt, Herodotus evidently knew perfectly from his friendship with the priests, but perpetually his conscience dictates silence—Amen, O venerable Father.

I knew some bold Howadji who essayed a crocodile banquet. They were served with crocodile chops and steaks, and crocodile boiled, roasted, and stewed. They talked very cheerfully of it afterward; but each one privately confessed that the flesh tasted like abortive lobster, saturated with musk.

Hadji Hamed cooked no crocodile, and had no golden-sleeved garment. He wore 'eree or cotton drawers, past their prime, and evidently originally made for lesser legs. That first evening he fluttered about the deck in a long white robe, like a solemn-faced wag playing ghost in a churchyard. By day he looked like a bird of prey, with long legs and a hooked bill.

IV.

The Ibis Sings.

While the Hadji Hamed fluttered about the deck, and the commander served his kara kooseh, the crew gathered around the bow and sang.

The stillness of early evening had spelled the river, nor was the strangeness dissolved by that singing. The men crouched in a circle upon the deck, and the reis, or captain, thrummed the tarabuka, or Arab drum, made of a fish-skin stretched upon a gourd. Raising their hands, the crew clapped them above their heads, in perfect time, not ringingly, but with a dead dull thump of the palms—moving the whole arm to bring them together. They swung their heads from side to side, and one clanked a chain in unison. So did these people long before the Ibis nestled to this bank, long before there were Americans to listen.

For when Diana was divine, and thousands of men and women came floating down the Nile in barges to celebrate her festival, they sang and clapped, played the castanets and flute, stifling the voices of Arabian and Lybian echoes with a wild roar of revelry. They, too, sang a song that came to them from an unknown antiquity, Linus, their first and only song, the dirge of the son of the first king of Egypt.

This might have been that dirge that the crew sang in a mournful minor. Suddenly one rose and led the song, in sharp jagged sounds, formless as lightning. "He fills me the glass full and gives me to drink," sang the leader, and the low measured chorus throbbed after him, "Hummeleager malooshee." The sounds were not a tune, but a kind of measured recitative. It went on constantly faster and faster, exciting them, as the Shakers excite themselves, until a tall gaunt Nubian rose in the moonlight and danced in the center of the circle, like a gay ghoul among his fellows.

The dancing was monotonous, like the singing, a simple jerking of the muscles. He shook his arms from the elbows like a Shaker, and raised himself alternately upon both feet. Often the leader repeated the song as a solo, then the voices died away, the ghoul crouched again, and the hollow throb of the tarabuka continued as an accompaniment to the distant singing of Nero's crew, that came in fitful gusts through the little grove of sharp slim masts—

> "If you meet my sweetheart,
> Give her my respects."

The melancholy monotony of this singing in unison, harmonized with the vague feelings of that first Nile night. The simplicity of the words became the perpetual childishness of the men, so that it was not ludicrous. It was clearly the music and words of a race just better than the brutes. If a poet could translate into sound the expression of a fine dog's face, or that of a meditative cow, the Howadji would fancy that he heard Nile music. For, after all, that placid and perfect animal expression would be melancholy humanity. And with the crew only the sound was sad; they smiled and grinned and shook their heads with intense satisfaction. The evening and the scene were like a chapter of Mungo Park. I heard the African mother sing to him as he lay sick upon her mats, and the world and history forgotten, those strange sad sounds drew me deep into the dumb mystery of Africa.

But the musical Howadji will find a fearful void in his Eastern life. The Asiatic has no ear and no soul for music. Like other savages and children, he loves a noise and he plays on shrill pipes—on the tarabuka, on the tár or tambourine, and a sharp one-stringed fiddle, or rabáb. Of course in your first oriental days, you will decline no invitation, but you will grow gradually deaf to all entreaties of friends or dragomen to sally forth and hear music. You will remind him that you did not come to the East to go to Bedlam.

This want of music is not strange, for silence is natural to the East and the tropics. When, sitting quietly at home, in midsummer, sweeping ever sunward in the growing heats, we at length reach the tropics in the fixed fervor of a July noon, the day is rapt, the birds are still, the wind swoons, and the burning sun glares silence on the world.

The Orient is that primeval and perpetual noon. That very heat explains to you the voluptuous elaboration of its architecture, the brilliance of its costume, the picturesqueness of its life. But no Mozart was needed to sow Persian gardens with roses breathing love and beauty, no Beethoven to build mighty Himalayas, on Rossini to sparkle and sing with the birds and streams. Those realities are there, of which the composers are the poets to Western imaginations. In the East, you feel and see music, but hear it never.

Yet in Cairo and Damascus the poets sit at the cafés, surrounded by the forms and colors of their songs, and recite the romances of the Arabian Nights, or of Aboo Zeyd, or of Antar, with no other accompaniment than the Tár or the Rabáb, then called the "Poet's Viol," and in the same monotonous strain. Sometimes the single strain is touching, as when on our way to Jerusalem, the too enamored camel-driver, leading the litter of the fair Armenian, saddened the silence of the desert noon with a Syrian song. The high shrill notes trembled and rang on the air. The words said little, but the sound was a lyric of sorrow. The fair Armenian listened silently as the caravan wound slowly along, her eyes musily fixed upon the East, where the flower-fringed Euphrates flows through Bagdad to the sea. The fair Armenian had her thoughts and the camel-driver his; also the accompanying Howadji listened and had theirs.

The Syrian songs of the desert are very sad. They harmonize with the burning monotony of the landscape in their long recitative and shrill wail. The camel steps more willingly to that music, but the Howadji swaying upon his back is tranced in the sound, so naturally born of silence.

Meanwhile our crew are singing, although we have slid upon their music, and the moonlight, far forward into the desert. But these are the forms and feelings that their singing suggested. While they sang I wandered over Sahara, and was lost in the lonely Libyan hills,—a thousand simple stories, a thousand ballads of love and woe trooped like drooping birds through the sky-like vagueness of my mind. Rosamond Grey, and the child of Elle passed phantom-like with vailed faces,—for love, and sorrow, and delight are cosmopolitan, building bowers indiscriminately of palm-trees or of pines.

The voices died away like the Muezzins', whose cry is the sweetest and most striking of all Eastern sounds. It trembles in long rising and falling cadences from the balcony of the Minaret, more humanly alluring than bells, and more respectful of the warm stillness of Syrian and Egyptian days. Heard in Jerusalem it has especial power. You sit upon your housetop reading the history whose profoundest significance is simple and natural in that inspiring clime—and as your eye wanders from the aeriel dome of Omar, beautiful enough to have been a dome of Solomon's Temple, and over the olives of Gethsemane climbs the Mount of Olives—the balmy air is suddenly filled with a murmurous cry like a cheek suddenly rose-suffused—a sound near, and far, and everywhere, but soft and vibrating and alluring, until you would fain don turban, kaftan, and slippers, and kneeling in the shadow of a cypress on the sun-flooded marble court of Omar, would be the mediator of those faiths, nor feel yourself a recreant Christian.

Once I heard the Muezzin cry from a little village on the edge of the desert, in the starlight before the dawn. It was only a wailing voice in the air. The spirits of the desert were addressed in their own language,—or was it themselves lamenting, like water spirits to the green boughs overhanging them, that they could never know the gladness of the green world, but were forever demons and denizens of the desert? But the tones trembled away without echo or response into the starry solitude;—Al-lâ-hu Ak-bar, Al-lâ-hu Ak-bar!

So with songs and pictures, with musings, and the dinner of a Mecca pilgrim, passed the first evening upon the Nile. The Ibis clung to the bank at Boulak all that night. We called her Ibis because the sharp lateen sails are most like wings, and upon the Egyptian Nile was no winged thing of fairer fame. We prayed Osiris that the law of his religion might yet be enforced against winds and waves. For whoever killed an Ibis, by accident or willfully, necessarily suffered death.

The Lotus is a sweeter name, but consider all the Poets who have so baptized their boats! Besides, soothly saying, this Dahabieh of ours, hath no flower semblance, and is rather fat than fairy. The zealous have even called their craft *Papyrus*, but poverty has no law.

V.

The Crew.

We are not quite off, yet. Eastern life is leisurely. It has the long crane neck of enjoyment—and you, impatient reader, must leave your hasty habits, and no longer bolt your pleasure as you do your Tremont or Astor dinner, but taste it all the way down, as our turbaned friends do. Ask your dragoman casually, and he will regale you with choice instances of this happy habitude of the Orientals—or read the Arabian Nights in the original, or understand literally the romances that the Poets recite at the Cafés, and you will learn how much you are born to lose—being born as you were, an American, with no time to live.

Your Nile crew is a dozen Nondescripts. They are Arabs—Egyptians—Nubians and half-breeds of all kinds. They wear a white or red cap, and a long flowing garment which the Howadji naturally calls "Night-gown," but which they term "Zaaboot"—although as Mrs. Bull said, she thought Night-gown the better name. It is a convenient dress for river mariners, for they have only to throw it off, and are at once ready to leap into the stream if the boat grounds—with no more incumbrance than Undine's uncle Kühleborn always had. On great occasions of reaching a town they wear the 'eree or drawers, and a turban of white cotton.

Our Reis was a placid little Nubian, with illimitable lips, and a round, soft eye. He was a feminine creature, and crept felinely about the boat on his little spongy feet, often sitting all day upon the bow, somnolently smoking his chibouque, and letting us run aground. He was a Hadji too; but, except that he did no work, seemed to have no especial respect from the crew. He put his finger in the dish with them, and fared no better. Had he been a burly brute, the savages would have feared him; and, with them, fear is the synonym of respect.

The grisly Ancient Mariner was the real captain—an old, gray Egyptian, who crouched all day long over the tiller, with a pipe in his mouth, and his firm eye fixed upon the river and the shore. He looked like a heap of ragged blankets, smoldering away internally, and emitting smoke at a chance orifice. But at evening he descended to the deck, took a cup of coffee, and chatted till midnight. As long as the wind held to the sail, he held to the tiller. The Ancient Mariner was the real worker of the Ibis, and never made faces at it, although the crew bemoaned often enough their hard fate. Of course, he tried to cheat at first, but when he felt the eye of the Pacha looking through him and turning up his little cunning, he tried it no more, or only spasmodically, at intervals, from habit.

Brawny, one-eyed Seyd was first officer, the leader of the working chorus and of the hard pulling and pushing. He had put out his own eye, like other Egyptians, many of whom did the same office to their children to escape Mohammad Alee's conscription. He was a good-natured, clumsy boor—a being in the ape stage of development. He proved the veracity of the "Vestiges," that we begin in a fishy state, and advance through the tailed and winged ones. "We have had fins, we may have wings." I doubt if Seyd had yet fairly taken in his tail—he was growing. Had I been a German naturalist, I should have seized the good Seyd and presented him to some "Durchlauchtiger," king or kaiser, as an ourang-outang from the white Nile; and I am sure the Teutons would have decreed it, a "sehr ausgezeichnete" specimen.

Seyd, I fear, was slightly sensual. He had ulterior views upon the kitchen drippings. While the Howadji dined, he sat like an ourang-outang, gazing with ludicrous intensity at the lickerous morsels, then shifted into some clumsier squat, so that the Howadji could not maintain becoming gravity. At times he imbibed cups of coffee privately in the kitchen regions, then gurgled his cocoanut nargileh with spasmodic vigor.

Seyd fulfilled other functions not strictly within his official walk. He washed the deck, brought coals to the chibouque, cleaned the knives and scraped kettles and pans. But after much watching, I feared that Seyd was going backward—developing the wrong way, for he became more baboonish and less human every day. His feet were incredible. I had not seen the colossi then. Generally, he was barefooted. But sometimes, O goddess of Paris kids! he essayed slippers. Then no bemired camel ever extricated himself more ponderously pedaled. These leather cases, that might have been heir-looms of Memnon, were the completion of his full dress. Ah! Brummell! Seyd *en grande tenue* was a stately spectacle.

There was Saleh or Satan, a cross between the porcupine and the wild-cat, whom I disliked as devoutly as the Rev. Dr. Duck did the devil. And Aboo Seyd, a little old-maidish Bedoueen, who told wonderful stories to the crew and prayed endlessly. He was very vain and direfully ugly, short and speckled and squat. On the Nile I believed in necromancy, and knew Aboo Seyd to be really a tree-toad humanized. I speculated vainly upon his vanity. It was the only case where I never could suspect the secret.

Great gawky Abdallah then, God's favorite as his name imports, and a trusty mastiff of a man. Abdallah had few human characteristics, and was much quizzed by the crew under Satan's lead. He was invaluable for plunging among the grass and bushes, or into the water for pigeons which the Pacha had shot. And he loved his townsman Aboo Tar, or Congo, as we called him, as if his heart were as huge as his body. Congo was the youngest and brightest of the crew. He was black and slim, and although not graceful, moved rapidly and worked well. The little Congo was the only one of the crew who inspired human interest.

They are all bad workers, and lazy exceedingly. Never was seen such confused imbecility of action and noise, as in the shifting of sail. The ropes are twisted and tangled, and the red and black legs are twisted and tangled in the trouble to extricate them. Meanwhile the boat comes into the wind, the great sails flap fiercely, mad to be deprived of it; the boats that had drifted behind come up, even pass, and the Pacha, wrapped in his capote, swears a little to ease his mind.

Yet that Nile poet, Harriet Martineau, speaks of the "savage faculty" in Egypt. But "faculty" is a Western gift. Savages with faculty may become a leading race. But a leading race never degenerates, so long as faculty remains. The Egyptians and Easterns are not savages, they are imbeciles. It is the English fashion to laud the Orient, and to prophesy a renewed grandeur, as if the East could ever again be as bright as at sunrise. The Easterns are picturesque and handsome, as is no nation with faculty. The coarse costume of a Nile sailor shames in dignity and grace the most elaborate toilet of Western saloons. It is drapery whose grace all men admire, and which all artists study in the antique. Western life is clean and comely and comfortable, but it is not picturesque.

Therefore, if you would enjoy the land, you must be a poet, and not a philosopher. To the hurrying Howadji, the prominent interest is the picturesque one. For any other purpose, he need not be there. Be a pilgrim of beauty and not of morals or of politics, if you would realize your dream. History sheds moonlight over the antique years of Egypt, and by that light you can not study. Believe before you begin, that the great Asian mystery which D'Israeli's mild-minded Tancred sought to penetrate, is the mystery of death. If you do not, then settle it upon the data you have at home, for unless you come able and prepared for profoundest research and observation, a rapid journey through a land whose manners and language you do not understand, and whose spirit is utterly novel to you, will ill qualify you to discourse of its fate and position.

That the East will never regenerate itself, cotemporary history shows; nor has any nation of history culminated twice. The spent summer reblooms no more—the Indian summer is but a memory and a delusion. The sole hope of the East is Western inoculation. The child must suckle the age of the parent, and even "Medea's wondrous alchemy" will not restore its peculiar prime. If the East awakens, it will be no longer in the turban and red slippers, but in hat and boots. The West is the sea that advances forever upon the shore, the shore can not stay it, but becomes the bottom of the ocean. The Western, who lives in the Orient, does not assume the kaftan and the baggy breeches, and those of his Muslim neighbors shrink and disappear before his coat and pantaloons. The Turkish army is clothed like the armies of Europe. The grand Turk himself, Mohammad's vicar, the Commander of the Faithful, has laid away the magnificence of Haroun Alrashid, and wears the simple red Tarboosh, and a stiff suit of military blue. Cairo is an English station to India, and the Howadji does not drink sherbet upon the pyramids, but champagne. The choice Cairo of our Eastern imagination is contaminated with carriages. They are showing the secrets of the streets to the sun. Their silence is no longer murmurous, but rattling. The Uzbeekeeyah, public promenade of Cairo, is a tea garden, of a Sunday afternoon crowded with ungainly Franks, listening to bad music. Ichabod, Ichabod! steam has towed the Mediterranean up the Nile to Boulak, and as you move on to Cairo, through the still surviving masquerade of the Orient, the cry of the melon-merchant seems the significant cry of each sad-eyed Oriental, "Consoler of the embarrassed, O Pips!"

The century has seen the failure of the Eastern experiment, headed as it is not likely to be headed again, by an able and wise leader. Mohammad Alee had mastered Egypt and Syria, and was mounting the steps of the sultan's throne. Then he would have marched to Bagdad, and sat down in Haroun Alrashid's seat, to draw again broader and more deeply the lines of the old Eastern empire. But the West would not suffer it. Even had it done so, the world of Mohammad Alee would have crumbled to chaos again when he died, for it existed only by his imperial will, and not by the perception of the people.

At this moment the East is the El Dorado of European political hope. No single power dares to grasp it, but at last England and Russia will meet there, face to face, and the lion and the polar bear will shiver the desert silence with the roar of their struggle. It will be the return of the children to claim the birthplace. They may quarrel among themselves, but whoever wins, will introduce the life of the children and not of the parent. A possession and a province it may be, but no more an independent empire. Father Ishmael shall be a sheikh of honor, but of dominion no longer, and sit turbaned in the chimney corner, while his hatted heirs rule the house. The children will cluster around him, fascinated with his beautiful traditions, and curiously compare their little black shoes with his red slippers.

Here, then, we throw overboard from the Ibis all solemn speculation, reserving only for ballast this chapter of erudite Eastern reflection and prophecy. The shade of the Poet Martineau moves awfully along these clay terraces, and pauses minatory under the palms, declaring that "He who derives from his travels nothing but picturesque and amusing impressions * * * uses like a child, a most serious and manlike privilege."

It is reproving, but some can paint, and some can preach, Poet Harriet, so runs the world away. That group of palms waving feathery in the moonlight over the gleaming river is more soul-solacing than much conclusive speculation.

VI.

The Ibis Flies.

At noon the wind rose. The Ibis shook out her wings, spread them and stood into the stream. Nero was already off.

Stretching before us southward were endless groups of masts and sails. Palms fringed the western shore, and on the east, rose the handsome summer palaces of Pachas and rich men. They were deep retired in full foliaged groves and gardens, or rose white and shining directly over the water. The verandahs were shaded with cool, dark-green blinds, and spacious steps descended stately to the water, as proudly as from Venetian palaces. Graceful boats lay moored to the marge, the lustrous darkness of acacias shadowed the shore, and an occasional sakia or water-wheel began the monotonous music of the river.

Behind us from the city, rose the alabaster minarets of the citadel Mosque—snow spires in the deep blue—and the aerial elegance of the minor minarets mingling with palms, that seemed to grow in unknown hanging-gardens of delight, were already a graceful arabesque upon the sky. The pyramids watched us as we went—staring themselves stonily into memory forever. The great green plain between us, came gently to the water, over whose calm gleam skimmed the Ibis with almost conscious delight that she was flying to the South. The Howadji, meanwhile, fascinated with the fair auspices of their voyage, sat cross-legged upon Persian carpets sipping mellow mocha, and smoking the cherry-sticked chibouque.

As life without love, said the Cairene Poet to me as I ordered his Nargileh to be refilled with Tumback—choice Persian tobacco—is the chibouque without coffee. And as I sipped that mocha, and perceived that for the first time I was drinking coffee, I felt that all Hadji Hamed's solemnity and painful Mecca pilgrimages were not purposeless nor without ambition. Why should not he prepare coffee for the choicest coterie of houris even in the Prophet's celestial pavilion? For a smoother sip is not offered the Prophet by his fairest favorite, than his namesake prepared, and his other namesake offered to us on each Nile day.

The mocha is so fragrant and rich, and so perfectly prepared, that the sweetness of sugar seems at length quite coarse and unnecessary. It destroys the most delicate delight of the palate, which craves at last the purest flavor of the berry, and tastes all Arabia Felix therein. A glass of imperial Tokay in Hungary, and a fingan of mocha in the East, are the most poetic and inspiring draughts. Whether the Greek poets, born between the two, did not foreshadow the fascination of each, when they celebrated nectar and ambrosia as divine delights, I leave to the most erudite Teutonic commentator. Sure am I that the delight of well-prepared mocha transcends the sphere of sense, and rises into a spiritual satisfaction—or is it that mocha is the magic that spiritualizes sense ?

Yet it must be sipped from the fingan poised in the delicate zarf. The fingan is a small blue and gold cup, or of any color, of an egg's caliber, borne upon an exquisitely wrought support of gold or silver. The mouth must slide from the cup's brim to the amber mouth-piece of the chibouque, drawing thence azure clouds of latakia, the sweet mild weed of Syria. Then, O wildered Western, you taste the Orient, and awake in dreams.

So waned the afternoon, as we glided gently before a failing breeze, between the green levels of the Nile valley. The river was lively with boats. Dignified Dahabieh sweeping along like Pachas of importance and of endless tails. Crafty little Cangie, smaller barques, creeping on like Effendi of lesser rank. The far rippling reaches were white with the sharp saucy sails, bending over and over, reproaching the water for its resistance, and, like us, pursuing the South. The craft was of every kind. Huge lumbering country boats, freighted with filth and vermin, covered with crouching figures in blankets, or laden with grain; or there were boats curiously crowded, the little cabin windows overflowing with human blackness and semi-naked boys and girls, sitting in close rows upon the deck.

These are first class frigates of the Devil's navy. They

are slave boats floating down from Dongola and Sennaar. The wind does not blow for them. They alone are not white with sails, and running merrily over the water, but they drift slowly, slowly with the weary beat of a few oars.

The little slaves stare at us with more wonder than we look at them. They are not pensive or silent. They smile and chat, and point at the Howadji and the novelties of the Nile very contentedly. Not one kneels and inquires if he is not a man and a brother, and the Venuses, "carved in ebony," seem fully satisfied with their crisp, closely curling hair, smeared with castor oil. In Egypt and the East generally, slavery does not appear so sadly as elsewhere. The contrasts are not so vivid. It seems only an accident that one is master and the other slave. A reverse of relations would not appear strange, for the master is as ignorant and brutal as the servant.

Yet a group of disgusting figures lean and lounge upon the upper deck, or cabin roof. Nature, in justice to herself, has discharged humanity from their faces—only the human form remains—for there is nothing so revolting as a slave-driver with his booty bagged. In the chase, there may be excitement and danger, but the chase once successful, they sink into a torpidity of badness. But this is only a cloud floating athwart the setting sun. To our new Nile eyes, this is only proof that there are crocodiles beyond—happily not so repulsive, for they are not in the human shape.

The slavers passed and the sun set over the gleaming river. A solitary heron stood upon a sandy point. In a broad beautiful bay beyond, the thin lines of masts were drawn dark against the sky. Palms, and the dim lines of Arabian hills dreamed in the tranquil air, a few boats clung to the western bank, that descended in easy clay terraces to the water, their sails hanging in the dying wind. Suddenly we were among them, close under the bank.

The moon sloped westward behind a group of palms, and the spell was upon us. We had drifted into the dream world. From the ghostly highlands and the low shore, came the baying of dogs, mellowed by distance and the moonlight into the weird measures of a black forest hunting. Drifted away from the world, yet, like Ferdinand, moved by voiceless music in the moonlight.

> "Come unto these yellow sands,
> And then take hands—
> Curtsied when you have, and list,
> (The wild waves whist,)
> Foot it featly here and there,
> And sweet sprites the burden bear.
> Hark, hark!
> The watch-dog's bark."

Such aerial witchery was in the night, for our Shakspeare was a Nile necromancer as well. Drifted beyond the world, yet not beyond the Poet. Flutes, too, were blown upon the shore, and horns and the chorus of a crew came sadly across the water with the faint throb of the tarabuka. Under those warm southern stars, was a sense of solitude and isolation. Might we not even behold the southern cross, when the clouds of Latakia rolled away? Our own crew were silent, but a belated boat struggling for a berth among our fleet, disturbed the slumbers of a neighboring crew. One sharp, fierce cackle of dispute suddenly shattered the silence like a tropical whirlwind, nor was it stiller by the blows mutually bestowed. Our chat of Bagdad and the desert was for a moment suspended. Nor did we wonder at the struggle, since Mars shone so redly over. But it died away as suddenly, and inexplicably mournful as the sphinx's smile, streamed the setting moonlight over the world. Not a ripple of Western feeling reached that repose. We were in the dream of the death of the deadest land.

VII.

The Landscape.

The Nile landscape is not monotonous, although of one general character. In that soft air the lines change constantly, but imperceptibly, and are always so delicately lined and drawn, that the eye swims satisfied along the warm tranquillity of the scenery.

Egypt is the valley of the Nile. At its widest part it is, perhaps, six or seven miles broad, and is walled upon the west by the Libyan mountains, and upon the east by the Arabian. The scenery is simple and grand. The forms of the landscape harmonize with the forms of the impression of Egypt in the mind. Solemn and still and inexplicable sits that antique mystery among the flowery fancies and broad green fertile feelings of your mind and contemporary life, as the sphinx sits upon the edge of the grain-green plain. No scenery is grander in its impression, for none is so symbolical. The land seems to have died with the race that made it famous—it is so solemnly still. Day after day unrolls to the eye the perpetual panorama of fields wide-waving with the tobacco, and glittering with the golden-blossomed cotton, among which half-naked men and women are lazily working. Palm-groves stand, each palm a poem, brimming your memory with beauty. You know from Sir Gardiner Wilkinson, whose volumes are here your best tutor, that you are passing the remains of ancient cities, as the Ibis loiters languidly before the rising and falling north wind, or is wearily drawn along by the crew filing along the shore. An occasional irregular reach of mounds and a bit of crumbling wall distract imagination as much with the future as the past, straining to realize the time when New York shall be an irregular reach of mounds, or a bit of crumbling wall.

Impossible? Possibly. But are we so loved of time, we petted youngest child, that the fate of his eldest gorgeous Asia, and Africa, its swart mysterious twin shall only frown at us through them and fly?

The austere Arabian mountains leave Cairo with us, and stretch in sad monotony of strength along the Eastern shore. There they shine sandily, the mighty advanced guard of the desert. "Here," say they, and plant their stern feet forever, and over their shoulders sweep and sing the low wild winds from mid Arabia, "sand-grains outnumbering all thy dear drops of water are behind us, to maintain our might and subdue thee, fond, fair river!"

But it glides unheeded at their base, lithely swinging its long unbroken phalanx of sweet water—waving gently against the immovable cliffs like palm branches of peace against a foe's serried front.

Presently the Libyan heights appear, and the river is invested. A sense of fate then spells you, and you feel that the two powers must measure their might at last, and go forward to the cataract with the feeling of one who shall behold terrible battles.

Yet the day, mindful only of beauty, lavishes all its light upon the mighty foes, adorning them each impartially for its own delight. Along the uniform Arabian highland, it swims and flashes, and fades in exquisite hues, magically making it the sapphire wall of that garden of imagination, which fertile Arabia is; or in the full gush of noon standing it along the eastern horizon as an image of those boundless deserts, which no man can conceive, more than the sea, until he beholds them.

But the advancing desert consumes cities of the river, so that fair fames of eldest history are now mere names. Even the perplexed river sweeps away its own, but reveals richer reaches of green land for the old lost, and Arabia and Lybia are foiled forever. Forever, for it must be as it has been, until the fertility of the tropics that floats seaward in the Nile, making the land of Egypt as it goes, is exhausted in its source.

But there is a profounder charm in the landscape, a beauty that grows more slowly into the mind, but is as perfect and permanent. Gradually the Howadji perceives the harmony of the epical, primitive, and grand character of the landscape, and the austere simplicity of the Egyptian art. Fresh from the galleries of Europe, it is not without awe that he glides far behind our known beginnings of civilization, and standing among its primeval forms, realizes the relation of nature and art.

There is no record of any thing like lyrical poetry in the history of the elder Egyptians. Their theology was the somber substance of their life. This fact of history the Howadji sees before he reads.

Nature is only epical here. She has no little lyrics of green groves, and blooming woods, and sequestered lanes—no lonely pastoral landscape. But from every point the Egyptian could behold the desert heights, and the river, and the sky. This grand and solemn Nature has imposed upon the art of the land, the law of its own being and beauty. Out of the landscape, too, springs the mystery of Egyptian character, and the character of its art. For silence is the spirit of these sand mountains, and of this sublime sweep of luminous sky—and silence is the mother of mystery. Primitive man so surrounded, can then do nothing but what is simple and grand. The pyramids reproduce the impression and the form of the landscape in which they stand. The pyramids say, in the Nature around them, "Man, his mark."

Later, he will be changed by a thousand influences, but can never escape the mystery that haunts his home, and will carve the Sphinx and the strange mystical Memnon. The Sphinx says to the Howadji what Egypt said to the Egyptian—and from the fascination of her face streams all the yearning, profound and pathetic power that is the soul of the Egyptian day.

So also from the moment the Arabian highlands appeared, we had in their lines and in the ever graceful and suggestive palms, the grand elements of Egyptian architecture. Often in a luminously blue day as the Howadji sits reading or musing before the cabin, the stratified sand mountain side, with a stately arcade of palms on the smooth green below, floats upon his eye through the serene sky as the ideal of that mighty Temple which Egyptian architecture struggles to realize—and he feels that he beholds the seed that flowered at last in the Parthenon and all Greek architecture.

The beginnings seem to have been, the sculpture of the hills into their own forms,—vast regular chambers cut in the rock or earth, vaulted like the sky that hung over the hills, and like that, starred with gold in a blue space.

From these came the erection of separate buildings—but always of the same grand and solemn character. In them the majesty of the mountain is repeated. Man cons the lesson which Nature has taught him.

Exquisite details follow. The fine flower-like forms and foliage that have arrested the quick sensitive eye of artistic genius, appear presently as ornaments of his work. Man as the master, and the symbol of power, stands calm with folded hands in the Osiride columns. Twisted water reeds and palms, whose flowing crests are natural capitals, are added. Then the lotus and acanthus are wreathed around the columns, and so the most delicate detail of the Egyptian landscape re-appeared in its art.

But Egyptian art never loses this character of solemn sublimity. It is not simply infancy, it was the law of its life. The art of Egypt never offered to emancipate itself from this character,—it changed only when strangers came.

Greece fulfilled Egypt. To the austere grandeur of simple natural forms, Greek art succeeded as the flower to foliage. The essential strength is retained, but an aerial grace and elegance, an exquisite elaboration followed; as Eve followed Adam. For Grecian temples have a fine feminineness of character when measured with the Egyptian. That hushed harmony of grace—even the snow-sparkling marble, and the general impression, have this difference.

Such hints are simple and obvious—and there is no fairer or more frequent flower upon these charmed shores, than the revelations they make of the simple naturalness of primitive art.

VIII.

Tracking.

Our angels of annunciation, this Christmas eve, were the crews of the boats at Benisoeth, the first important town upon the river. They blew pipes, not unlike those of the Pifferari in Rome, who come from the Abruzzi at the annunciation, and play before the Madonna shrines until her son is born. The evening was not too cool for us to smoke our chibouques on the upper deck. There in the gray moonlight too, Aboo Seyd was turned to Mecca, and genuflexing and ground-kissing to a degree that proved his hopeless sinfulness.

Courteous reader, that Christmas eve, for the first time the Howadji went to bed in Levinge's bag. It is a net, warranted to keep mosquitoes out, and the occupant in, and much recommended by those who have been persuaded to buy, and those who have them to sell. I struggled into mine, and was comfortable. But the Pacha of two shirt tails was in a trying situation. For this perplexing problem presented itself—the candle being extinguished to get in, or being in, to blow out the candle. "'Peace on earth' there may be," said the Pacha, holding with one hand the candlestick, and with the other the chimney of the bag, "but there is none upon the water," and he stood irresolute, until, placing the candlestick upon the floor, and struggling into the bag, as into an unwilling shirt, the hand was protruded—seized the candlestick, and Genius had cut the Gordian knot of Doubt.

A calm Christmas dawned. It was a day to dream of the rose-radiance that trembles over the Mountains of the Moon: a day to read Werne's White Nile Journal, with its hourly record of tropical life among the simple races of the Equator, and enchanting stories of acres of lotus bloom in Ethiopia. It was not difficult to fancy that we were following him, as we slid away from the shore and saw the half-naked people, the mud huts, and every sign of a race forever young.

We sprang ashore for a ramble, and the Pacha took his gun for a little bird-murder. Climbing the bank from the water we emerged upon the level plain covered with an endless mesh of flowering lupin. The palm-grove beckoned friendlily with its pleasant branches, through which the breath of the warm morning was whispering sweet secrets. I heard them. Fine Ear had not delicater senses than the Howadji may have in Egypt. I knew that the calm Christmas morning was toying with the subtle-winged Summer, under those palms—the Summer that had fled before me from Switzerland over the Italian vintage. Over my head was the dreamy murmurousness of summer insects swarming in the warm air. The grain was green, and the weeds were flowering at my feet. The repose of August weather brooded in the radiant sky. Whoso would follow the Summer will find her lingering and loitering under the palm-groves of the Nile, when she is only a remembrance and a hope upon the vineyards of the Rhine, and the gardens of the Hudson.

Aboo Seyd followed us, and we suddenly encountered a brace of unknown Howadji. They proved to be Frenchmen, and had each a gun. Why is a Frenchman so unsphered, out of Paris? They inquired for their boat with a tricolor, which we had not seen, and told us that there were wild boars in the palm-groves. Then they stalked away among the coarse, high, hilfeh grass, with both gun-barrels cocked. Presently the charge of one of them came rustling around our legs, through the grass. We hailed, and informed the hunters that we were pervious to shot. They protested and demanded many thousand pardons, then discovered their boat and embarked to breakfast, to recount over their Bordeaux the morning hunt of *sangliers* and *Anglais*, for one of which, they probably mistook us.

We returned too, and eat pomegranates, but went ashore again, for this was a tracking day—a day when there is no wind, but the boat is drawn a few miles by the crew. There was a village near us under the palms, and the village smoke, aerialized into delicate blue haze, made with the sunset a glowing atmosphere of gold and blue, in which a distant palm-grove stood like a dream of Faery. Querulous dogs were barking in the vicinity of the mud city, for it deserved that name, a chaos of mud huts and inclosures, built apparently at random, and full of an incredible squalor, too animal to be sad. The agile Gauls were plunging across the plain, scrambling up little hillocks with their cocked muskets, causing us rueful reflections upon the frailty of human legs. Pop-pop, went the desperadoes of hunters at the tame pigeons on the palms. We wended through the fields of sprouting beans. A few women and children lingered still, others were driving donkeys and buffaloes homeward—for these hard clay hovels were homes too.

I foresee that the Egyptian sunsets will shine much, too much, along these pages. But they are so beautiful, and every sunset is so new, that the Howadji must claim the law of lovers, and perpetually praise the old beauty forever young.

This evening the sun swept suddenly into the west, drawing the mists in a whirlpool after him. The vortex of luminous vapor gradually diffused itself over the whole sky, and the Ibis floated in a mist of gold, its slim yards and masts sculptured like Claude's vessels in his sunsets. It paled then, gradually, and a golden gloom began the night.

We emerged from the palms, on whose bending boughs doves sat and swung, and saw the gloom gradually graying over the genial Nile valley. As we neared the Ibis we met our third Mohammad, a smooth Nubian of the crew, and Seyd, the one-eyed first officer, whom the Commander had sent to search for us. They carried staves like beadles or like Roman consuls, for they were to see that we "took no detriment"—"for the dogs and the impudent people," said Golden-sleeve, with bodeful head-shakings.

Thou timorous Commander! Hath not the Pacha a one-barreled gun and tales innumerable? He said that Nero had passed the mud city only the night before. But did the moonlight show him what we saw—two Ibis perched, snowy white, upon the back of a buffalo?

Then, for the first time in their lives, the Howadji sat quietly smoking in the open air upon Christmas evening: but hunted no slipper, nor was misletoe hung in the cabin.

IX.

Flying.

The wind rose cheerly, the tricolor fluttered and dropped behind, and leaving all rivals, the eager Ibis ran wing and wing before the breeze.

The bold mountains did not cease to bully. Sometimes they receded a little, leaving spaces of level sand, as if the impatient desert behind had in some spots pressed over and beyond them ; but they drew out again quite to the stream, and rose sheerly in steep, caverned cliffs from the water, housing wild fowl innumerable, that shrieked and cried like birds of prey before the mighty legions.

Over these mountain shoulders, the winds not only sing, but bloated into storms and sudden tempests, they spring upon the leaning lateen sails that fly with eagerly pointing yards beneath, as if to revenge themselves upon the river, in the destruction of what it bears. Under the Aboofeyda and the Gebel Shekh Hereedee, and the Gebel Tookh, and wherever else the mountains pile their frowning fronts in precipices along the shore, are the dangers of Nile navigation.

A tranquil twilight breath wafted us beneath the first,

and another sunset breeze ran us dashingly toward the Shekh Hereedee. But just when the evening was darkest, a sudden gust sprang upon us from the mountain. It shook the fleet bold Ibis into trembling, but she succeeded in furling her larger wing, and struggling through she fled fast and forward in the dark, until under Orion in the zenith, and his silent society, she drew calmly to the shore, and dreamed all night of the serpent of Shekh Hereedee, who cured all woes but those of his own making.

Neither was the Gebel Tookh our friend. The mountainous regions are always gusty, and the Ibis had been squall-struck several times, but ran at last free and fair before the wind, between shores serene, on which we could hear the call of women to each other, and not seeing their faces, could fancy their beauty at will, and their worthiness to be nymphs of the Nile.

We were still slipping swiftly along under the foresail, and the minarets of Girgeh glittered on the southern horizon.

"Why not the mainsail," cried the Pacha, "in this lulling wind?"

The Ibis shook out her great wing, and stood across, bending with the river, straight toward the Gebel Tookh. She plowed the water into flashing foam-furrows as we swept on. The very landscape was sparkling and spirited for that exciting speed. The half human figures upon the shore paused to watch us as we passed. But in the dark gulf under the mountain, where, on the steep strip of shore, the Nile had flung down to its foe a gauntlet of green, the gale that lives in Arab tradition along those heights, like an awful Afreet, plunged suddenly upon us, and for a few moments the proud Ibis strained and quivered in its grasp.

The dark waves dashed foam-tipped against her side, and seethed with the swell of a small sea, as the Ibis spurned them and flew on. Behind, one solitary Cangie was struggling with a loosely flapping sail, through a narrow channel, and before us was the point, round which, once made, we should fly before the wind. It was clear that we had too much canvas for the pass. The crew squatted imbecile, wrapped in their blankets, and stared in stupid amazement at the cliff and the river. The ancient mariner, half crouching over the tiller, and showing his two surviving teeth to the gale, fastened his eye upon the boat and the river, while the wild wind danced about his drapery, fluttering all his rags, and howling with delight as it forced him to strain at his tiller, or with rage as it feared his mastery.

I did not observe that the Muslim were any more fatalists than the merest Christians. Mere Christians would have helped themselves a little, doubtless, and so would the Muslim, if they had known how to do it. Their resignation was not religion, but stupidity. The golden-sleeved Commander was evidently averse to a sloping deck, at least to slopes of so aggravated an angle ; and the crew were clearly wondering how infidels could rate their lives so justly as the Howadji did, in suggesting the mainsail at the very feet of the inexorable Gebel Tookh.

Twice the squall struck the Ibis, and twice pausing and shivering a moment, she stretched her wings again, and fled foamingly mad before it. Then she rounded the point, and passing a country boat fully laden with men and produce, lying to under a bank, drove on to Girgeh. The baffled gale retreated to its mountain cavern to lie in awful ambush for Nero, and the blue pennant, whom we had passed already—yes, O Osiris! possibly to hunt the hunting Messieurs, nor to let them off for their legs alone. Then the Ibis furled neatly and handsomely her wild wings before the minarets of Girgeh.

X.

Verde Ginnane and Fellow Mariners.

As we drift along, and the day paints its placid picture upon the eye, each sail shining in the distance, and fading beyond the palm-groved points, recalls our fellow-mariners. You may embark on the same day that others embark from Boulak, and be two months upon the Nile, yet never meet or only so rarely, as to make parting, sorrow. Yet as the charm of new impressions and thoughts is doubled by reflection in a friend's mind, you scan very curiously upon your arrival in Cairo, the groups who are to form the society of the River. Usually, however, you will come with one friend, nor care much for many others. Once in Egypt, you are so far removed from things familiar, that you wish to unsphere yourself entirely, to lose all trace of your own nationality, and to separate yourself from the past. In those dim, beautiful bazaars of Cairo, where all the wares of the most inventive imagination should be, you dream vaguely that some austere astrologer sitting cross-legged before his odorous crucibles, and breathing contemplative smoke, must needs be Icarian progeny, and can whisper the secret of those wings of the morning which shall bear you to the uttermost parts of the earth.

All things seem possible when you actually see the pyramids and palms. Persia is then very probable,—and you are willing to propose the Ganges as your next river voyage. Yet the first Cairo eve, as the Howadji sat in Shepherd's dining-room, that long large hall opening upon the balcony, of whose stability some are suspicious, which overhangs the Uzbeekeeyah,—massively foliaged with December-blooming acacias,—there as they sat tranquilly smoking chibouques, detecting an unwonted tendency in the legs to curl, and cross themselves upon the cushions, and inwardly congratulating themselves that at length they were oriental, a brisk little English officer suddenly spoke, and said—" When I was in the East." Heavens! the Howadji legs uncurled immediately, and the words shoved them deep into the West—" when I was in the East!"

" And *where* were you then, Major Pendennis?"

For it was plain to see that it was Major Pendennis—wearied of Pall Mall—and recruiting from the fatigues of Indian service in a little Western recreation in Syria and Egypt.

" Ah! my dear sir, it was when I was in Persia,"—and the worthy Major waxed warm in his tales of Persian life, especially of that horsemanship whereof Apollo seems to have been the God—so graceful, so poetic, so perfect is its character. But no listener, listened so lovingly and long, as Verde Giovane. I thought him a very young grandson of my elderly friend Bull. Verde was joyous and gay. He had already been to the pyramids, and had slept in a tomb, and had his pockets picked as he wandered through their disagreeable darkness. He had come freshly and fast from England, to see the world, omitting Paris and Western Europe on his way,—as he embarked at Southampton for Alexandria. Being in Cairo, he felt himself abroad. Sternhold and Hopkins were his Laureates, for perpetually on all kinds of wings of mighty winds he came flying all abroad. He lost a great deal of money at billiards to "jolly" fellows whom he afterward regaled with cold punch and choice cigars. He wrangled wildly with a dragoman of very imperfect English powers, and packed his tea for the voyage in brown paper parcels. He was perpetually on the point of leaving. At breakfast, he would take a loud leave of the "jolly" fellows, and if there were ladies in the room, he slung his gun in a very abandoned manner over his shoulder, and while he adjusted his shot-pouch with careless heroism, as if the enemy were in ambush on the stairs,—as who should say, "I'll do their business easily enough," he would remark with a meaning smile, that he should stop a day or two at Esne, probably, and then go off humming a song from the Favorita,—or an air whose words were well known to the jolly fellows, but would scarcely bear female criticism.

After this departure, he had a pleasant way of reappearing at the dinner-table, for the pale ale was not yet aboard, or the cook was ill, or there had been another explosion with the dragoman. Verde Giovane found the Cairene evenings "slow." It was astonishing how much execution he accomplished with those words of very moderate caliber, "slow," "jolly," and "stunning." The universe arranged itself in Verde Giovane's mind, under those three heads. Presently it was easy to predicate his criticisms in any department. He had lofty views of travel. Verde Giovane had come forth to see the world, and vainly might the world seek to be unseen. He wished to push on to Sennaar and Ethiopia. It was very slow to go only to the cataracts. Ordinary travel, and places already beheld of men, were not for Verde. But if there were any Chinese wall to be scaled, or the English standard were to be planted upon any vague and awful Himalayan height, or a new oasis were to be revealed in the desert of Sahara, here was the heaven-appointed Verde Giovane, only awaiting his pale ale, and determined to dally a little at Esne. After subduing the East by travel, he proposed to enter the Caucasian Mountains, and serve as a Russian officer. These things were pleasant to hear, as to behold at Christmas those terrible beheadings of giants by Tom Thumb, for you enjoyed a sweet sense of security and a consciousness that no harm was done. They were wild Arabian romances, attributable to the inspiration of the climate, in the city he found so slow. The Cairenes were listening elsewhere to their poets, Verde Giovane was ours; and we knew very well that he would go quietly up to the first cataract, and then returning to Alexandria, would steam to Jaffa, and thence donkey placidly to Jerusalem, moaning in his sleep of Cheapside and St. Paul's.

His chum, Gunning, was a brisk little barrister, dried up in the Temple like a small tart sapson. In the course of acquaintance with him, you stumbled surprised upon the remains of geniality and gentle culture, as you would upon Greek relics in Greenland. He was a victim of the Circe, Law, but not entirely unhumanized. Like the young king, he was half marble, but not all stony. Gunning's laugh was very ludicrous. It had no fun in it —no more sweetness than a crow's caw, and it sprang upon you suddenly and startling, like the breaking down of a cart overloaded with stones. He was very ugly and moody, and walked apart muttering to himself, and nervously grinning ghastly grins, so that Gunning was suspected of insanity—a suspicion that became certainty when he fringed his mouth with stiff black bristles, and went up the Nile with Verde Giovane.

For the little Verde did say a final farewell at last, and left the dining-room gayly and gallantly, as a stage bandit disappears down pasteboard rocks to desperate encounters with mugs of beer in the green-room.

XI.

Verde piu Giovane.

I KNEW at Cairo, too, another youth, whom I was sure was a Verde. I thought him brother of the good Verde Giovane, but he denied all relationship, although I am convinced he was at least first cousin. Possibly, you know not the modesty of the Indian Englishman.

It was in the same dining-room, and the youth was expatiating to Major Pendennis upon his braving the desert dangers from Suez, of his exploits of heroism, and endurance upon the Nile voyage, which he had already made, and was again projecting, and generally of things innumerable, and to lesser men insuperable, undergone or overborne.

"And up the Nile, too," said he, "I carried no bed, and slept upon the bench; over the desert I go with one camel, and she carries every thing. Why will men travel with such retinues, caring for their abominable comfort;" and the young gentleman ordered his nargileh.

"But, my dear sir," said Major Pendennis, "why rough it here upon the Nile? It is harder to do that than to go comfortably. You might as well rough it through England. The bottle, if you please."

"Why, Major," returned the youth, smiling in his turn, and crowding his body into his chair, so that the back of his head rested upon the chair-back, "it is well enough for some of you, but we poor East India subalterns! Besides, you know, Major, *discipline*—not only military, which is in our way, but moral. For what says the American poet, who, I doubt not, lives ascetically in some retired cave :

> "Know how sublime a thing it is
> To suffer and be strong."

So saying, the young man clapped his hands, and a Hindoo boy in his native costume appeared. The youth addressed some words to him in an unknown tongue, which produced no effect until he pointed to his nargileh, and rising at the same time, the slave removed the nargileh a few steps toward his master, who curled up his feet and prepared to suffer and be strong in the sofa corner.

By this time Galignani and the French news were entirely uninteresting to me. Who this was ?—this personage who modestly styled himself we "poor East India subalterns," and summoned Hindoo servants to turn round his nargileh, and hob-nobbed with Major Pendennises, and who suffered and was strong in such pleasant ways.

Major Pendennis shoving his chair a little back, said, "When I was in the East," and compared experience of travel with his young friend.

The Major, truly a gallant gentleman, related the Roman hardihood of those British officers who advance into the heart of Hindostan and penetrate to Persia, reclining upon cushioned camels, resting upon piles of Persian carpets on elevated frameworks under silken tents, surrounded by a shining society of servants and retinue, so that, to every effective officer, every roaring and rampant British Lion of this caliber, go eight or ten attendant supernumeraries, who wait upon his nargileh, coffee, sherbet, and pale ale, and care generally for his suffering and strength.

In the dim dining-room, I listened wondering to these wild tales of military hardship sung by a soldier-poet. I fancied as the periods swelled, that I heard the hoary historian reciting the sparkling romance of Xerxes' marches and the shining advance of Persian arms. But no sooner had the Major ceased his story, than " we poor East India subalterns" " took up the wondrous tale."

The Howadji weltered then in a whirlpool of brilliant confusion. Names of fair fame bubbled up from the level tone of his speech, like sudden sun-seeking fountains from bloom-matted plains. I heard Bagdad, Damascus, Sinai, and farther and fairer, the Arabian Gulf, Pearls and Circassians. I knew that he was telling of where he had been, or might have been, or wished to have been. The rich romance reeled on. The fragrant smoke curled in heavier clouds. I felt that my experience was like a babe unborn, beside that of this mighty man, who knew several things, and had brushed the bloom from life with the idle sweep of his wings, and now tossed us the dull rind for our admiring.

The silence of the room was only more rapt by his voice meshing about our attention its folds of fascination, when the good Verde Giovane, who sat next to me, and who, I fear, was not lending that length of admiring ears, of which he was certainly capable, suddenly asked the subaltern, "Pray, is the tobacco you are smoking—"

"Pardon me, sir, this is not tobacco. I am smoking coffee leaves."

Unhappy Giovane! The subaltern looked upon him with eyes that said, "Unworthy fellow-countryman, do you imagine that men live a brace of years in the H. E. I. C.'s service and then smoke tobacco—talk of Arabia and pearls, and yet smoke tobacco—of Circassians and Lahore, and still smoke tobacco?"

In the amazement of that interruption the last whiff of the smoke of coffee leaves curled scornfully away over Giovane's diminished head. Hands were clapped again, servants appeared and replaced with a chibouque the Persian nargileh of the disciplinarian.

The mere American Howadji was fascinated with the extent and variety of knowledge acquired by the "poor subalterns." "Never," mused he, in a certain querulousness of spirit, "never, until we too have an H. E. I. C., can we hope to rear such youths as this. Happy country, imperial England, that at home fosters young men like my excellent Verde Giovane, and in distant India, a race of Verdes, piu Giovane.

The "poor subaltern" gradually melted, and at length even smiled benignly upon Giovane, as he suddenly clapped his hands again and summoned the Hindoo. "Mr. Verde, do you smoke paper?" inquired he.

"No—why—yes, I should be very happy," replied the appalled Giovane, who told me later, that he considered the subaltern a right "jolly" fellow, with a "stunning" way with him, in which latter half of praise I was entirely of Verde's opinion.

Turning to his servant, the youth said something probably in refined Hindostanee, which the boy, speaking only a patois, of course could not understand. But "make a cigarette" in pure English, resembled his patois to that degree that he understood at once, and rolled the cigarette, which the youth handed to Giovane with an air of majestic forgiveness, and then taking a candle, he left the room, wishing us good night, as who should say, "My Lords, farewell;" leaving the party still as champagne when the gas has bubbled briskly away.

And yet, with that unmistakable family likeness, he could deny that he was of the great Verde family!

The mental shock of subsiding into my own thoughts, at once, after that evening would have been too much. I therefore sought to let myself down by delicate degrees, and thinking that I had seized a volume of Hafiz, I stepped upon the balcony to read by moonlight songs of love and wine. But I found that I had a natural history by an unknown Arabian author. My finger was on this passage—

"This is a species of the John Bull which now for the

first time falls under the author's observation. Great is Allah and Mohammad his prophet for these new revelations. I am told," he continues, "that it is not uncommon in the mother country. It is there gregarious in its habits, and found in flocks in the thickets of Regent and Oxford streets, in the paddock of Pall Mall, and usually in any large herd of Bulls.

"Its horns are enormous and threatening, but very flexible and harmless. Its ears and tail are of uncommon length, but adroitly concealed, and it comes to luxuriant perfection in the southern parts of India, and in fact, wherever the old herds obtain a footing.

"It is very frisky and amusing, and delights to run at the spectator with its great horns branching. If he is panic-stricken and flies, the Bull pursues him roaring like a mighty lion, and with such energy, that the more ingenious naturalists suppose, that for the moment, the animal really fancies his horns to be hard and pointed, and serviceable. If, however, the spectator turns, and boldly takes the animal by the horns, they will bend quite down—in fact, with a little squeezing will entirely disappear, and the meek-faced Bull will roar you as gently as any sucking dove."

Nor wonder at such figures in our Nile picture, for here are contrasts more profound, lights lighter and shadows more shaded, than in our better balanced West. Believe that you more truly feel the picturesqueness of that turban and that garb moving along the shore, because Verde Giovane's "wide-awake" and checked shooting-jacket are hard before us. We overhauled them one afternoon, and while Verde Giovane stood in a flat cap and his hands in the shooting-jacket's pocket, and told us that Nero was just ahead and in sight that morning, Gunning suddenly sprang upon deck, blew off his two barrels, laughed hysterically, and glaring full at us, we saw—O Dolland! that he had succumbed to blue spectacles.

XII.

Asyoot.

SHERBET OF ROSES in a fountained kiosk of Damascus can alone be more utterly oriental to the imagination and sense than the first interior view of many-minareted Asyoot.

Breathe here, and reflect that Asyoot is a squalid mud town, and perceiving that, and the other too, as you must needs do when you are there, believe in magic for evermore.

Under Aboofeyda, from the dragoman of a Dahabieh whose Howadji were in the small boat shooting ducks and waking all the wild echoes of the cliffs, we had heard of Nero just ahead, again, and had left Verde and Gunning far behind. As the Ibis flew on with favoring gales, the river became more and more winding, and the minarets of Asyoot were near across the land, long before the river reached the port of the town. Rounding one of the points we descried two boats ahead, and we could at length distinguish the Italian tricolor of Nero. His companion bore an immensely blue pennant that floated in great bellying folds upon the wind, like a huge serpent. Suddenly we came directly into the wind and threw the men ashore to track along a fine bank of acacias. This passed, we saw the blue pennant standing across into the reach of the stream that stretches straight to Asyoot, and a few moments after Nero emerged and strained canvas after, and we, piling in our men as soon as possible, drew round, with the wind upon our quarter, in hot pursuit. The Ibis had not time to win a victory so sure, for Nero's "Kid" frisked by the proud pennant, and mooring first to the bank, was quiet as the dozing donkeys on the shore, by the time that the Ibis touched the bank, and the Howadji landed under a salute of one gun from the Kid. Salutatory Nero had an arsenal on board, but in that hour, only one gun would go.

We were yet a mile or two from the town, which lies inland, and we took our way across the fields in which a few of the faithful stared sedately upon the green-vailed Nera, by whose side rode the Pacha,—Nero and I, and a running rabble of many colors, bringing up the rear. Herons floated snowily about the green, woodpeckers, sparrows, and birds of sunset plumage, darted and fluttered over the fields, deluged with the sunlight; and under a gate of Saracenic arch, heralded by the golden-sleeved Commander, we entered a cool shady square.

It was the court of the Pacha's palace, the chief entrance of the town. A low stone bench ran along the base of the glaring white walls of the houses upon the square, whose windows were screened by blinds, as dark as the walls were white, and sitting, and lounging upon this bench, groups of figures,—smoking, sipping coffee, arrayed in gorgeous stuffs—for there in sober sadness was the court circle, with the long beards flowing from the impassible dark faces,—gazed with serious sweet Arabian eyes upon the Howadji. The ground was a hard smooth clay floor, and an arcade of acacias on either hand, walled and arched with grateful cool green, the picturesque repose of the scene.

This was a small square, and faded upon the eye, forever daguerreotyped on the memory, as we passed over a bridge by a Shekh's tomb, a mound of white plaster, while under an arch between glaring white walls, stood a vailed woman with a high water jar upon her head.

Threading the town, which is built entirely of the dark mud brick, we emerged upon the plain between the houses and the mountains. Before us a funeral procession was moving to the tombs, and the shrill, melancholy cry of the wailers rang fitfully upon the low gusts that wailed more grievously, and for a sadder sorrow. We could not overtake the procession, but saw it disappear among the white domes of the cemetery, as we began to climb the hills to the caves—temples, I might say, for their tombs are temples who reverence the dead, and these were built with a temple grandeur by a race who honored the forms that life had honored, beyond the tradition or conception of any other people. Great truths, like the Gods, have no country or age, and over these ancient Egyptian portals might have been carved the saying of the modern German Novalis, the body of man is the temple of God.

These tombs of Stabl Antar, are chambers quarried in

the rock. They are not vast, only, but stately. The elevation of the entrances and the proportion of the chambers are full of character. The entrance is not merely a way to get in, but attracts the eye by its grand solemn loftiness. It harmonizes in sentiment with the figures sculptured upon its side—those mysterious high-shouldered profile figures, whose secret is hidden forever. The caves do not reach far into the hills, and there are square pits at intervals upon the ground which the donkey boys called baths. Haply without authority.

About these caves are many bones, and a few mummied human members, whereover many Nile poets wax melodious. Eliot Warburton speaks of "the plump arms of infancy,"—O poet Eliot, were they plump when you saw them? When your pen slipped smoothly into that sentence, were you not dreaming of those Egyptian days, when doubtless babes were plump, and mothers fair, or had you clearly in your eye that shrunken, blackened, shapeless and unhuman mummied hand or foot, that your one-eyed donkey boy held in his hand? We must after all confess, O Eliot, that three-thousand-yeared mummied maidens and Verde Giovanes of yesterday are not poetic, though upon the Nile.

There is a broad platform in front of the caves, overlooking the valley of the river, the few white tombs of shekhs, which dot the solitary places and the town below with palms and acacias, and the slim minarets spiring silverly and strangely from the undefined dark mass of mud houses. The Arabian mountain line, stretched straightly and sadly into the southern horizon. Was it the day or the place, was it some antique ghost haunting its old haunts mournfully, and charming us with its presence, that made that broad, luxuriant landscape, with its endless dower of spots and objects of fame, so sad?

Yet, if ghost it were, Verde Giovane laid him—Verde and Gunning mounting breathlessly on donkeys, with handkerchiefs tied around their wide-awakes, or slouch-hats, to "do" the Stabl Antar. The donkey-boys chewed sugar-cane as they clucked and chirruped us back to the city, we, galloping riotously over the plain, but gliding slowly through the streets, wondering if every woman were not the Princess of China—though which Howadji was the Prince of Persia? The city was simply an illuminated chapter of the Arabian Nights. The people were doing just what they do there, sitting in the same shops in the same dresses, the same inscriptions from the Koran straggled about the walls, blurred, defaced, and dim—too much, I fear me, as the morals of the Koran straggle about Mohammadan brains. There were water-carriers, and fruit-carriers, and bread-carriers. The dark turbaned Copt, the wily eyed Turk, the sad-eyed swarthy Egyptian, half curious, half careless, smoking, sipping, quarreling, cross-legged, parboiled, and indolent.

Through the narrow bazaar pressed demure donkeys, with panniers pregnant of weeds and waste. Camels, with calm contemptuous eyes, swung their heads over all others, and trod on no naked feet in the throng with their own huge, soft, spongy pedals. Little children straddled the maternal right shoulder, and rode triumphant over turbaned men, unabashed by the impending camels. The throng was immense, but no sense of rush or hurry heated the mind. There was a constant murmur, but that and the cool shade were only the sound and the atmosphere of the Arabian Nights.

We stepped into smaller side passages—veins leading to the great artery of the bazaar—where, through some open door, the still, bright court of a Mosque was revealed, like the calm face of a virgin. In one niche stood a child so handsome, with eyes that were not devoured by flies, but round and softly lashed, and very deep and tender, that I began to feel that, after all, I might be the Prince of Persia.

Yet it was strange how the scene separated itself from the actors. They were essential as picturesque objects, but slovenly, ugly, and repugnant as fellow-men. The East, like the natures which it symbolizes, is a splendid excess. There is no measure, no moderation in its richness and beauty, or in its squalor and woe. The crocodile looks out from a lotus bank, the snake coils in the corner of the hareem, and a servant who seems slave from the soul out, conducts you to the most dream-like beautiful of women. So, as we sauntered through the bazaar of Asyoot, we passed the figures of men with no trace of manliness, but with faces full of inanity and vice. The impression would be profoundly sad, if you could feel their humanity. But they are so much below the lowest level known to a Western, that they disappear from sympathy.

Then suddenly passes a face like a vision, and your eyes turn, fascinated, to follow, as if they had seen the realized perfection of an ideal beauty.

Oriental masculine beauty is so mild and feminine, that the men are like statues of men seen in the most mellowing and azure atmosphere. The forms of the face have a surprising grace and perfection. They are not statues of heroes and gods so seen, but the budding beauty of Antinous, when he, too, had been in this soft climate, the ripening, rounding lip, the arched brow, the heavy drooping lid, the crushed closed eye, like a bud bursting with voluptuous beauty, the low broad brow; these I remember at Asyoot, and remember forever. There is nothing Western comparable with this. Some Spanish and Italian faces suggest it. But they lack the mellow harmony of hue and form. Western beauty is intellectual, but intellect has no share in this oriental charm. It is in kind the same superiority which the glowing voluptuousness of color of the Venetian school of painting, in which form is secondary and subdued, has over the serenity of the Roman and Tuscan schools, which worship form. And, according as a man is born with an Eastern or Western nature, will he prefer this or that beauty. The truest thing in Byron was his great oriental tendency. Men of profoundly passionate natures, instinctively crave the East, or must surround themselves with an Eastern atmosphere and influence. The face of every handsome Oriental is the face of a passionate poet in repose, and if you have in yourself the key of the mystery, you will perceive poems there that never have been and never can be written, more than the sad sweet strength of the Sphinx's beauty can be described. Yet, young yearner for the East, do not fancy that you shall always walk glorious among silent poets when you touch that land, so golden-shored and houri-peopled in our cold imaginations. The handsome of whom I speak, are rare as poets are.

Not only will you find the faces revolting, but the body is maimed to a frightful degree. Every second man lacks an eye or forefinger, or he is entirely blind. The Egyptians maimed themselves to escape Mohammad Alee's conscription. Seyd, the first officer of the Ibis, as we have seen, had put out his right eye, that he might have no aim, others chop off their forefinger, that they may not pull a trigger.

But more than all disgusting, is the sight of flies feeding upon the acrid humors that exude from diseased eyes; a misery that multiplies itself. The natives believe that to wash this away will produce blindness. So it remains, and nine tenths of the young children whom you pass, are covered, like carrion, with the pertinacious flies, so that your own eyes water, though the children seem not to heed it. Thus accustomed to that point and that food, the fly makes directly for the eye upon every new face that he explores, not without vivid visions to the proprietor, of imported virus, borne by these loathsome bees of disease.

We tasted sweets at a Turkish Greybeard's—a fire-worshiper, I doubt not, from the intense twinkling redness of his mole eyes; then through the slave market—

empty, for the caravan from Darfour was not yet arrived; then went on to the bath and were happy.

Yet, while we lie turbaned and luxurious upon these cushions of the Bagnio, inhaling the pleasant tobacco of these lands, fancy for a moment our sensations, when, in the otiose parboiled state, we raised vague eyes through the reeking warm mist of the Sudarium, and beheld Verde Giovane, gazing semi-scornfully through the door! To the otiose parboiled, however, succeeds the saponaceous state, in which all merely human emotion slips smoothly away.

The crew returned at midnight to the Ibis, and tumbled their newly-baked bread upon the deck over our heads, with a confused shouting and scramble, in the midst of which I heard the gurgling water, and knew that the famed Lycopolis of old Greece (why "upstart Greeks," Poet Harriet?) was now set away as a choice bit of memory, which no beautiful Damascus, nor storied Cairo, could displace, although they might surpass.

But while the Ibis spreads her wings southward under the stars, let us recall and believe the fair tradition that makes many-minareted Asyoot the refuge of Mary and her child, during the reign of Herod. So is each lovely landscape adorned with tales so fair, that the whole land is like a solemn-browed Isis, radiantly jeweled.

XIII.

The Sun.

THE sun is the secret of the East. There seems to be no light elsewhere. Italy simply preludes the Orient. Sorrento is near the secret. Sicily is like its hand stretched forth over the sea. Their sunsets and dreamy days are delicious. You may well read Hafiz in the odorous orange darkness of Sorrento, and believe that the lustrous leaves languidly moving over you, are palms yielding to the wooing of Arabian winds. The song of the Syrens, heard by you at evening, from these rocks, as you linger along the shore, is the same that Ulysses heard, seductive sweet, the same that Hadrian must have leaned to hear, as he swept, silken-sailed, eastward, as if he had not more than possible Eastern conquest in his young Antinous!

But the secret sweetness of that song is to you what it was to Ulysses. Son of the East, it sang to him his native language, and he longed to remain. Son of the West, tarry not thou for that sweet singing, but push bravely on and land where the song is realized.

The East is a voluptuous reverie of nature. Its Egyptian days are perfect. You breathe the sunlight. You feel it warm in your lungs and heart. The whole system absorbs sunshine, and all your views of life become warmly and richly voluptuous. Your day-dreams rise, splendid with sun-sparkling aerial architecture. Stories are told, songs are sung in your mind, and the scenery of each, and the persons, are such as is Damascus seen at morning from the Salaheeyah, or Sala-ed-Deen, heroic and graceful, in the rosy light of chivalric tradition.

The Egyptian sun does not glare, it shines. The light has a creamy quality, soft and mellow, as distinguished from the intense whiteness of our American light. The forms of our landscape stand sharp and severe in the atmosphere, like frost-work. But the Eastern outlines are smoothed and softened. The sun is the Mediator, and blends beautifully the separate beauties of the landscape. It melts the sterner stuff of your nature. The intellect is thawed and mellowed. Emotions take the place of thought. Sense rises into the sphere of soul. It becomes so exquisite and refined, that the old landmarks in the moral world begin to totter and dance. They remain nowhere, they have no permanent place. Delight and satisfaction, which are not sensual, but sensuous, become the law of your being; conscience, lulled all the way from Sicily in the soft rocking lap of the Mediterranean, falls quite asleep at Cairo, and you take your chance with the other flowers. The thoughts that try to come, masque no more as austere and sad-browed men, but pass as large-eyed, dusky maidens, now, with fair folding arms that fascinate you to their embrace. Even old thoughts throng to you in this glowing guise. The Howadji feels once more, how the Nile flows behind history, and he glides gently into the rear of all modern developments, and stands in the pure presence of primitive feeling—perceives the naturalness of the world's first worship, and is an antique Arabian, a devotee of the sun, "as he sails, as he sails."

For sun-worship is an instinct of the earliest races. The sun and stars are the first great friends of man. By the one he directs his movements, by the light of the other, he gathers the fruit its warmth has ripened. Gratitude is natural to the youth, and he adores where he loves—and of the God of the last and wisest faith, the sun is still the symbol.

This sun shines again in the brilliance of the colors the Easterns love. The sculptures upon the old tombs and temples, are of the most positive colors—red, blue, yellow, green and black, were the colors of the old Egyptians—and still the instinct is the same in their costume. The poetic Howadji would fancy they had studied the beauty of rainbows against dark clouds. For golden and gay are the turbans wreathed around their dusky brows, and figures—the very people of poetry—of which Titian and Paul divinely dreamed, but could never paint, sit forever in crimson turbans—yellow, blue and white robes with red slippers crossed under them, languidly breathing smoke over Abana and Parphar, rivers of Damascus. And the buildings in which they sit, the walls of baths and cafés and mosques, are painted in the same gorgeous taste, with broad bars of red and blue, and white. Over all this brilliance streams the intense sunshine, and completes what itself suggested. So warm, so glowing, and rich is the universal light and atmosphere, that any thing less than this in architecture would be unnatural. Strange and imperfect as it is, you feel the heart of nature throbbing all through Eastern art. Art there follows the plainest hints of nature in costume and architecture now, as in the antique architecture. The fault of oriental art springs from the very excess, which is the universal law of Eastern life. It is the apparent attempt to say more than is sayable. In the infinite and exquisite elaborations of Arabian architecture, there is the evident effort to realize all the subtle and strange whims of a luxuriously inspired imagination; and hence results an art that lacks large features and character, like the work of a man who loves the details of his dreams.

The child's faith that the East lies nearer the rising sun is absurd until you are there. Then you feel that it was his first born and inherits the elder share of his love and influence. Wherever your eye falls it sees the sun and the sun's suggestion. Egypt lies hard against its heart. But the sun is like other fathers, and his eldest is spoiled.

As you sweep sun-tranced up the river, the strongest, most distinct desire of being an artist, is born of silence and the sun. So saturated are you with light and color, that they would seem to flow unaided from the brush. But not so readily, importunate reader, from the pen. Words are worsted by the East. *Chiaro 'scuro* will not give it. A man must be very cunning to persuade his pen to reveal those secrets. But, an artist, I would tarry and worship a while in the temples of Italy, then hurry across the sea into the presence of the power there adored. There I should find that Claude was truly a consecrated priest. For this silence and sun breathe beauty along his canvas. His pictures are more than Italian, more than the real sunset from the Pincio, for they are ideal Italy which bends over the Nile and fulfills the South. The cluster of boats with gay streamers at Luxor, and the turbaned groups under the temple columns on the shore, do justify those sunset dreams of Claude Lorraine, that stately architecture upon the sea.

I was lost in a sun-dream one afternoon, wondering if, Saturn-like, the sun would not one day utterly consume his child, when I heard the Commander exclaim, "El Karnak!" much as Columbus might have heard "land" from his mast-head.

"There," said the Commander; and I could scarcely believe such a confirmation of my dreams of palm architecture, as my eye followed the pointing of his finger to a dim, distant point.

"Those?" said I.

"Those," said he.

I looked again with the glass and beheld, solitary and stately upon the distant shore, a company of most undoubted trees! The Pacha was smiling at my side, and declaring that he saw some very fine palms. The Commander looked again, confessed his mistake, and in extenuation, I remarked that he was not golden-sleeved. And, after all, what was Alà-ed-deen, if Mr. Lane will spell it so, without his lamp?

A few moments after, a small boat drew up to us and an Emerald Howadji stepped on board. He had left Thebes at two o'clock, which sounded strangely to me when he said it, for I fancied Thebes already to have done with time, and become the property of eternity. He coffeed and smoked, and would leave a duck for dinner, gave us all the last news from Thebes, then shook hands and went over the side of the Ibis, and out of our knowledge forever.

Bon voyage, Emerald Howadji, and as he pulled rapidly away with the flowing stream toward his descending Dahabieh, he fired at a heron that was streaming whitely over him across the stream, a parting salute, possibly, and the dead heron streamed whitely after him upon the river.

XIV.

Thebes Triumphant.

THE warm vaporous evening gathered, and we moored in a broad, beautiful bay of the river. Far inland over the shore, the mountain lines differently dark, waved away into the night. There were no masts upon the river but our own, and only one neighboring Sakia moaned to the twilight. Groups of turbaned figures crouched upon the bank. They looked as immovable forms of the landscape as the trees. Molded of mystery, they sat like spirits of the dead land personified. In the south, the Libyan mountains came to the river, vague and dim, stealthily approaching, like the shy monsters of the desert. The eye could not escape the fascination of those fading forms, for those mountains overhung Thebes.

Moored under the palm-trees in the gray beginnings of the evening, by the sad mud huts and the squalid Fellah, and within the spell of the sighing Sakia, I remembered Thebes and felt an outcast of time.

A world died before our history was born. The pomp and splendor had passed along—the sounds that were the words of a great life had swept forward into silence, and I lingered in the wake of splendor, like a drowning child behind a ship, feeling it fade away. I remembered the West too, and its budding life, its future, an unrolled heaven of new constellations. But it was only a dream dizzying the brain, as a man, thirst-stricken, dreams of flowing waters. Here for the first time, probably the only time of a life, I felt the grandeur and reality of the past preponderate over all time. It was the success of Egypt and the East. A fading, visionary triumph, as of a dumb slave who wins for a single night the preference of her master.

But in that mountain shadow sat Memnon, darling of the dawn, drawing reverence backward to the morning of Time. I felt the presence of his land and age, sitting solemn, saddening but successful, in the hush of my mind, as he sat, marvelous, but melodious no longer, rapt in the twilight repose. It was not a permanent feeling. The ever young stars looked out, and smiled away antiquity as a vapor. They who have visions of the dead floating fair in their old beauty and power, do not see them so always, probably never again. They repair like all men to their tombs, and dream vaguely of the departed. But those tombs are temples to them, forever after.

XV.

The Crocodile.

> " Where naked boys, bridling tame water snakes,
> Or charioteering ghastly alligators,
> Had left on the sweet waters mighty wakes
> Of those huge forms———"

DAY and night the Ibis did not rest, except when the wind fell, and her wings fell with it. She passed Dendereh—Thebes—Luxor. A light breeze wafted her along, and those sites of fame grew fair and faded, like pictures on the air. The upward Nile voyage is a Barmecide feast. You do not pause, except at Asyoot for the crew to bake bread, and at Esne, dear to Verde Giovane—so you enjoy the great fames and places by name only; as Shacabac, the Barber's sixth brother, delighted in the sweet bread, and the chicken stuffed with pistachio, and the golden cups of wine, although they did not appear until he had rehearsed his emotions. So finally, you, having partaken the Barmecide feast of the ascent, and passed Memphis—Abydos—Dendereh—Edfoo, and Kalabsheh, clap your hands at Aboo Simbel, and returning—taste the reality of Egypt.

But we were to stop at Esne, for another bread-baking

for the crew. There was an unwonted display of fine raiment as the afternoon waned—coarse hempen blankets gave place to blue cotton kaftans—the same that the female Bull insisted upon calling Nightgowns. Under these, the white vest, with the row of close set buttons, was not unhandsome. But when the ample turban went round the head—how great was that glory! With horror I beheld Seyd contemplating his slippers, and thence knew that Esne was a place of especial importance.

Strange is the magic of a turban. Eastern garments are always graceful, and truly the turban is the crown of grace, and honored as the protector of the human head should be. There are fashions and colors, in turbans. The Turkish is heavy and round—the Syrian broad and flat, roll outside roll of rich Cashmere. A special chair is consecrated to the repose of the turban—and losing the substance in the form, when an irreverent donkey threw a Shekh of dignity into the dirt, and among the camel legs of a bazaar, causing him to shed his turban in tumbling, the reverent crowd eagerly pursued the turban, and rescuing it, bore it with care in their hands, shouting "lift up the crown of El Islam"—while the poor neglected Shekh angrily cried from the dirt, "lift up the *Shekh* of El Islam." The lords of the land, and the luxurious, wreathe around their heads Cashmere shawls of texture so delicate, that they may be drawn through a thin signet ring, yet they are as full, and rich upon the head, as the forms of sunset clouds whose brilliance they emulate.

This day before Esne, Abdallah, our Samsonian Abdallah, sat glorious in the sunset in an incredible turban. He was not used to wear one, content on ordinary days with a cap that had been white. At first, as if to break his head gently into the unaccustomed luxury, I saw him sitting upon the boatside very solemnly—his brows cinctured with what seemed to be a mighty length of dish-clout. I fancied that having assisted at the washing of the dishes, he had wreathed his brows triumphantly with the clouts, as Indian warriors girdle themselves with scalps. But presently stationing the weasen-faced crew's cook near the mainmast, with one end of a portentously long white robe of cotton, he posted himself with the other end by the foremast, and then gradually drew the boy toward him, as he turned his head like a crank, and so wound himself up with glory. Afterward I saw him moving with solemn cautiousness, and with his hands ready—as if he were the merest trifle top-heavy. Fate paints what it will upon the canvas of memory, and I must forever see the great, gawky, dog-faithful, abused Samsonian Abdallah, sitting turbaned on the boatside in the sunset.

"A crocodile," shouted the Commander. And the Howadji saw for the first time the pet monster of the Nile.

He lay upon a sunny sand shore, at our right, a hideous, horrible monster—a scaled nightmare upon the day. He was at least twenty feet long; but seeing the Ibis with fleet wings running, he slipped, slowly soughing, head foremost and leisurely, into the river.

It was the first blight upon the beauty of the Nile. The squalid people were at least picturesque, with their costume and water-jars on the shore. But this mole-eyed, dragon-tailed abomination, who is often seen by the same picturesque people, sluggishly devouring a grandam or child on the inaccessible opposite bank, was utterly loathsome. Yet he too had his romantic side, the scaly nightmare! so exquisite and perfect are the compensations of nature. For if, in the perpetual presence of forms and climate so beautiful, and the feeling of a life so intense as the Egyptian, there is the constant feeling that the shadow must be as deep as the sun is bright, and that weeds must foully flaunt where flowers are fairest; so, when the shadow sloped and the weed was seen, they had their own suggestions of an opposite grace, and in this loathsome spawn of slime and mystic waters, it was plain to see the Dragon of oriental romance. Had the Howadji followed this feeling and penetrated to Buto, they might have seen Sinbad's valley. For there Herodotus saw the bones of winged snakes, as the Arabians called them. These, without doubt, were the bones of serpents, which, being seized by birds and borne aloft, seemed to the astonished people to be serpents flying, and were incorporated into the Arabian romances as worthy wonders.

The Pacha felt very like St. George, and longed to destroy the dragon; but having neither sword, spear, nor shield—only that trusty one-barreled gun, and no jolly-boat (I understood then why all our English friends have that boat), he was obliged to see the enemy slinking untouched into the stream, and relieve his mind by rehearsing to me the true method of ending dragons—opportunity and means *volentibus*. You do not see the crocodile without a sense of neighborhood to the old Egyptians, for they are the only live relics of that dead time, and Ramses the Great saw them sprawled on the sunny sand as Howadji the Little sees them to-day.

The crocodile was not universally honored. In Lower Egypt was it especially sacred, and it was buried with dead kings in the labyrinth—too sacred in death even for Herodotus to see—and doubtless quite as much to our advantage unseen by him, for had he been admitted to the tombs, our reverent and reverend father would probably have "preferred" to say nothing about them.

In some regions, however, there were regular crocodile hunts, and the prey was eaten—a proceeding necessarily so disgusting to the devotees of the dragon, that they were obliged to declare war against the impious, and endeavor to inhibit absolutely the consumption of crocodile chops. They did not regard Dragon himself as a God, but as sacred to the God Savak, who was crocodile-headed, and a deified form of the sun.

For, in the city of crocodiles, founded gratefully by King Menas, whom a crocodile ferried over the lake Mœnis upon his back, when the disloyal hunting-hounds drove royalty into the water, was a crocodile so sacred, that it was kept separately in an especial lake, and suffered the touching of the priests, with a probable view to touching them effectually on some apt occasion. This was the crocodile Sachus, says Sir Gardner, quoting Strabo, and Strabo's host, a man of mark—"one of our most distinguished citizens" in the city of crocodiles—showed him and his friends the sacred curiosities, conducting them to the brink of the lake, on whose bank the animal was extended. While some of the priests opened its mouth, one put in the cake, and then the meat, after which the wine was poured in. The crocodile then dived and lounged to the other side of the lake for a similar lunch, offered by another stranger. It has no tongue, says Plutarch, speaking through Sir Gardiner, and is therefore regarded as an image of the Deity itself—"the divine reason needing not speech, but going through still and silent paths, while it administers the world with justice."

Who shall say that the Egyptians of old were not poets? The ears of crocodiles were decked with ear-rings, and the fore feet with bracelets. They loved life too well, those elder brethren of ours, to suffer any refuse in their world. As with children, every thing was excellent and dear. If they hated, they hated with Johnsonian vigor, and which of the Persian poets is it who says that hate is only love inverted? Nor revile their animal worship, since they did not make all Dragons Gods, but had always some sentiment of gratitude and reverence in the feeling which consecrated any animal. There were but four animals universally sacred—the Ibis, Hawk, Cynocephalus and Apis.

Animal worship was only a more extended and less poetic Manicheism. Simple shepherds loved the stars and worshiped them. But shepherds lose their simplicity in towns, and their poetic worship goes out through prose to a machinery of forms. The distance from the Arabian worship of stars to the mystic theology of Egypt, is no greater than from the Syrian simplicity of Jesus Christ to the dusky dogmas of Rome or Geneva.

But what right have our pages to such names as Apis and Cynocephalus? The symmetry, not the significance of hieroglyphs, is the shrine of our worship. Feebly flies the Ibis while the sun sets in a palm-grove, and long sad vapors, dashed with dying light, drift and sweep formlessly through the blue, like Ossianic ghosts about a dying hero, who wail by waving mournfully their flexile length. The Reis beat the tarabuka. Abdallah blew the arghool, a reedy pipe that I dreamed might draw Pan himself to the shore, or a nymph to float in a barque of moon-pearled lotus, across the calm. Aboo Seyd clinked the castanets, and the crew sang plaintively, clapping their hands. So we slid into Esne, and as the Ibis nestled in the starlight to the shore, she shook poor little lithe Congo from her wing. He fell with a cry and a heavy plunge upon the deck. The Howadji ran forward, but found no bones broken, only cuts and bumps, and bruises, which the Pacha knew how to treat. The crew shook doleful heads, and were sure that it was the work of the evil eye—the glance of envy cast upon the Ibis by a neighboring dragoman, when he heard that she was only eighteen days from Cairo. Congo was brought to the rear and laid upon a matress and cushions. All that Pachalic skill could do was done, and you, ye Indian youths and maidens, sages and hags of the West, sing to the sleeping Congo, the Pacha's salvatory successes.

I saw dimly a mud town, and on the bank under a plane-tree a little hut, yclept by the luxurious Orientals, coffee-shop. Thither, being robed with due magnificence, the Commander proceeded, and bestowed the blessing of the golden-sleeved bournouse upon the undeserving Esnians.

XVI.

Getting Ashore.

GREAT is travel! Yesterday Memnon, to-day a crocodile, to-morrow dancing-girls—and all sunned by a January, whose burning brilliance shames our fairest June fervors. This comes of going down to the sea in ships, and doing business upon the great waters, and Sinbading round the world generally.

Yet there are those who cultivate chimney corners, and chuckle that a rolling stone gathers no moss, who fillip their fingers at Memnon and the sources of the white Nile, who order warm slippers and declare that traveling is a fool's paradise. Yes. But, set in the azure air of that paradise stands the Parthenon, perfect as Homer. There are the Coliseum, the Forum, and the earth-quaking memories of Rome. There Memnon sings and the Gondolier. There wave palms, and birds of unimagined plumage float. There are the mossy footsteps of history, the sweet sources of song, the sacred shrines of religion.

Objective all, I know you will respond, fat friend of the warm slippers, and you will take down your Coleridge and find,

"O lady, we receive but what we give,
And in our life alone does nature live."

Yes—again, but I mistrust your poet was abroad when he sang these numbers. The melodious mystic could not reach the fool's paradise through the graceful Grecian gate, or the more congenial Egyptian Pylon—so through rainbow airs, opium-pinioned, he overflew the walls, and awhile breathed other airs. The lines are only partially true. Elia, copying accounts in the India House, could not enjoy in the wood upon which he wrote, the charm of the Tree which had "died into the desk." And though nature be the mirror of our moods—we can yet sometimes escape ourselves—as we can sometimes forget all laws. "Go abroad and forget yourself," is good advice. The Prodigal was long and ruinously abroad before he came to himself. And poets celebrate the law unlimited, which circumstances constantly limit. You would fancy Thomson an early riser. Yet that placid poet, who rented the castle of indolence, and made it the House Beautiful, so that all who pass are fain to tarry, used to rise at noon, and sauntering into the garden eat fruit from the trees with his hands in his pocket, and then and there composed sonorous apostrophes to the rising sun.

Traveling is a fool's paradise, to a fool. But to him, staying at home is the same thing. A fool is always in paradise. But into that delight a wise man can no more penetrate, than a soul into a stone. If you are a fool, O friendly reader of the rolling stone theory, you are in the paradise you dread, and hermetically closed in. The great gates clanged awful behind you at your birth. But if you are wise, you can never by any chance get in. Allons, take your slippers, I shall take passage with the fool.

All this we say being somewhat sleepy, under the bank at Esne, on the verge of tumbling in. Good night! But one word! You facetious friends in the hot slippers, what is our so stable-seeming, moss-amassing Earth doing? Truly what Rip Van Winkle heard the aged men do among the mountains—rolling, rolling, rolling forever.

O friends of the Verde family, have you duly meditated these things?

XVII.

Fair Frailty.

FRAIL are the fair of Esne. Yet the beauty of gossamer webs is not less beautiful, because it is not sheet-iron. Let the panoplied in principle pass Esne by. There dwell the gossamer-moraled Ghawazee. A strange sect the Ghawazee—a race dedicate to pleasure.

Somewhere in these remote regions lay the Lotus islands. Mild-eyed and melancholy were the forms that swam those calm waters to the loitering vessel, and wooed the Mariners with their heart's own longings soothlier sung—

> "Here are cool mosses deep
> And through the moss the ivies creep,
> And in the stream the long-leaved flowers weep,
> And from the craggy ledge the Poppy hangs in sleep."

To those enchanted islands and that summer sea, is not this river of unknown source the winding avenue? Through its silence, ever silenter—along the peaceful waving of its palms—azure-arched and lotus-shored, leads it not backward to that dream?

Yes—the Howadji felt it. The day whispered it at

noon. The palms at sunset waved it from the shore. The stars burning ever brighter with the deepening south, breathed it with their greater beauty all night long, " Mild-eyed, melancholy" were the men. But along the shores of this Labyrinth which we so dreamily thread, are stations posted, to give exquisite earnest of our borne. And here are maidens, not men, vowed to that fair forgetfulness of yesterday and to-morrow which is the golden garland of to-day.

These azure airs, soft and voluptuous, are they not those that blew beyond the domain of conscience—remote region of which Elia dreamed? Is not the Bishop of that diocese unmitred here? For the nonce I renounce my fealty, and air myself beyond those limits; and when I return, if mortal may return from the Lotus islands, and from streams enchanted, that good Bishop shall only lightly touch me with his crosier for the sake of bright Kushuk Arnem, and the still-eyed Xenobi.

Did you sup at the Barmecide's in Bagdad, with Shacabac and myself, that Arabian night? Well, the Ghazeeyah Kushuk Arnem, a girl of Palestine, claims descent from him. Or did you assist at Herodias' dancing before the royal Herod? Well, the Ghazeeyah Kushuk Arnem dances as Herodias danced. Or in those Pharaoh days, something musty now, did you frequent the court balls? Well, this is the same dancing, and needless was it to have lived so long ago, for here you have the same delight in Kushuk Arnem. Or seated under olives-trees in stately Spain, with Don Quixote de la Mancha, were your eyes enamored of the Fandango? That was well, but January is not June in Spain, and in Esne the Howadji saw Kushuk Arnem, and the gracious Ghazeeyah's dance was the model of the Spanish.

For the Egyptian dancing-girls are of a distinct race, and of an unknown antiquity. The Egyptian gipsys, but not unanimously, claim the same Barmecidian descent, and the Ghawazee, or dancing-girls, each one of which is termed Ghazeeyah, wear divers adornments, like those of the gipsys. They speak the language and profess the faith of the Egyptians—nay, like Hadji Hamed, the long cook of the Ibis, they perform the pilgrimage to Mecca for the solace of their own souls and bodies, or those of some accompanying ascetic. The race of Ghawazee is kept distinct. They marry among themselves, or some Ghazeeyah, weary of those sunny slopes, *fuori le mure* of conscience, wondering haply whither they do slope, retreats into the religious retirement of the hareem. When she has made a vow of repentance, the respectable husband is not considered disgraced by the connection.

For the profession of the Ghawazee is dancing *ed altri generi*. They are migratory, moving from town to town with tents, slaves, and cattle, raising readily their homely home, and striking it as speedily. In the large cities, they inhabit a distinct quarter of the region especially consecrate to pleasure. In villages, they sojourn upon the outskirts. At all fairs, they are the fairest and most fascinating. But they mostly affect religious festivals—the going out to tombs in the desert a few miles from the cities. For on the natal days of saints inhabiting those tombs, a religious spree takes place upon the spot, and scenes are presented to the contemplative eye, not unlike those of Methodist camp-meetings. At such times and places they are present "by thousands, by millions," cried the unmathematical Commander, ecstatic with his theme, but again without the golden sleeve.

In golden sleeves alone, O Commander, is dignity and wisdom.

I said it was a sect vowed to pleasure. From earliest youth they are educated to their profession. They do not marry until they have commenced a public career. Then the husband is the grand Vizier and Kapellmeister of his wife's court.

Let the moralizing mind reflect here, that the pursuit of pleasure is an hereditary tenet, dear to the husband as to the wife, who can not be false, because there is no such thing as faithfulness. And let the Moral Reform Society carefully avoid judging this frailty on principle, for in tribes, traditions of usage become principle, by the vice of enlightened lands, where it is a very sorrowful and shameful thing, bred in deceit and ending in despair. In Europe, society squeezes women into this vortex. Then it is a mere *pis-aller* for existence, and loathsome much more to the victims themselves than to others. In America, a fair preludes the foul. Seduction smooths the slopes of the pit, although once in, society here, as there, seals inexorably the doom of the fallen. For the Ghazeeyah who turns from her ways, there is the equality with other wives, and no taunting for the Past. For the woman who once falls in England or America, there is no resurrection to sympathy and regard. The world, being without sin, casts endless paving-stones, until hope, heart, and life are quite crushed out.

Moralizing at Esne!

Although the Ghawazee, when they marry out of the tribe, do not dishonor their husbands in public estimation, they are by no means held honorable while they practice their profession. This is for many reasons. But let no moral reformer flatter himself upon the moral sense of the East. "No," said the Golden-sleeve, "I wouldn't trust my own mother." The Ghawazee are not honorable, because, being, as Mr. Lane says, the most beautiful of Egyptian women, they show to the sun, moon, stars, and all human eyes, their unvailed faces. Then they receive men into their own apartments—let us not desecrate the sacred name of hareem. And they dance unvailed in public, and if you may believe the shuddering scandal of the saints at Cairo, each of whom has a score of women to dance for him alone, they adorn with nude grace the midnight revels of the Cairene rakes.

Mohammad Alee's mercury of virtue rose in his impotent age to such a height of heat, that he banished all the Cairene Ghawazee to Esne, which sounded morally, until the curious discovered that Esne was the favorite river retreat of the Pacha, and the moment they disappeared from Cairo, they were replaced by boys dressed like women, who danced as the Ghawazee danced, and imitated their costume, and all the womanliness of a woman, growing their thair, vailing their faces, kohling their eyelashes, hennaing their finger and toe nails.

And there was also another set of boy-dancers, called Gink, into the melancholy mystery of which name the discreet and virtuous refrain from prying. The Howadji, too, is Herodotean for the nonce, and "thinks it better it should not be mentioned."

XVIII.

Fair Frailty—Continued.

And so frailty was all boated up the Nile to Esne. Not quite, and even if it had been, Abbas Pacha, grandson of Mohammad Alee, and at the request of the old Pacha's daughter, has boated it all back again. Abbas Pacha heritor of the shreds and patches of the Pharaohs' throne, and the Ptolemies and the Cleopatras. He did well to honor the Ghawazee by his permission of return, for what was the swart queen but a glorious Ghazeeyah? Ask Marc Antony and Julius Cesar. Nor shall Rhodopis be forgotten, centuries older than Cleopatra, supposed to be the builder of one of the pyramids, and of wide Grecian fame.

Herodotus tells her story. She was a Thracian and fellow-servant of Esop. Xanthus the Samian brought her to Egypt, and Charaxus, brother of Sappho, ransomed her, for which service when Charaxus returned, Sappho grievously gibed him in an ode. Rhodopis became very rich and very famous, and sent gifts to Delphi. "And now," says our testy and garrulous old guide, as if to wash his hands of her iniquity, "I have done speaking of Rhodopis."

Even grandfather Mohammad did not boat all the frailty up the Nile. That would have been, if the beautiful Ghazeeyah had been the sole Egyptian sinner. But this especial sin pays a tenth of the whole tax of Egypt, and the Ghawazee are but the most graceful groups of Magdalens, not at all the crowd. The courtesans who went with vailed faces discreetly, who were neither handsome nor of any endowment of grace or charm to draw the general eye;—widows and wives, who, in the absence of their lords, mellowed their morals for errant cavaliers;—the dead-weighted, sensual, ungraceful, inexcusable, and disgusting mass remained, and flourished more luxuriantly.

The solidest sin always does remain;—the Houris as more aerial are blown away, the sadder sinners cling. Law and propriety yearly pour away into perdition a flowing surface of addled virtue, vice-stained, and a small portion of veritable vice. But the great, old, solid sin, sticks steadfastly, like the lump of ambergris in the Sultan's cup, flavoring the whole draught. For not even the friend of the warm slippers and rolling stone theory, can suppose that the Muslim are a continent race, or that Mohammad Alee was Simeon Stylites, because he exported the dancing-girls.

Hear what Abu Taib said in the gardens of Shubra.

Once there was a Pacha, who, after drinking much wine all his days, lost his taste, and fell in danger of his life if he drank of it any more. And the Pacha ordered all the wine in the country to be cast into the river. And the fair fountains that flowed sweet wine of exquisite exhilaration before the mosques, and upon the public place, were seized and utterly dried up. But the loathsome, stagnant tanks, and ditches of beastly drunkenness that festered concealed behind white walls, were untouched, and flowed poison. And the Pacha heard what had been done, and said, it was well. And far lands heard of the same thing, and said, "Lo! a great prince, who removes sores from his inheritance, and casts out vice from his dominions."

There are English poets who celebrate the pleasant position of the Eastern woman, and it is rather the Western fashion of the moment to fancy them not so very miserably situated. But the idea of woman disappears entirely from your mind in the East except as an exquisite and fascinating toy. The women suggest houris, perhaps, but never angels. Devils, possibly, but never friends. And now, Pacha, as we stroll slowly by starlight under the palms, by the mud cabins round which the Fellaheèn, or peasants, sit, and their fierce dogs bark, and see the twin tombs of the shekhs gleaming white through the twilight, while we ramble toward the bower of Kushuk Arnem and the still-eyed Xenobi, tell me truly by the sworded Orion above us, if you cherish large faith in the virtue of men, who, of a voluptuous climate, born and nursed, shut up dozens of the most enticing women in the strict and sacred seclusion of the hareem, and keep them there without knowledge, without ambition—petted girls with the proud passions of Southern women, seeing him only of men, jealous of each other, jealous of themselves, the slaves of his whims, tender or terrible, looking to him for their sole excitement, and that solely sensual—rarely tasting the bliss of becoming a mother, and taught to stimulate in indescribable ways the palling and flagging passions of their keeper.

Individually, I lay no great stress on the objections of such gentry to the unvailed dancing of beautiful women, or to their pleasurable pursuit of pleasure ; nor do I find much morality in it. I am glad to grant the Oriental great virtue ; and do not wish to whine at his social and national differences from the West. At Alexandria, let the West fade from your horizon, and you will sail fascinated forever. This Howadji holds that the Ghawazee are the true philosophers and moralists of the East, and that the hareem and polygamy in general, are without defense, viewed morally. Viewed picturesquely under palms, with delicious eyes melting at lattices, they are highly to be favored and encouraged by all poets and disciples of Epicurus.

Which, as you know as well as I, we will not here discuss. But, as I am out of breath, toiling up that steep sentence of the hareem, while we more leisurely climb the last dust heap toward that bower, the sole white wall of the village (how Satan loves these dear deceits, as excellent Dr. Bunyan Cheever would phrase it) soothe me soothly with those limpid lines of Mr. Milnes, who holds strongly to the high human and refining influence of the hareem. Does Young England wish to engraft polygamy among the other patriarchal benefits upon stout old England?

"Thus in the ever-closed hareem,
As in the open Western home,
Sheds womanhood her starry gleam,
Over our being's busy foam.
Through latitudes of varying faith,
Thus trace we still her mission sure,
To lighten life, to sweeten death;
And all for others to endure."

Every toad carries a diamond in its head, says Hope and the Ideal. But in any known toad was it ever found? retorted the Howadji cutting adrift his Western morals.

XIX.

Kushuk Arnem.

The Howadji entered the bower of the Ghazeeyah. A damsel admitted us at the gate, closely vailed, as if women's faces were to be seen no more forever. Across a clean little court, up stone steps that once were steadier, and we emerged upon a small inclosed stone terrace, the sky-vaulted anti-chamber of that bower. Through a little door that made us stoop to enter, we passed into the peculiar retreat of the Ghazeeyah. It was a small, white, oblong room, with but one window, opposite the door, and that closed. On three sides there were small holes to admit light as in dungeons, but too lofty for the eye to look through, like the oriel windows of Sacristies. Under these openings were small glass vases holding oil, on which floated wicks. These were the means of illumination.

A divan of honor filled the end of the room—on the side was another, less honorable, as is usual in all Egyptian houses—on the floor a carpet, partly covering it. A straw matting extended beyond the carpet toward the door, and between the matting and the door was a bare space of stone floor, whereon to shed the slippers.

Hadji Hamed, the long cook, had been ill, but hearing of music and dancing and Ghawazee, he had turned out for the nonce, and accompanied us to the house, not all unmindful possibly of the delectations of the Mecca pilgrimage. He stood upon the stone terrace afterward, looking in with huge delight. The solemn, long tomb-pilgrim! The merriest lunges of life were not lost upon him, notwithstanding.

The Howadji seated themselves orientally upon the divan of honor. To sit as Westerns sit, is impossible upon a divan. There is some mysterious necessity for crossing the legs, and this Howadji never sees a tailor now in lands civilized, but the dimness of Eastern rooms and bazaars, the flowingness of robe, and the coiled splendor of the turban, and a world reclining leisurely at ease, rise distinct and dear in his mind—like that Sicilian mirage seen on divine days from Naples—but fleet as fair. To most men a tailor is the most unsuggestive of mortals. To the remembering Howadji he sits a poet.

The chibouque and nargileh and coffee belong to the divan, as the parts of harmony to each other. I seized the flowing tube of a brilliant amber-hued nargileh, such as Hafiz might have smoked, and prayed Isis that some stray Persian might chance along to complete our company. The Pacha inhaled at times a more sedate nargileh, at times the chibouque of the Commander, who reclined upon the divan below.

A tall Egyptian female, filially related I am sure to a gentle giraffe who had been indiscreet with a hippopotamus, moved heavily about, lighting the lamps, and looking as if her bright eyes were feeding upon the flame, as the giraffes might browse upon lofty autumn leaves. There was something awful in this figure. She was the type of those tall, angular, Chinese-eyed, semi-smiling, wholly homely and bewitched beings who sit in eternal profile in the sculptures of the temples. She was mystic, like the cow-horned Isis. I gradually feared that she had come off the wall of a tomb, probably in Thebes hard by, and that our Ghawazee delights would end in a sudden embalming, and laying away in the bowels of the hills with a perpetual prospect of her upon the walls.

Avaunt, Specter! The Fay approaches, and Kushuk Arnem entered her bower. A bud no longer, yet a flower not too fully blown. Large laughing eyes, red pulpy lips, white teeth, arching nose, generous-featured, lazy, carelessly self-possessed, she came dancing in, addressing the Howadji in Arabic—words whose honey they would not have distilled through interpretation. Be content with the aroma of sound, if you can not catch the flavor of sense—and flavor can you never have through another mouth. Smiling and Pantomime were our talking, and one choice Italian word, she knew—*buono.* Ah! how much was *buono* that choice evening. Eyes, lips, hair, form, dress, every thing that the strangers had or wore, was endlessly *buono.* Dancing, singing, smoking, coffee,—*buono, buono, buonissimo!* How much work one word will do!

The Ghazeeyah entered—not mazed in that azure mist

of gauze and muslin wherein Cerito floats fascinating across the scene, nor in the peacock plumage of sprightly Lucille Grahn, nor yet in that June cloudiness of aery apparel which Carlotta affects, nor in that sumptuous Spanishness of dark drapery wherein Fanny is most Fanny.

The glory of a butterfly is the starred brilliance of its wings. There are who declare that dress is divine, who aver that an untoileted woman is not wholly a woman, and that you may as well paint a saint without his halo, as describe a woman without detailing her dress. Therefore, while the coarser sex vails longing eyes, will we tell the story of the Ghazeeyah's apparel.

Yellow morocco slippers hid her feet, rosy and round. Over these brooded a bewildering fullness of rainbow silk. Turkish trowsers we call them, but they are shintyan in Arabic. Like the sleeve of a clergyman's gown, the lower end is gathered somewhere, and the fullness gracefully overfalls. I say rainbow, although to the Howadji's little cognizant eye was the shintyan of more than the seven orthodox colors. In the bower of Kushuk, nargileh-clouded, coffee-scented, are eyes to be strictly trusted?

Yet we must not be entangled in this bewildering brilliance. A satin jacket striped with velvet and of open sleeves, wherefrom floated forth a fleecy cloud of undersleeve, rolling adown the rosy arms, as June clouds down the western rosiness of the sky, inclosed the bust. A shawl twisted of many folds cinctured the waist, confining the silken shintyan. A golden necklace of charms girdled the throat, and the hair much unctuated, as is the custom of the land, was adorned with a pendent fringe of black silk, tipped with gold, which hung upon the neck behind.

Let us confess to a dreamy vaporous vail, overspreading, rather suffusing with color, the upper part of the arms and the lower limits of the neck. That rosiness is known as tób to the Arabians—a mystery whereof the merely masculine mind is not cognizant. Beneath the tób, truth allows a beautiful bud-burstiness of bosom. Yet I swear, by John Bunyan, nothing so aggravating as the Howadji beholds in saloons unnamable nearer the Hudson than the Nile. This brilliant cloud, whose spirit was Kushuk Arnem, our gay Ghazeeyah, gathered itself upon a divan, and she inhaled vigorously a nargileh. A damsel in tób and shintyan, exhaling azure clouds of aromatic smoke, had not been displeasing to that Persian poet, for whose coming I had prayed too late.

But more welcome than he, came the still-eyed Xenobi. She entered timidly like a bird. The Howadji had seen doves less gracefully sitting upon palm-boughs in the sunset, than she nestled upon the lower divan. A very dove of a Ghazeeyah, a quiet child, the last born of Terpsichore. Blow it from Mount Atlas, a modest dancing-girl. She sat near this Howadji, and handed him, O Haroun Alrashid! the tube of his nargileh. Its serpentine sinuosity flowed through her fingers, as if the golden gayety of her costume were gliding from her alive. It was an electric chain of communication, and never until some Xenobi of a houri hands the Howadji the nargileh of Paradise, will the smoke of the weed of Shiraz float so lightly, or so sweetly taste.

Xenobi was a mere bud, of most flexile and graceful form—ripe and round as the Spring fruit of the tropics. Kushuk had the air of a woman for whom no surprises survive. Xenobi saw in every new day a surprise, haply in every Howadji a lover.

She was more richly dressed than Kushuk. There were gay gold bands and clasps upon her jacket. Various necklaces of stamped gold and metallic charms clustered around her neck, and upon her head a bright silken web, as if a sun-suffused cloud were lingering there, and dissolving, showered down her neck in a golden rain of pendants. Then, O Venus! more azure still, that delicious gauziness of tób, whereof more than to dream is delirium. Wonderful the witchery of a tób! Nor can the Howadji deem a maiden quite just to nature, who glides through the world, unshintyaned and untóbed.

Xenobi was perhaps sixteen years old, and a fully developed woman. Kushuk Arnem, of some half-dozen Summers more. Kushuk was unhennaed. But the younger, as younger maidens may, graced herself with the genial gifts of nature. Her delicate filbert nails were rosily tinted on the tips with henna, and those pedler poets meeting her in Paradise would have felt the reason of their chant—"Odors of Paradise, O flowers of the henna!" But she had no kohl upon the eyelashes, nor like Fatima of Damascus, whom the Howadji later saw, were her eyebrows shaved and replaced by thick, black arches of kohl.

Yet fascinating are the almond-eyes of Egyptian women, bordered black with the kohl, whose intensity accords with the sumptuous passion that mingles moist and languid with their light. Eastern eyes are full of moonlight—Eastern beauty is a dream of passionate possibility, which the Howadji would fain awaken by the same spell with which the Prince of faery dissolved the enchanted sleep of the princess. Yet kohl and henna are only beautiful for the beautiful. In a coffee-shop at Esne, bold-faced among the men, sat a coarse courtesan sipping coffee and smoking a nargileh, whose kohled eyebrows and eyelashes made her a houri of hell.

"There is no joy but calm," I said, as the moments, brimmed with beauty, melted in the starlight, and the small room became a bower of bloom and a Persian garden of delight. We reclined, breathing fragrant fumes, and interchanging, through the Golden-sleeved, airy nothings. The Howadji and the Houris had little in common but looks. Soulless as Undine, and suddenly risen from a laughing life in watery dells of lotus, sat the houris, and, like the mariner, sea-driven upon the enchanted isle of Prospero, sat the Howadji, unknowing the graceful gossip of Faery. But there is a faery always folded away in our souls, like a bright butterfly chrysalised, and sailing eastward, layer after layer of propriety, moderation, deference to public opinion, safety of sentiment, and all the thick crusts of compromise and convention roll away, and bending southward up the Nile, you may feel that faery fairly flutter her wings. And if you pause at Esne, she will fly out, and lead you a will-o'-the-wisp dance across all the trim sharp hedges of accustomed proprieties, and over the barren flats of social decencies. Dumb is that faery, so long has she been secluded, and can not say much to her fellows. But she feels and sees and enjoys all the more exquisitely and profoundly for her long sequestration.

Presently an old woman came in with a tár, a kind of tambourine, and her husband, a grisly old sinner, with a rabáb, or one-stringed fiddle. Old Hecate was a gone Ghazeeyah—a rose-leaf utterly shriveled away from rosiness. No longer a dancer, she made music for dancing. And the husband, who played for her in her youth, now played with her in her age. Like two old votaries who feel when they can no longer see, they devoted all the force of life remaining, to the great game of pleasure, whose born thralls they were.

There were two tarabukas and brass castanets, and when the old pair were seated upon the carpet near the door, they all smote their rude instruments, and a wild clang raged through the little chamber. Thereto they sang. Strange sounds—such music as the angular, carved figures upon the Temples would make, had they been conversing with us—sounds to the ear like their gracelessness to the eye.

This was Egyptian Polyhymnia preluding Terpsichore.

XX.

Terpsichore.

> "The wind is fair,
> The boat is in the bay,
> And the fair mermaid Pilot calls away———"

Kushuk Arnem quaffed a goblet of hemp arrack. The beaker was passed to the upper divan, and the Howadji, sipping, found it to smack of aniseed. It was strong enough for the Pharaohs to have imbibed—even for Herod before beholding Herodias, for these dances are the same. This dancing is more ancient than Aboo Simbel. In the land of the Pharaohs, the Howadji saw the dancing they saw, as uncouth as the temples they built. This dancing is to the ballet of civilized lands, what the gracelessness of Egypt was to the grace of Greece. Had the angular figures of the Temple sculptures preluded with that music, they had certainly followed with this dancing.

Kushuk Arnem rose and loosened her shawl girdle in such wise, that I feared she was about to shed the frivolity of dress, as Venus shed the sea-foam, and stood opposite the divan, holding her brass castanets. Old Hecate beat the tár into a thunderous roar. Old husband drew sounds from his horrible rabáb, sharper than the sting of remorse, and Xenobi and the Giraffe each thrummed a tarabuka until I thought the plaster would peel from the wall. Kushuk stood motionless, while this din deepened around her, the arrack aerializing her feet, the Howadji hoped, and not her brain. The sharp surges of sound swept around the room, dashing in regular measure against her movelessness, until suddenly the whole surface of her frame quivered in measure with the music. Her hands were raised, clapping the castanets, and she slowly turned upon herself, her right leg the pivot, marvelously convulsing all the muscles of her body. When she had completed the circuit of the spot on which she stood, she advanced slowly, all the muscles jerking in time to the music, and in solid, substantial spasms.

It was a curious and wonderful gymnastic. There was no graceful dancing—once only there was the movement of dancing when she advanced, throwing one leg before the other as gipsys dance. But the rest was most voluptuous motion—not the lithe wooing of languid passion, but the soul of passion starting through every sense, and quivering in every limb. It was the very intensity of motion, concentrated and constant. The music still swelled savagely in maddened monotony of measure. Hecate and the old husband, fascinated with the Ghazeeyah's fire, threw their hands and arms excitedly about their instruments, and an occasional cry of enthusiasm and satisfaction burst from their lips. Suddenly stooping, still muscularly moving, Kushuk fell upon her knees, and writhed with body, arms and head upon the floor, still in measure—still clanking the castanets, and arose in the same manner. It was profoundly dramatic. The scenery of the dance was like that of a characteristic song. It was a lyric of love which words can not tell—profound, oriental, intense and terrible. Still she retreated, until the constantly down-slipping shawl seemed only just clinging to her hips, and making the same circuit upon herself, she sat down, and after this violent and extravagant exertion was marbly cold.

Then timid but not tremulous, the young Xenobi arose bare-footed, and danced the same dance—not with the finished skill of Kushuk, but gracefully and well, and with her eyes fixed constantly upon the elder. With the same regular throb of the muscles she advanced and retreated, and the Paradise-pavilioned prophet could not have felt his heavenly hareem complete, had he sat smoking and entranced with the Howadji.

Form so perfect was never yet carved in marble—not the Venus is so mellowly molded. Her outline has not the voluptuous excess which is not too much—which is not perceptible to mere criticism, and is more a feeling flushing along the form, than a greater fullness of the form itself. The Greek Venus was sea-born, but our Egyptian is sun-born. The brown blood of the sun burned along her veins—the soul of the sun streamed shaded from her eyes. She was still, almost statuesquely still. When she danced it was only stillness intensely stirred, and followed that of Kushuk as moonlight succeeds sunshine. As she went on, Kushuk gradually rose, and joining her they danced together. The Epicureans of Cairo indeed, the very young priests of Venus, assemble the Ghawazee in the most secluded Adyta of their dwellings, and there eschewing the mystery of the Hintyan, and the gauziness of the tôb, they behold the unencumbered beauty of these beautiful women. At festivals so fair, arrack, raw brandy, and "depraved human nature," naturally improvise a ballet whereupon the curtain here falls.

Suddenly, as the clarion call awakens the long-slumbering spirit of the war-horse, old Hecate sprang to her feet, and loosening her girdle, seized the castanets, and with the pure pride of power advanced upon the floor, and danced incredibly. Crouching before like a wasted old willow, that merely shakes its drooping leaves to the tempest—she now shook her fibers with the vigor of a nascent elm, and moved up and down the room with a miraculous command of her frame.

In Venice I had heard a gray Gondolier, dwindled into a Ferryman, awakened in a moonlighted midnight, as we swept by with singers chanting Tasso, pour his swan-song of magnificent memory into the quick ear of night.

In the Champs Elysées I had heard a rheumy-eyed Invalide cry with the sonorous enthusiasm of Austerlitz, "Vive Napoleon," as a new Napoleon rode by.

It was the Indian summer goldening the white winter—the Zodiacal light far flashing day into the twilight. And here was the same in dead old Egypt—in a Ghazeeyah who had brimmed her beaker with the threescore and ten drops of life. Not more strange, and unreal, and impressive in their way, the inscrutable remains of Egypt, sand-shrouded but undecayed, than in hers this strange spectacle of an efficient Coryphée of seventy.

Old Hecate! thou wast pure pomegranate also, and not banana, wonder most wonderful of all—words which must remain hieroglyphics upon these pages—and whose explication must be sought in Egypt, as they must come hither who would realize the freshness of Karnak.

Slow sweet singing followed. The refrain was plaintive, like those of the boat songs—soothing, after the excitement of the dancing, as nursery lays to children after a tired day. "Buono," Kushuk Arnem! last of the Arnems, for so her name signified. Was it a remembering refrain of Palestine, whose daughter you are? "Taib," dove Xenobi! Fated, shall I say, or favored? Pledged life-long to pleasure! Who would dare to be? Who but a child so careless would dream that these placid ripples of youth will rock you stormless to El Dorado?

O Allah! and who cares? Refill the amber nargileh, Xenobi—another fingan of mellow mocha. Yet another strain more stirring. Hence, Hecate! shrivel into invisibility with the thundering tár, and the old husband with his diabolical rabáb. Waits not the one-eyed first officer below, with a linen lantern, to pilot us to the boat? And the beak of the Ibis points it not to Syene, Nubia, and a world unknown?

Farewell, Kushuk! Addio, still-eyed dove! Almost thou persuadest me to pleasure. O Wall-street, Wall-street! because you are virtuous, shall there be no more cakes and ale?

XXI.

Sakias.

We departed at dawn. Before a gentle gale the Ibis fleetly flew, in the starlight, serenaded by the Sakias.

These endless sighing Sakias! There are fifty thousand of them in Egypt, or were, when Grandfather Mohammad was. They required a hundred and fifty thousand oxen to work them. But the murrain swept away the cattle, and now the Nile shores are strewn with the falling mud walls of Sakias, ruins of the last great Egyptian reign. Like huge summer insects, they doze upon the bank, droning a melancholy, monotonous song. The slow, sad sound pervades the land—one calls to another, and he sighs to his neighbor, and the Nile is shored with sound no less than sand. Their chorus is the swan-song of Egypt. For Egypt is effete. The race is more ruined than the temples. Nor shall there be a resurrection of an exhausted people, until fading roses, buried in the ground, take root again, or Memnon calls musically once more, down the far glad valley of the Nile.

The Sakia is the great instrument of irrigation. It is a rude contrivance of two perpendicular wheels, turned by a horizontal cog. The outer wheel is girdled with a string of earthen jars, which descend with every revolution into the pit open to the river, in which the wheel turns. As the jars ascend, they empty themselves into a trough, thence conducted away, or directly into a channel of earth; and the water flowing into the fields, by little canals, invests each separate small square patch. There are no fences, and the valley of the Nile is divided into endless inclosures by these shallow canals. The surface of the country is regularly veined, and the larger channels are the arteries fed by the great Sakia heart. Overflowing or falling, the Nile is forever nourishing Egypt, and far forth-looking from the propylons of temples, you may see the land checkered with slight silver streaks—tokens of its fealty and the Nile's devotion.

The Sakia is worked by a pair of oxen. Upon the tongue of the crank which they turn, sits a boy, drowsing and droning, and beating their tail-region all day long. Nor is the sad creak of the wheel ever soothed by any unctuous matter, which the proprietor appropriates to his own proper person, and which would also destroy the cherished creak. So sit the boys along the Nile, among the cotton, tobacco, corn, beans, or whatever other crop, and by beating the tail-region of many oxen, cause the melancholy music of the river. It has infinite variety, but a mournful monotony of effect. Some Sakias are sharp and shrill; they almost shriek in the tranced stillness. These you may know for the youth—these are the gibes of greenness. But sedater creaks follow. A plaintive monotony of moan that is helpless and hopeless. This is the general Sakia sigh. It is as if the air simmered into sound upon the shore. It is the overtaxed labor of the land complaining, a slave's plaining—low and lorn and lifeless. Yet as the summer seems not truly summer, until the locusts wind their dozy reeds, so Egypt seems not truly Egypt, except when the water-wheels sadden the silence. It is the audible weaving of the spell. The stillness were not so still without it, nor the temples so antique, nor the whole land so solitary and dead.

In books I read that it is the Ranz des Vaches of the Fallaheen, and that away from the Nile they sigh for the Sakia, as it sighs with them at home. And truly no picture of the river would be perfect that had not the water-wheels upon the shore. They abound in Nubia, and are there taxed heavily—some seventeen of our dollars each one. The Howadji wonders how such a tax can be paid, and the Nubian live. But if it be not promptly rendered the owner is ejected. He may have as much land as he can water, as much Arabian sand or Libyan, as he can coax the Nile to fructify. And there nature is compassionate. For out of what seems sheer sand you will see springing a deep-green patch of grain.

In upper Egypt and Nubia the Shadoof is seldom seen. That is a man-power Sakia, consisting simply of buckets swinging upon a pole, like a well bucket, and dipped into the river and emptied above by another into the channel. There are always two buckets, and the men stand opposite, only girded a little about the loins, or more frequently not at all, and plunging the bucket rapidly. It is exhausting labor, and no man is engaged more than two or three hours at a time. If the bank is very high, there are two or more ranges of Shadoofs, the lower pouring into the reservoirs of the upper. The Shadoofs abound in the sugar-cane region about Minyeh. They give a spectral life to the shore. The bronze statues moving as by pulleys, and the regular swing of the Shadoof. There is no creak, but silently in the sun the poles swing and the naked laborers sweat.

Sakia-spelled the Ibis flew, and awakening one midnight, I heard the murmurous music of distant bells filling all the air. As one on Summer Sundays loiters in flowery fields suburban, and catches the city chimes hushed and far away, so lingered and listened the Howadji along the verge of dreaming. Has the ear mirages, mused he, like the eye?

He remembered the day, and it was Sunday—Sunday morning across the sea. Still the clanging confusion, hushed into melody, rang on. He heard the orthodox sonorousness of St. John's, the sweet solemnity of St. Paul's, then the petulant peal of the dissenting bells dashed in. But all so sweet and far, until the belfry of the old Brick bellowed with joy, as if the head of giant Despair were now finally broken. Had Nilus wreathed these brows with magic lotus?

Now, mused the Howadji, haply dreaming still, now contrite Gotham, in its Sunday suit of sackcloth and ashes, hies humbly forth to repentance and prayer. Perchance some maiden tarries that her hair may be fitly folded, that she may wait upon the Lord *en grande tenue.* In godly Gotham such things have been. Divers of its daughters once tarried from the service and sermon that a French barber might lay his hand upon their heads, before the bishop. Then, like coiffed cherubim, they stole sweetly up the church-aisle, well named of grace, if its God must abide such worship, and were confirmed—in what? demanded the now clearly dreaming Howadji.

Belfry of old Brick, clang not so proudly! Haply the head of the giant Despair is only cracked, not yet broken.

Still trembled the melodious murmur of bells through the air, sweet as if the bells rang of the shining city, to Christian lingering on the shore. It was the marvel of many marvels of travel. The dawn opened dim eyes at length, still dreaming of that sound, when the golden-sleeved Commander opened the blue door of the cabin, and the Howadji then heard the mingled moaning of many Sakias, but the sweet, far bells no more.

XXII.

Under the Palms.

"A motion from the river won,
Ridged the smooth level, bearing on
My shallop through the star-strown calm,
Until another night in night
I entered, from the clearer light,
Imbowered vaults of pillar'd Palm."

HUMBOLDT, the only cosmopolitan and a poet, divides the earth by beauties, and celebrates as dearest to him, and first fascinating him to travel, the climate of palms. The palm is the type of the tropics, and when the great Alexander marched triumphing through India, some Hindoo, suspecting the sweetest secret of Brama, distilled a wine from the palm, the glorious fantasy of whose intoxication no poet records.

I knew a palm-tree upon Capri. It stood in select society of shining fig-leaves and lustrous oleanders; it overhung the balcony, and so looked, far overleaning, down upon the blue Mediterranean. Through the dream-mists of southern Italian noons, it looked up the broad bay of Naples and saw vague Vesuvius melting away; or at sunset the isles of the Syrens, whereon they singing sat, and wooed Ulysses as he went; or in the full May moonlight the oranges of Sorrento shone across it, great and golden, permanent planets of that delicious dark. And from the Sorrento where Tasso was born, it looked across to pleasant Posylippo, where Virgil is buried, and to stately Ischia. The palm of Capri saw all that was fairest and most famous in the bay of Naples.

A wandering poet, whom I knew—sang a sweet song to the palm, as he dreamed in the moonlight upon that balcony. But it was only the free-masonry of sympathy. It was only syllabled moonshine. For the palm was a poet too, and all palms are poets.

Yet when I asked the bard what the palm-tree sang in its melancholy measures of waving, he told me that not Vesuvius, nor the Syrens, nor Sorrento, nor Tasso, nor Virgil, the stately Ischia nor all the broad blue beauty of Naples bay, was the theme of that singing. But partly it sang of a river forever flowing, and of cloudless skies, and green fields that never faded, and the mournful music of water-wheels, and the wild monotony of a tropical life—and partly of the yellow silence of the Desert, and of drear solitudes inaccessible, and of wandering caravans, and lonely men. Then of gardens overhanging rivers, that roll gorgeous-shored through Western fancies—of gardens in Bagdad watered by the Euphrates and the Tigris, whereof it was the fringe and darling ornament—of oases in those sere sad deserts where it overfountained fountains, and every leaf was blessed. More than all, of the great Orient universally, where no tree was so abundant, so loved and so beautiful.

When I lay under that palm-tree in Capri in the May moonlight, my ears were opened, and I heard all that the poet had told me of its song.

Perhaps it was because I came from Rome, where the holy week comes into the year as Christ entered Jerusalem, over palms. For in the magnificence of St. Peter's, all the pomp of the most pompous of human institutions is on one day charactered by the palm. The Pope borne upon his throne, as is no other monarch,—with wide-waving Flabella attendant, moves, blessing the crowd through the great nave. All the red-legged cardinals follow, each of whose dresses would build a chapel, so costly are they, and the crimson-crowned Greek patriarch with long silken black beard, and the crew of motley which the Roman clergy is, crowded after in shining splendor.

No ceremony of imperial Rome had been more imposing, and never witnessed in a temple more imperial. But pope, patriarch, cardinals, bishops, ambassadors, and all the lesser glories, bore palm branches in their hands. Not veritable palm branches, but their imitation in turned yellow wood; and all through Rome that day, the palm branch was waving and hanging. Who could not see its beauty, even in the turned yellow wood? Who did not feel it was a sacred tree as well as romantic?

For palm branches were strewn before Jesus as he rode into Jerusalem, and forever, since, the palm symbolizes peace. Wherever a grove of palms waves in the low moonlight or starlight wind, it is the celestial choir chanting peace on earth, good-will to men. Therefore is it the foliage of the old religious pictures. Mary sits under a palm, and the saints converse under palms, and the prophets prophesy in their shade, and cherubs float with palms over the Martyr's agony. Nor among pictures is there any more beautiful than Correggio's Flight into Egypt, wherein the golden-haired angels put aside the palm branches, and smile sunnily through, upon the lovely Mother and the lovely child.

The palm is the chief tree in religious remembrance and religious art. It is the chief tree in romance and poetry. But its sentiment is always Eastern, and it always yearns for the East. In the West it is an exile, and pines in the most sheltered gardens. Among Western growths in the Western air, it is as unsphered as Hafiz in a temperance society. Yet of all Western shores it is happiest in Sicily, for Sicily is only a bit of Africa drifted westward. There is a soft Southern strain in the Sicilian skies, and the palms drink its sunshine like dew. Upon the tropical plain behind Palermo, among the sun-sucking aloes, and the thick, shapeless cactuses, like elephants and rhinoceroses enchanted into foliage, it grows ever gladly. For the aloe is of the East, and the prickly pear, and upon that plain the Saracens have been, and the palm sees the Arabian arch, and the oriental sign-manual stamped upon the land.

In the Villa Serra di Falco, within sound of the vespers of Palermo, there is a palm beautiful to behold. It is like a Georgian slave in a Pacha's hareem. Softly shielded from eager winds, gently throned upon a slope of richest green, fringed with brilliant and fragrant flowers, it stands separate and peculiar in the odorous garden air. Yet it droops and saddens, and bears no fruit. Vain is the exquisite environment of foreign fancies. The poor slave has no choice but life. Care too tender will not suffer it to die. Pride and admiration surround it with the best beauties, and feed it upon the warmest sun. But I heard it sigh as I passed. A wind blew warm from the East, and it lifted its arms hopelessly, and when the wind, love-laden with most subtle sweetness, lingered, loth to fly, the palm stood motionless upon its little green mound, and the flowers were so fresh and fair—and the leaves of the trees so deeply hued, and the native fruit so golden and glad upon the boughs—that the still warm garden air, seemed only the silent, voluptuous sadness of the tree; and had I been a poet my heart would have melted in song for the proud, pining palm.

But the palms are not only poets in the West, they are prophets as well. They are like heralds sent forth upon the farthest points to celebrate to the traveler the glories they foreshow. Like spring birds they sing a summer unfading, and climes where Time wears the year as a queen a rosary of diamonds. The mariner, eastward-sailing, hears tidings from the chance palms that hang along the southern Italian shore. They call out to him across the gleaming calm of a Mediterranean noon, "Thou happy mariner, our souls sail with thee."

The first palm undoes the West. The Queen of Sheba and the Princess Shemselnihar look then upon the most

Solomon of Howadji's. So far the Orient has come—not in great glory, not handsomely, but as Rome came to Britain in Roman soldiers. The crown of imperial glory glittered yet and only upon the seven hills, but a single ray had penetrated the northern night—and what the golden house of Nero was to a Briton contemplating a Roman soldier, is the East to the Howadji first beholding a palm.

At Alexandria you are among them. Do not decry Alexandria as all Howadji do. To my eyes it was the illuminated initial of the oriental chapter. Certainly it reads like its heading—camels, mosques, bazaars, turbans, baths and chibouques: and the whole East rows out to you, in the turbaned and fluttering-robed rascal who officiates as your pilot and moors you in the shadow of palms under the Pacha's garden. Malign Alexandria no more, although you do have your choice of camels or omnibuses to go to your hotel, for when you are there and trying to dine, the wild-eyed Bedoueen who serves you, will send you deep into the desert by his masquerading costume and his eager, restless eye, looking as if he would momently spring through the window, and plunge into the desert depths. These Bedoueen or Arab servants are like steeds of the sun for carriage horses. They fly, girt with wild fascination, for what will they do next?

As you donkey out of Alexandria to Pompey's Pillar, you will pass a beautiful garden of palms, and by sunset nothing is so natural as to see only those trees. Yet the fascination is lasting. The poetry of the first exiles you saw, does not perish in the presence of the nation, for those exiles stood beckoning like angels at the gate of Paradise, sorrowfully ushering you into the glory whence themselves were outcasts forever :—and as you curiously looked in passing, you could not believe that their song was truth, and that the many would be as beautiful as the one.

Thenceforward, in the land of Egypt, palms are perpetual. They are the only foliage of the Nile, for we will not harm the modesty of a few Mimosas and Sycamores by foolish claims. They are the shade of the mud villages, marking their site in the landscape, so that the groups of palms are the number of villages. They fringe the shore and the horizon. The sun sets golden behind them, and birds sit swinging upon their boughs and float glorious among their trunks; on the ground beneath are flowers; the sugar-cane is not harmed by the ghostly shade nor the tobacco, and the yellow flowers of the cotton-plant star its dusk at evening. The children play under them, the old men crone and smoke, the donkeys graze, the surly bison and the conceited camels repose. The old Bible pictures are ceaselessly painted, but with softer, clearer colors than in the venerable book.

The palm-grove is always enchanted. If it stretch inland too alluringly, and you run ashore to stand under the bending boughs to share the peace of the doves swinging in the golden twilight, and to make yourself feel more scripturally, at least to surround yourself with sacred emblems, having small other hope of a share in the beauty of holiness—yet you will never reach the grove. You will gain the trees, but it is not the grove you fancied—that golden gloom will never be gained—it is an endless El Dorado gleaming along these shores. The separate columnar trunks ray out in foliage above, but there is no shade of a grove, no privacy of a wood, except, indeed, at sunset,

"A privacy of glorious light."

Each single tree has so little shade that the mass standing at wide ease can never create the shady solitude, without which, there is no grove.

But the eye never wearies of palms more than the ear of singing birds. Solitary they stand upon the sand, or upon the level, fertile land in groups, with a grace and dignity that no tree surpasses. Very soon the eye beholds in their forms the original type of the columns which it will afterward admire in the temples. Almost the first palm is architecturally suggestive, even in those Western gardens—but to artists living among them and seeing only them! Men's hands are not delicate in the early ages, and the fountain fairness of the palms is not very flowingly fashioned in the capitals, but in the flowery perfection of the Parthenon the palm triumphs. The forms of those columns came from Egypt, and that which was the suspicion of the earlier workers, was the success of more delicate designing. So is the palm inwound with our art and poetry and religion, and of all trees would the Howadji be a palm, wide-waving peace and plenty, and feeling his kin to the Parthenon and Raphael's pictures.

But nature is absolute taste, and has no pure ornament, so that the palm is no less useful than beautiful. The family is infinite and ill understood. The cocoa-nut, date and sago, are all palms. Ropes and sponges are wrought of the tough interior fiber. The various fruits are nutritious, the wood, the roots and the leaves are all consumed. It is one of nature's great gifts to her spoiled sun-darlings. Whoso is born of the sun is made free of the world. Like the poet Thomson, he may put his hands in his pockets and eat apples at leisure.

I do not find that the Egyptians ever deified the palm, as some of them did the crocodile. And therein I find a want of that singular shrewdness of perception which the Poet Martineau perpetually praises in that antique people. It was a miserably cowardly thing to make a God of a Dragon, who dined and supped upon you and your friends whenever he could catch you; who did nothing but stretch his scales upon the sand in the sun; and left only suspicious musk-balls as a legacy to his worshipers. To deify that mole-eyed monster, and then carefully embalm the dead abomination, looked very like fear, spite of Thothmes, Psamitticus, and Ramses the Great. For meanwhile, the land entertained angels unawares. They were waving gracious wings over the green fields, and from the womb of plenty dropped the sweet nutritious dates, and from the plumage of those wings were houses thatched. And every part of the beautiful body, living or dead, was a treasure to the mole-eyed Crocodile-worshipers. The land was covered with little Gods, whispering peace and plenty, but they were no more deified than the sweet stray thoughts of the villagers. Indeed, Poet Harriet, your erudite Egyptians went out of their way to worship devils.

They do better even to this day, higher up the river. Along the remote shores of the white Nile, are races wild and gentle, who extract the four lower front teeth for beauty, and worship the great trees. And truly, in the Tropics, the great tree is a great God. Far outspreading shielding arms, he folds his worshipers from the burning sun, and wrestles wondrously with the wildest gales. Birds build in the sweet security of his shade. Fruit ripens and falls untended from his beneficent boughs. At midnight the winds converse with him, and he hides the stars. He outlives generations, and is a cherished tradition.

There is a Godlike God! A great tree could proselyte even among Christians. The Boston elm has moved hearts that Park-street and Brattle-street have never intenerated. There is a serious, sensible worship! The God hath duration, doth nothing harm, and imparts very tangible blessings. The Egyptian worship of the crocodile is very thin, measured by this Dinka religion of the tree. And is the crocodile's a loftier degree of life than the tree's?

It is the date-palm which is so common and graceful in Egypt. Near Asyoot, the ascending Howadji sees for the first time the Dôm palm. This is a heavier, huskier tree, always forked. It has a very tropical air, and solves the mystery of gingerbread nuts. For if the hard, brown fruit of the Dôm be not the hard, brown nuts which our credulous youth ascribed to the genius of the baker at the corner, they are certainly the type of those gingered blisses, and never did the Howadji seem to himself more hopelessly lost in the magic of Egypt and the East, than when he plucked gingerbread from a palm-tree.

The Dôm is coarse by the side of the feathery date-palm, like a clumsy brake among maiden hair ferns. It is tropically handsome, but is always the plebeian palm. It has clumsy hands and feet, and, like a frowsy cook, gawks in the land. But, plumed as a prince and graceful as a gentleman, stands the date, and whoever travels among palms, travels in good society. Southward stretches the Ibis, and morning and evening sees few other trees. They sculpture themselves upon memory more fairly than upon these old columns. The wave of their boughs henceforward, wherever you are, will be the wave of the magician's wand, and you will float again upon the Nile, and wonder how were shaped the palms upon the shore when Adam sailed with Eve down the rivers of Eden.

XXIII.

Alms! O Shopkeeper.

THERE are but two sounds in Egypt, the sigh of the Sakia and the national cry of "Bucksheesh, Howadji"—Alms, O Shopkeeper! Add the ceaseless bark of curs, if you are Trinitarian, and you will find your mystic number everywhere made good.

"Bucksheesh Howadji," is the universal greeting. From all the fields, as you stroll along the shore or sail up the river, swells this vast shout. Young and old and both sexes, in every variety of shriek, whine, entreaty, demand, contempt, and indifference, weary the Howadji's soul with the incessant cry. Little children who can not yet talk, struggle to articulate it. Father and mother shout it in full chorus. The boys on the tongues of Sakias, the ebony statues at the Shadoofs, the specters in the yellow-blossomed cotton-field, or standing among the grain, break their long silence with this cry only, "Alms, O Shopkeeper."

It is not always a request. Girls and boys laugh as they shout it, nor cease picking cotton or cutting stalks. Groups of children with outstretched hands, surround you in full chorus, if you pause to sketch or shoot or loiter. They parry your glances with the begging. Have the sleepy-souled Egyptians learned that if Howadji have evil eyes, there is no surer spell to make them disappear than an appeal to their pockets? Like a prayer, the whole land repeats the invocation, and with the usual amount of piety and the pious.

Yet sometimes it is an imperial demand, and you would fancy Belisarius or Ramses the Great sat begging upon the bank. Sauntering in a golden sunset along the shore at Edfoo, a wandering minstrel in the grass tapped his tarabuka as the Howadji passed, that they should render tribute. The unnoting Howadji passed on. Thankless trade the tax-gatherer, thou tarabuka thrummer!—and he looked after us with contempt for the Christian dogs.

Farther on a voice shouted, as if the Howadji had passed a shrine unkneeling, "Shopkeepers! Shopkeepers!" But dignity is deaf, and they sauntered on. Then more curtly and angrily, "Shopkeepers! Shopkeepers!"—as if a man had discovered false weight in his wares. And constantly nearing, the howl of Howadji grew intolerable, until there was a violent clapping of hands, and a blear-eyed Egyptian ran in front of us like a ragingly mad emperor, "Alms! O Shopkeeper!" "To the devil, O Egyptian!"

For no shopkeeper on record ever gave alms except to the miserable, deformed, old, and blind. They are the only distinctions you can make or maintain in an otherwise monotonous mass of misery. Nation of beggars, effortless, effete, bucksheesh is its prominent point of contact with the Howadji, who, revisiting the Nile in dreams, hears far-sounding and forever, "Alms, O Shopkeeper."

XXIV.

Syene.

> "Some from farthest South—
> Syene, and where the shadow both way falls,
> Meroe, Nilotick isle."

APPROACHING Assouan, or the Greek Syene, which we will henceforth call it, as more graceful and musical, the high bluffs with bold masses of rock heralded a new scenery—and its sharp lofty forms were like the pealing trumpet tones, announcing the crisis of the struggle. It was a pleasant January morning, that the Ibis skimmed along the shore. The scenery was bolder than any she had seen in her flight. Rocks broke the evenness of the river's surface, and in the heart of the hills the river seemed to end, it was so shut in by the rocky cliffs and points.

The town Syene is a dull mud mass, like all other Egyptian towns. But palms spread luxuriantly along the bank, and on the shores of Elephantine, the island opposite—sweeps and slopes of greenery stretched westward from the eye.

Upon that shore the eye lingers curiously upon the remains of a Christian convent, where there are yet grottoes, formerly used as chapels and shrines, and still as you look and linger, the forms and faces of Christian lands begin to rise, and reel before your fancy, and you half fear, while you are fascinated, that the East will fade in that Western remembrance, until some Arab beldame—brown and unhuman as a mummy from the hills, and fateful as Atropos, peers into your dreaming eyes, and tells you that on that site, an old King of the land buried incredible treasure, before he went to war against the Nubians. The miserly monarch left nothing for his family or friends, and all was committed to the charge of an austere Magician. Years passed, and the King came no more. The relatives sought to obtain the treasure, and foiling the Magician slew him upon the shore. But dying, he lived more terribly—for he rose a huge serpent, that devoured all his assailants. Years pass, and the King comes no more. Yet the serpent still watches the treasure, and once every midnight, at the culmination of certain stars, he descends to the Nile to drink, while so wonderful a light streams from his awful head—that if the King comes not, it is not because he can not see the way. Were the Aurora in the East, the Howadji would suspect the secret, and when it shone no more, know that the King had returned to Syene.

It is the city of the cataract. Built at the entrance of the rapids, it is the chief point for the Nubian-bound voyager, and is the borne of most Nile travelers. The Ibis had flown hither from Cairo in twenty-two days—a flight well flown, for we had met melancholy Howadji, who had been fifty days from Alexandria. And the Ancient Mariner of the Nile—will he ever behold Syene, or see it only a palm-fringed mirage upon the shore, as he dashes up and down the cataract? But do not turn there, reflective reader, when you ascend the Nile. Believe no Verde Giovanes who give breakfasts on Philæ, and decry Nubia. Push on, farther and faster—as if you must ride the equator before you pause—as if you could not sink deep enough in the strangeness and sweetness of tropical travel. Believe an impartial Howadji who has no Cangie or other boats to let at Mahratta, that Nubia is a very different land from Egypt, and that you have not penetrated antiquest Egypt, until you have been awe-stricken by the silence which was buried ages ago in Aboo Simbel, and by the hand-folded Osiride figures, that people, like dumb and dead Gods, that dim, demonic hall.

The beach of Syene was busy. Small craft were loading, and swarms of naked boys were driving little donkeys laden with sacks of dates, gum-arabic, tamarinds and other burdens, from Sennaar, and the tropical interior, pleasant to the imagination as to the taste. Huge camels loomed in the background, sniffing serenely, and growling and grumbling, as they were forced to kneel, and ponderous loads were heaped upon their backs. Shattered hulks of Dahabieh and Cangie lay, bare-ribbed carcasses, upon the sand, and deformed and blear-eyed wrecks of men and women crept, worm-like, in and out of them. Men and women, too, in coarse blankets, or Mrs. Bull's blue night-gowns, brought all kinds of savage spears, and clubs, and ostrich eggs, and gay baskets, and clustered duskily on the shore opposite the boat, and waited silently and passionlessly until they could catch the eye of the Howadji—then as silently elevated their wares with one hand, and with the other held up indicative fingers of the price. Unless trade more active goes on with other Dahabieh than with the Ibis, the Howadji suspects the blanketed and night-gowned Syenites do not live solely by such barter. Behind this activity, unwonted and unseen hitherto, a grove of thick palms broad-belted the beach—over which in a blue sky burned the noonday sun.

The Howadji landed, nevertheless, and rode through the town on donkeys. Dry dust under foot, yellow, ratty-looking dogs barking from the mud-caked roofs, women unutterable, happily hiding their faces, men blanketed or naked, idly staring, sore-eyed children beseeching buck-sheesh, woeless want everywhere, was the sum of sight in Syene. Thither, in times past, Juvenal was banished, and, dungeoned in Africa, had leisure to repent his satire and remember Rome. For the Romans reared a city here, and Sir Gardiner found remains some years since. But it was hard to believe that any spot could so utterly decay, upon which Rome had once set its seal. To a tourist from the lost Pleiad, there would have been very little difference between the brown mummies who stood silent among the huts of Syene and the yellow ratty curs that barked peevishly, as our donkeys trotted along. Brutes can never sink beneath a certain level. But there is no certain level of degradation beneath which men may not fall. The existence of the Syenites is as morally inexplicable as that of loathsome serpents in lonely deserts. In these lands you seem to have reached the outskirts of creation—the sink of nature—and almost suspect that its genius is too indolent ever to be entirely organized. For all strength should be sweet, and all force made fair—a fact which is clearly forgotten or disproved in Syene.

The Howadji left the houses, and were instantly in the desert—the wild, howling wilderness, that stretches ungreened to the Red Sea. It was not a plain of sand, but a huge hilliness of rock and sand commingled. There was none of the grandeur of the sand-sea, for there was no outlet for the eye to the horizon. It was like that craggy, desolate, diamond-strewn valley, into which Sinbad was carried by the Roc. All around us there was much glittering, but I saw few gems. One solitary man was watering with a Shadoof a solitary inclosure of sand. A few spare blades of grass, like the hairs on a bald head, were visible here and there, but nothing to reward such toil. It faintly greened the sand, that small inclosure, but the man at his hopeless labor was a fitting figure for the landscape.

Among the tombs, grouped together in the desert, the Howadji seemed hundreds of miles from men. There is nothing so dreary as an Egyptian burial-place. It is placed always on the skirts of the desert, where no green thing is. Huge scaly domes, like temples where ghouls worship, were open to the wild winds, and the stones lay irregularly scattered, buried in the sand. It was Lido-like, because it was sand, but inexpressibly sadder than those Hebrew graves upon the Adriatic shore, for here the desert, illimitable, stole all hope away.

A solitary camel passed, phantom-like, with his driver. Noiseless their tread. No word was spoken, no sign made. The Muslim looked at us impassibly, as if we had been grotesque carvings upon the tombs. The low wind went pacing deliriously through the defiles. The silent solitude stifled thought, and seemed to numb the soul with its deadness. But suddenly palms waved over us like hands of blessing, and, caressing the shore of Syene, ran the victor of the desert, blue-armored from his cataract triumph.

XXV.

The Treaty of Syene.

At sunset a cloud of dust.

It was a donkey cavalcade, descending the beach. Foremost rode the Captain of the Cataract, habited blackly, with a white turban. The pilotage through the cataract is the monopoly of a club of pilots (Mercury, God of commerce, forgive the name!) with some one of which the bargain must be concluded. They all try to cheat each other, of course; and probably manage the affairs of the partnership, by allowing each member in turn an illimitable chance of cheating. The white-turbaned, black-habited donkestrian, was the very Reis of Reises, the sinfulest sinner.

Behind him thronged a motley group, cantering upon small donkeys. At length the spell was successful, and the spirits were coming. Black spirits and white, blue spirits and gray, were mingled and mingling. Long men and short, bald and grisly, capped and turbaned variously, and swathed in ungainly garments, that flew and fluttered in the breeze of their speed, and blent with the dust of the donkeys, made great commotion in the golden quiet of sunset.

The cavalcade was magically undonkeyed, the savages sprang and shambled, and tumbled off, while their beasts were yet in full motion, and were mounting the plank and plunging upon the Ibis, before the animals had fairly halted. Then ensued the greeting, the salaaming. This is an exquisitely ludicrous ceremony to the spectator. It commences with touching hands and repeating some formula of thanksgiving and prayer. It continues by touching hands and repeating the formula, which is by no means brief, and is rattled off as unconcernedly as Roman priests rattle off their morning masses, looking all around and letting the words run. When it is finished, the parties kiss their own hands and separate. Generally having nothing to say, they go apart after this elaborate greeting, and separate silently at last, unless as usual they quarrel stoutly before parting.

It was amusing to see the Commander conducting this ceremony with several. The point seemed to be, who should have the last word. When the innocent spectator supposed the How-d'ye-do already said, the actors burst forth again, and kept bursting forth until kissing time. It shows the value of time to a people who are fifteen minutes saying, "how are you." And yet the Syenites and all other Egyptians have the advantage of us in some ways. They salaam at great length, and then having nothing to say, are silent. We salaam very briefly, and then having nothing to say, talk a great deal. After all, some Howadji doubt whether a Syenite Reis, sitting silent in the sunset smoking his pipe, is not as fair a figure to imagination as

Verde Giovane, or all the Piu Giovanes sitting in white gloves and bright boots, and talking through an act in an opera-box.

The salaaming accomplished, the savages seated themselves about the deck. The Captain of the Cataract, as one of the high contracting parties, sat next the cabin, before which sat the other party—the Howadji. The Commander of the Faithful, in full pontificals, enthroned himself upon a chair in the center of the deck. Chibouques were lighted, coffee brought by the Hadji Hamed, whose solemnity was not softened as on that Terpsichorean night at Esne, and zealously puffing and sipping, the council commenced.

The Howadji knows no occasion, except similar diplomatic assemblies, which could present a group of more imbecile faces. The want of pride, of manliness, of dignity, of force, of all that makes the human face divine, was supplied by an expression of imbecile cunning, ridiculously transparent. The complexions were of every color, from yellow copper to Nubian deadness of blackness. It was as hateful to be treating with such human caricatures, as it would have been with apes. The natural savage may be noble—certainly the records of Indian life are rich in dignity, heroism and manliness. But a race effete—the last lees of what was a nation, are not to be gilded when they have sunken into imbecility, because the elder inhabitants of the land were noble. Howbeit the poet Martineau could watch these men and sing rapturously of "the savage faculty." Learn at Syene, O unpoetic Howadji! that not the savage faculty of a dotard race, but the pure providence of God, takes you up and down the Cataract.

The conditions of the treaty, as of many others, were mostly understood before the Congress assembled. Prolix palaver and the dexterous seizing of chance advantages, were the means of attaining those conditions, and the Commander shook out his golden-sleeves, as Metternich his powdered wig at Vienna, then crossed his eyes like the arbiter of many fates, and said, pleasantly puffing, in Arabic—

"You took up an English boat this morning?"

The Captain of the Cataract responded "Taib," meaning, "yes, very true;" and the high contractors smoked significantly.

"A good wind for passing the Cataract," continued the Commander. No answer, but a ceaseless puffing, and a dubious, indifferent shrug. The fact being so, and the passage much depending upon the wind, it was an advantage, say the five of trumps, for the Commander, and there was a brief silence. Not to irritate by following up advantages, Golden-sleeve suggested mildly, "Quite a pleasant day," and smiled benignly upon the last rosy blushings of the West.

"Quite a pleasant day," retorted the Reis, without showing his hand, but meditating a play.

The Captain of the Cataract raised his eyes carelessly to the far outspreading yards of the Ibis, glanced along her deck with his shrunken, soulless orbs, puffed portentously, then slowly said, "Your boat is too large to go up the

Cataract." The Knave of Trumps, for the boat was very large.

But the Commander puffed, and the Reis puffed, and we all puffed, as if nothing had been said. The motley cavalcade of the Reis squatted upon the deck, stared at the Howadji, and listened to the talk, while they passed a nargileh around the circle, and grunted and groaned intense satisfaction and delight.

"This boat went up the Cataract last year," commenced the Commander, as if opening up an entirely new topic, and quite ignoring the knave. Silence again, and great cloudiness from the chibouques.

"Many boats pass up this year?"

"Many, and pay high." The Commander lost that lift.

Gradually the face of Golden-sleeve settled into a semi-sternness of expression. He exhaled smoke with the air of a man whose word was final, and in whose propositions the finger of fate was clearly to be discerned, and whom to withstand, would be the sin against the Pacha. Curious to contemplate! In the degree that the Commander's face waxed stern, and his eyes darkened with decision, crept a feline softness of sweetness over the visage of the Reis of Reises, and his mole eyes more miserably dwindled, and the smoke curled more lightly from his pipe. His body squirmed snake-like as he glanced, sycophantically entreating, at the Howadji. How clearly the crisis was coming! Astute Commander in full pontificals!

At length like a bold lover the Golden-sleeve popped the question. Then what smiling, what snaky sweetness, what utter inability to reply.

"Tell him," said the Pacha, "that going or staying is quite indifferent to us—"

The Captain of the Cataract received the interpretation like glad tidings, and smiled as if it would solace his soul, te embrace the company.

The question was popped again—

"Six hundred piasters," simpered, almost inaudibly, the old sinner.

"Damn! Six hundred devils," exclaimed the Commander in English, shoving his chair back—frowning and springing up. "We'll not go." And the golden-sleeved cloak became suddenly a gilt-edged cloud, pregnant with the maddest tempests.

But unconcerned puffed the Captain of the Cataract, smoking as serenely as Vesuvius during a Norway gale—and unconcerned puffed all the lieutenants and majors and under-scrubbery of the cataract, as if the world were not about to end.

Innocent Howadji! It was only part of the play. The Commander's face and manner said plainly enough all the time, "If you think I come hither as a lion it were pity of my life," and presently he sat down again with a fresh pipe, and another fingan of mocha, calmly as any other actor who has made a point, but will waive your approbation. Mildly smoking, he suggested pleasantly,

"We don't pay six hundred piasters."

Smoky silence—

"We pay about four hundred and fifty."

Smoky silence—

" Taib—good," said the Captain of the Cataract, that being the preconceived price of both parties.

A general commotion ensued,—an universal shaking as after sermon in Christian churches,—when this word was said. Followed much monosyllabic discourse, also grave grunting, and a little more salaaming among the belated sinners. Chibouques were refilled, fingans freely circulated, and the resonance of satisfactory smacks clearly excited the wonder and envy of the unfavored pedlars who still stood along the beach. The Reis of Reises looked about him with a great deal of expectation and anxiety, of which no notice was taken, until he made bold to suggest interrogatively, " A little something else ?"—meaning brandy, which the Commander brought, and of which the Reis emptied two such mighty measures, that if there be virtue in Cognac, he was undonkeyed before that hour of night when the serpent-magician glares glorious over Syene.

Suddenly the Congress rose. The Reis of the Cataract smiled approvingly upon the Howadji as if they were very pretty men, to be very prettily done by a grisly old mummy of an Egyptian, then salaamed, kissed his hand and stepped ashore. When he was fairly landed, I saw the Commander assisting the confused crowd of underscrubbery out of the boat, with his kurbash or whip of hippopotamus hide. They all clattered out, chattering and fluttering; and tumbling on to their donkeys, one of the high contracting parties shambled up the beach, and disappeared in a cloud of dust among the palms

And the Treaty of Syene was concluded.

XXVI.

The Cataract.

The Ibis went up the cataract.

In that pleasant, spacious dining-room of Shepherd's at Cairo, after billiard-exhilaration of a pleasant morning, men ask each other, over a quiet tiffin, "You went up the cataract?" as if boats leaped cataracts, as lovers scale silken ladders to their ladies.

The Ibis, however, went up the cataract. Imaginative youth will needs picture the Ibis dashing dexterously up a Nile Niagara, nor deem that in mystic Egypt is any thing impossible. Nor can that imagination picture scenes more exciting. Only now let us more sedately sail, for stranger scenery than this, no man sees in long voyaging.

Early on the morrow of the Treaty, a mad rabble took possession of the Ibis. They came tumbling and pitching in, wild and wan and grotesque as the eager ghosts that file into Charon's barque when it touches the Stygian shore. The Captain of captains had gone round by land to meet us at a certain point in the rapid, but had sent a substitute to pilot our way until we met him. The new rabble ran around the deck tumbling over each other, shouting, chattering, staring at the Hadji Hamed's kitchen arrangements, and the peculiarities of the Howadji—and the whole devil's row was excited and stirred up constantly by a sagacious superintendent with a long kurbash, who touched the refractory where cherubs are intangible, taking good care that the row should be constantly more riotous, and nothing be effected but his abundant castigation. Our own crew were superfluous for the nonce, and lay around the deck useless as the Howadji. A bright sun shone—a fair breeze blew, and we slipped quietly away from the shore of Syene.

The Ibis rounded a rock, and all greenness and placid palm beauty vanished. We were on the outskirts of the seething struggle between the two powers. Narrow and swift, and dark and still, like a king flying from a terrible triumph, flowed our royal river. Huge hills of jagged rock impended. Boulders lay in the water. White sand shored the stream, stretching sometimes among the rocks in short sweeps, whose dazzling white contrasted intensely with the black barriers of rock. High on a rocky peak glared a shekh's white tomb, the death's-head in that feast of terrible fascination and delight, and smoothly sheering precipices below, gave Hope no ledge to grasp in falling, but let it slip and slide inevitably into the black gulf beneath. The wreck of a Dahabieh lay high-lifted upon the rocks in the water, against the base of the cliff, its sycamore ribs white-rotting, like skeletons hung for horror and warning around the entrance of Castle Despair. All about us was rock ponderously piled, and the few sand strips. Every instant the combinations changed, so narrow was the channel, and every moment the scenery was more savage.

The wind blew us well, and the sharp quick eye of the pilot minded well our course. Sometimes we swept by rocks nearly enough to touch them. Sometimes the doubtful Ibis seemed inevitably driving into a cliff, but bent away as she approached, and ran along the dark, solemn surface of the river. Three miles of such sailing, then the cataract.

It is a series of rocky rapids. There is no fall of water, only a foaming, currenty slope, as in all rapids. The cataract is the shock of the struggle between the desert and the river. The crisis announced long since by the threatening sand-heights, has arrived. Through your dreamy avenue of palm twilight and silence, you have advanced to no lotus isles, but to a fierce and resounding battle—that sense of fate announced it in the still sunniness of the first mornings. But it seemed then only shadowy, even seductive in awfulness, like death to young imaginations. At Syene, this sunny morning, it has become a stirring reality. Pressing in from Libya and Arabia, the intervening greenness overwhelmed, the insatiate rocks and sands here grasp the shoulders of the river, and hurl their shattered crags into its bosom.

Bleak, irregular mounds and hills and regularly layered rock, rise and slope and threaten all around. Down the steep sides of the mountains, here reaching the river, like a headlong plunge of disordered cavalry, roll fragments of stone of every size and shape. Like serried fronts, immovable, breasting the burden of the battle, the black smooth precipices stand in the rushing stream. Then pile upon pile, fantastic, picturesque, strange, but never sublime, like foes lifted upon foes to behold the combat, the intricate forms of rock crowd along the shore.

It is the desert's enthusiastic descent—its frenzied charge of death or victory. Confusion confounded, desolated desolation, never sublime, yet always solemn, with a sense of fate in the swift-rushing waters, that creates a somber interest, not all unhuman, but akin to dramatic intensity.

The Nile, long dallying in placid Nubia, lingers lovingly around templed Philæ—the very verge of the vortex. It laves the lithe flowers along its shore, and folds it in a beautiful embrace. It sees what it saw there, but what it sees no longer. Is its calm the trance of memory or of love? What were the Ptolemies and their temples and their lives; what those of all their predecessors there, but various expressions sweet and strange, that flushed along the face of the Nile's idol, but fleetly faded? It lingers on the very verge of the vortex, then, unpausing, plunges in. Foamingly furious, it dashes against the sharp rocks and darts beyond them. Scornfully sweeping, it seethes over ambuscades of jagged stone below. Through tortuous channels here, through wild ways there, it leads its lithe legion undismayed, and the demon desert is foiled forever.

Then royally raging, a king with dark brows thoughtful, the Nile sweeps solemnly away from the terrible triumph—but caresses palm-belted Syene as it flies, and calms itself gradually beyond, among serene green shores.

The Ibis reached the first rapid. The swift rush of the river and the favoring wind held it a long time stationary. Had the wind lulled, she would have swung round suddenly with the stream, and plunged against the rocks that hemmed her—rocks watching the Ibis as inexorably as desert monsters their prey.

Suddenly a score of savages leaped shouting and naked into the water, and buffeting the rapid, reached a rock with a rope. This they clumsily attached to a stump, and the yelling savages on board pulled at it and drew us slowly up. Like imps and demons, the black sinners clambered over the sharp points and along the rocks, shouting and plunging into the rapid, to reach another rock—at home as much in the black water as out of it—madly dancing and deviling about; so that, surveying the mummy-swathed groups on deck, and the hopeless shores and the dark devils, the Nile was the Nile no longer, but the Styx, and the Ibis, Charon's barque of death. The tumult was terrible. No one seemed to command, and the superintendent kept up a vigorous application of the kurbash to the adjacent shoulders, but without the slightest practical influence upon the voyage. In the hellish howling of the rabble, and sure swiftness and dash of the stream, a little silent sense had been heavenly. For the channels are so narrow that it needs only a strong rope and a strong pull to insure the ascent. A few blocks, beams, and pulleys, upon points where a purchase is necessary, would make the ascent rapid and easy. There are, at this point, not more than four or five rapids, a few yards wide each one, at the narrowest. Between these hell-gates, there is room to sail, if there be wind enough, and if not, the tracking, with many men, is not arduous.

The poet Martineau and Belzoni are at issue upon the "savage faculty." This mystery, of which the Howadji could never discover the slightest trace, charmed the poet Harriet particularly at this point. Belzoni says of these men, that their utmost sagacity reaches only to pulling a rope, or sitting on the extremity of a lever as a counterpoise; and he also, in a very unpoetic fervor, declares that in point of skill, they are no better than beasts. Certainly it would be strange if a race so ignorant and clumsy in all things else, should develop fine faculties here. These demons drew the Ibis up the rapids, as they would have drawn a wagon up a hill—the success and the Io pæans are due to the strength of the rope. Had the poet Harriet ever shot the Sault Sainte Marie with a silent Indian in a birch shell, she might have beheld and chanted the "savage faculty." But this immense misdirection of the force of an hundred or more men, deserves no lyric.

The Ibis was drawn through two rapids, and then the Captain of the Cataract appeared upon the shore, mounted on a donkey and surrounded by a staff or a council of ministers, similarly mole-eyed and grisly. I fancied, at first, the apparition was only a party of mummies donkeying along through the cataract, to visit some friendly Nubian mummies in the hills beyond. For the cataract is a kind of "wolf's glen," and phantoms and grotesque ghosts of every kind are to be expected; but they slid off their beasts and shuffled down the sand slope to the shore and sprang aboard, helping up the most shriveled of mummies, who was presented to the Howadji as the father of the Captain of the Cataract, and it was clearly expected by the Captain and the crew that that fact would be recognized in a flowing horn of brandy, as partly discharging the world's debt to old grisly, for begetting that pilot and very Reis of very Reises—

> "Sing George the Third, and not the least in worth,
> For graciously begetting George the Fourth."

The brandy was served, and the Howadji stepped ashore to visit Philæ, while the Ibis cleared the rest of the rapids and met them at Mahratta, the first Nubian village.

XXVII.

Nubian Welcome.

"BUCKSHEESH HOWADJI—Buchsheesh Howadji," welcomed us to Nubia. A group of naked little negroes with donkeys awaited us on the bank, and intoned the national hymn, "Alms, O Shopkeeper," as we mounted through the sand. The Howadji straddled the donkeys, for you do not mount a donkey more than you would a large dog, and sitting upon a thick cloth, the steed's only trapping, and nothing but the Howadji's nimble management of his legs to keep that on, away we went, helter skelter, over the sand—shamble, trot, canter, tumble, up again and ahead, jerking and shaking upon the little beasts, that balanced themselves along as if all four legs at once were necessary to support such terrible Howadji weights.

Away we dashed, scrambling along the bank. The sky cloudless—burning the sun—wild the waste shore. Ledges of rock lay buried in the sand, and at the head of the cataract, its Nubian mouth, a palm-shaded village. Fantastically frowning everywhere, the chaos of rock, and beyond and among, the river in shining armor, sinuous in the foaming struggle.

It was pure desert—a few patches of green grew miserable in the sand, forlorn as Christian pilgrims in Saracen Jerusalem. The bold formlessness of the cliffs allured the eye. Seen from the shore they are not high, but the mighty masses, irregularly strewn and heaped, crowding and concentrating upon the river, shrinking along the shores, yet strewn in the stream, and boldly buffeting its fury, are fascinatingly fantastic. Your eye, so long used to actual silence, and a sense of stillness in the forms and characters of the landscape, is unnaturally excited, and bounds restlessly from rock to river, as if it had surprised Nature in a move, and should see sudden and startling changes. The Howadji has caught her in this outlawed corner before her arrangments were completed. She is setting up the furniture of her scenery. This rock is surely to be shifted there, and that point to be swept away, here. There is intense expectation. Ah! if the Howadji had not traveled in vain, but should really see something and understand the secret significance of cataracts!

But a sudden donkey-quake wrecked all speculation, and like a tower shaken, but recovering itself from falling, the Howadji allowed the quake to "reel unheededly away," and alighted quietly upon his left leg, while the liberated donkey smelt about for food in the sand, like an ass. The soaring speculations of the moment upon the text of the prospect, had made the Howadji too unmindful that the nimble clinging of his legs to the donkey's ribs was the sole belly-band of his cloth and warrant of his seat; so the three went suddenly asunder, donkey, Howadji and cloth, but reuniting, went forward again into Nubia, an uncertain whole.

The barking of dogs announced our arrival at Mahratta, the first Nubian village. Dull, mud Syene was only three miles distant over the desert. Yet here mud was plaster, smooth and neat, and the cleanliness of the houses—a certain regular grace in them—the unvailed faces of the women, and their determined color, for they were emphatically black—made Nubia pleasant, at once and forever. These women braiding baskets, or busily spinning in the sun, with mild features, and soft eyes—their woolly hair frizzling all over their heads, and bright bits of metal glittering around their necks and in their noses and ears, were genuine Ethiopians in their own land. At once the Howadji felt a nobler, braver race. The children were gayer and healthier. I saw no flies feeding upon Nubian eyes. The Nubian houses are square and flat-roofed, and often palm-thatched. Grain jars stood around them, not unhandsomely, and mud divans built against the outer walls were baked by the sun into some degree of comfort We paused in a group of women and children, and they gave us courteously to drink. Then we rode on, our route reeling always between the rocky hills and the rocky river.

Suddenly at high noon, at the end of a tortuous rocky vista, and a mile or two away, stood Philæ—form in formlessness, measured sound in chaotic discord. For a moment it was Greece visible—all detail was devoured by distance, which is enamored of general effect, and loves only the essential impression. It was a more wonderful witchery of that wild scenery, a rich revelation of forms as fair as Prospero could have built before Ferdinand's eyes. For the beauty and grace of Philæ, so seen, in that stern and vivid contrast of form and feeling, are like the aerial architecture which shone substantial before the Magician's eyes, as imaging the glory of the world—and whose delicacy sang to Ferdinand, when he knew not if it were "i' the air or the earth."

Philæ, so delicately drawn upon that transparent noon air, was an ecstasy of form. There were only architraves and ranges of columns among the black beetling rocks. It soothed the eye, for in chaos here was creation. And even broken columns, stately, still—ranging along a river, are as pleasant to the eye as water flowers.

XXVIII.

Philæ.

I WISH Philæ were as lovely as the melody of its name imports.

But I do not dare to call Isis by the name of Venus—or if the Palmyrene Zenobia, following the triumph of Aurelian, was pretty—then is Philæ chained to the car of Time, lovely. Poet Eliot Warburton, indeed, speaks of its "exquisite beauty." What shall the Howadji do with these poets?

Girdled with the shining Nile, Philæ is an austere beauty—Isis-like, it sits solemn-browed, column crushing column, pylons yet erect, and whole sides of temple courts yet standing with perfect pillars—huge decay, wherein grandeur is yet grand. It is strange to see human traces so lovely in a spot so lonely. Strange, after the death in life of the Nile valley, to emerge upon life in death so imperial as Philæ. For you remember that the Ibis did not pause at the temples, but beheld Thebes and Dendereh, as she flew, like pictures fading on the air.

Seen from the shore, a band of goldenest green surrounds the island. The steep bank is lithe with lupin and flowering weeds. Palms are tangled, as they spring, with vines and creepers, dragon-flies float sparkling all over it—and being the sole verdure in that desolation, the shores of Philæ are gracious as blue sky after storms. A party of naked young Nubians rowed us over in a huge tub of a boat, which, with their bent boughs of trees for oars, they could scarcely keep against the current. They had a young crocodile for toy, with which they played with as much delight as with a kitten. The infant dragon was ten days old, and about a foot long. It sprawled sluggishly about the bottom of the boat, as its mature relatives stretch indolently along the sandy shores, and the boys delighted to push it back with a stick as it crawled feebly up the side. There was no special malice in it at this treatment. Dragon seemed to know perfectly that he was born heir to a breakfast upon some of his tormentors, or their near relatives, and that the fun would be one day quite the other side of his mouth, into which our young friends thrust sticks and stones, not perceiving, the innocents! that they were simply rehearsing their own fate. The Howadji wished to sacrifice it to Osiris as they stepped ashore upon his island, but reflected that it was a bad precedent to sacrifice one God to another,—and wound through the crimson-eyed lupin, the wild bean, and a few young palms that fringe the island, up to the ruins.

The surface of the island is a mass of ruin. But the great temple of Isis yet stands, although it is shattered, and a smaller Hypethral temple overhangs the river. It is not inarticulate ruin, but while whole walls and architraves and column ranges remain, several buildings are shattered, and their fallen walls are blended.

Philæ was the holy island of old Egypt. Thither sailed processions of higher purpose, in barques more gorgeous than now sail the river, and deep down-gazing in the moonlight Nile, the Poet shall see the vanished splendor of a vanished race, centering solemnly here, like priestly pomp around an altar. Hither, bearing gifts, came kneeling Magi, before they repaired to the Bethlehem manger. And kings, not forgotten of fame, here unkinged themselves before a kinglier. For the island was dedicate to Osiris, the great God of the Egyptians, who were not idolaters, as far as appears, but regarded Osiris as the incarnation of the goodness of the unutterable God of Gods.

But it were easier for a novice to trace the temple lines among these ruins, than for an ordinary Howadji to evolve lucidity from the intricacy of the old Egyptian theology. And we who stroll these shores, pilgrims of beauty only, can not pause to lose ourselves in the darkness and ruin and inodorous intricacy of the labyrinth, like mere explorers of the pyramids. We know very little of the Egyptian theology, and that little is ill told. Had I graduated at Heliopolis, I would have revealed to you all. But many there be, who not having taken degrees at Heliopolis or Memphis, do yet treat of these things. Books abound wherewith the Howadji, in his Dahabieh on the Nile, or in the warm slippers at home, may befog his brain, and learn as much of the religious as of the political history of Egypt.

What did the tenth king of the seventeenth dynasty for the world? nay, why was Ramses great? Ah, confess that you love to linger with Cleopatra more than with Isis, and adore Memnon more willingly than Amun Re! Swart Cleopatra, superbly wound in Damascus silks and Persian shawls, going gorgeously down the Nile in a golden gondola to meet Marc Antony, had more refreshed my eyes than Sesostris returning victorious from the Ganges. Ramses may have sacrificed to Isis, as Cleopatra to Venus. But in the highest heaven all divinities are equal.

Isis was the daughter of Time, and the wife and sister of Osiris. Horus was their child, and they are the Trinity of Philæ. Osiris and Isis finally judged the dead, and were the best beloved Gods of the ancients, and best known of the moderns. Yet the devil Typhoo vanquished Osiris, who lies buried in the cataract, which henceforth will be an emblem to the poetic Howadji of the stern struggle of the Good and Bad Principle. And gradually, as he meditates upon Osiris and Egypt and a race departed, one of the fine old fancies of the elder Egyptians will grow into faith with him, and he will see in the annual overflow of the river the annual resurrection of the good Osiris to bless the land. Tradition buried Osiris in the cataract, and the solemn Egyptian oath, was "by him who sleeps in Philæ." Here was the great temple erected to his mourning widow, and sculptured gigantically upon the walls, the cow-horned, ever mild-eyed Isis, holds her Horus and deplores her spouse.

Very beautiful is Isis in all Egyptian sculptures. Tenderly tranquil her large generous features, gracious her full-lipped mouth, divine the dignity of her mien. In the groups of fierce fighters and priests, and beasts and bird-headed Gods that people the walls, her aspect is always serene and solacing—the type of the feminine principle in the beast and bird chaos of the world.

The temples are of Ptolemaic times, and of course modern for Egypt, although traces of earlier buildings are still discoverable. The cartouche, or cipher of Cleopatra, *our* Cleopatra, among the many of Egypt, appears here. The ruins are stately and imposing, and one range of thirty columns yet remains. The capitals, as usual, are different flowers. The lotus, the acacia and others, are wreathed around and among them. Desaix's inscription is upon the wall with its republican date, and that of Pope Gregory XVI.—the effete upon the effete.

The Howadji wandered among the temples. The colored ceilings, the columned courts, the rude sculptures of beasts and birds and flowers—rude in execution, but in idea very lofty—the assembling and consecration of all nature to the rulers of nature—these were grand and imposing. Nor less so in their kind, the huge masses of stone so accurately carved, whereof the temples were built. For the first time, at Philæ, we practically felt the massiveness of the Egyptian architecture. These temples scorn and defy time, as the immovable rocks the river. Yet the river and time wear them each slowly, but how slowly, away. We saw the singular strength of the buildings and the precision of their construction by climbing the roof by a narrow staircase, built in the wall of the great temple. The staircase emerges upon the roof over the Adytum, or Holy of Holies, with which singular, small apertures communicate. Conveniences for the Gods were these? Divine whispering-tubes? Private entrances of the spirit? Scuttles for Osiris and the fair Isis, or part of the stage-scenery of the worship, wherethrough priests whispered for Gods, and men were cozened by men?

Ah! Verde Giovane! fragments of whose pleasant Philæ breakfast are yet visible on this roof—Time loves his old tale and tells it forever over. Has not the Howadji seen in Rome the Pope, or spiritual papa of the world, sitting in a wooden kneeling figure, and playing pray under that very burning eye of heaven—an Italian sun of a June noonday?

The Arab boys crouched in their blankets in the sun, upon the roof, as if it were cold, for to the Egyptian clothes are too much a luxury not to be carefully used when he has any. They smoked their pipes carelessly, incuriously, as if they were sculptures upon one wall and the Howadji upon another. Pleasant, the sunny loitering, with no Cicerone to disgust, lost in mild musing meditation, the moonlight of the mind. You will have the same red book or another, when you loiter, and thence learn the details and the long list of Ptolemies and Euergetes, who built and added and amended. Thence, too, you will learn the translations of hieroglyphics—the theories and speculations and other dusty stuff inseparable from ruins.

You will be grave at Philæ, how serenely sunny soever the day. But with a gravity graver than that of sentiment, for it is the deadness of the death of the land that you will feel. The ruins will be to you the remains of the golden age of Egypt, for hither came Thales, Solon, Pythagoras, Herodotus and Plato, and from the teachers of Moses learned the most mystic secrets of human thought. It is the faith of Philæ that, developed in a thousand ways, claims our mental allegiance to-day—a faith transcending its teachers, as the sun the eyes which it enlightens. These wise men came—the wise men of Greece, whose wisdom was Egyptian, and hither comes the mere American Howadji and learns, but with a difference. He feels the greatness of a race departed. He recognizes that a man only differently featured from himself, lived and died here two thousand years ago.

Ptolemy and his Cleopatra walked these terraces, sought shelter from this same sun in the shade of these same columns, dreamed over the calm river, at sunset, by moonlight, drained their diamond-rimmed goblet of life and love, then embalmed in sweet spices, were laid dreamless in beautiful tombs. Remembering these things, glide gently from Philæ, for we shall see it no more. Slowly, slowly southward loiters the Ibis, and leaves its columned shores behind. Glide gently from Philæ, but it will not glide from you. Like a queen, crowned in death among her dead people, it will smile sadly through your memory forever.

XXIX.

A Crow that flies in Heaven's Sweetest Air.

Fleetly the Ibis flew. The divine days came and went. Unheeded the longing sunrise, the lingering eve. Unheeded the lonely shore of Nubia that swept, Sakia-singing, seaward. Unheeded the new world of African solitude, the great realm of Ethiopia. Unheeded the tropic upon which, for the first time, we really entered, and the pylons, columns and memorial walls that stood solitary in the sand. The Howadji lay ill in the blue cabin, and there is no beauty, no antiquity, no new world to an eye diseased.

Yet illness, said a white-haired form that sat shadowy by his side, hath this in it, that it smooths the slope to death. The world is the organization of vital force, but when a man sickens, the substantial reality reels upon his brain. The cords are cut that held him to the ship that sails so proudly the seas, and he drifts lonely in the jolly-boat of his own severed existence, toward shores unknown. Drifts not unwillingly, as he sweeps farther away and his eyes are darkened.

After acute agony, said still the white-haired shadow,

pausing slowly, as if he too were once alive and young, death is like sleep after toil. After long decay, it is as natural as sunset. Yet to sit rose-garlanded at the feast of love and beauty, yourself the lover, and the most beautiful, and hearing that you shall depart thence in a hearse, not in a bridal chariot, to rise smilingly and go gracefully away, is a rare remembrance for any man—an heroic death that does not often occur, nor is it to be rashly wished. For the heroic death is the Gods' gift to their favorites. Who shall be presumptuous enough to claim that favor? Nay, if all men were heroes, how hard it would be to die and leave them, for our humanity loves heroes more than angels and saints. It would be the discovery of a boundless California, and gold would be precious no more.

The shadow was silent, and the Nubian moonlight crept yellow along the wall; then, playing upon the Howadji's heartstrings vaguely and at random, as a dreaming artist touching the keys of an instrument, he proceeded. Yet we may all know how many more the dead are than the living, nor be afraid to join them. Here, in Egypt, it is tombs which are inhabited, it is the cities which are deserted. The great Ramses has died, and all his kingdom—why not little you and I? Nor care to lie in a tomb so splendid. Ours shall be a sky-vaulted Mausoleum, sculptured with the figaries of all life. No man of mature years but has more friends dead than living. His friendly reunion is a shadowy society. Who people for him the tranquil twilight and the summer dawn? In the woods we knew, what forms and faces do we see? What is the meaning of music, and who are its persons? What are the voices of midnight, and what words slide into our minds, like sudden moonlight into dark chambers, and apprise us that we move in the vast society of all worlds and all times, and that if the van is lost to our eyes in the dazzling dawn, and the rear disappears in the shadow of Night our Mother, and our comrades fall away from our sides—the van, and the rear, and the comrades are yet, and all, moving forward like the water-drops of the Amazon to the sea. It is not strange that when severe sickness comes, we are ready to die. Long buffeted by bleak, blue icebergs, we see at last with equanimity that we are sailing into Symmes' hole.

The Nubian moonlight crept yellow along the wall, but the monotonous speech of the white-haired mystery went sounding on, like the faint far noise of the cataract below Philæ.

Otherwise Nature were unkind. She smooths the slope, because she is ever gentle. For to turn us out of doors suddenly and unwillingly into the night, were worse than a cursing father. But Nature can never be as bad as man. What boots it that Faith follows our going with a rush lantern, and Hope totters before with a lucifer? Shrewd, sad eyes have scrutinized those lights, and whispered only, "It is the dancing of will-o'-the-wisps among the tombs." It is only the gift of Nature that we die well, as that we are born well. It is Nature that unawes death to us, and makes it welcome and pleasant as sleep.

A mystery!

But if you say that it is the dim dream of the future, wrought into the reality of faith, that smooths death—then that dream and faith are the devices of nature, like these enticing sculptures upon tomb avenues, to lead us gently down. For I find that all men are cheered by this dream, although its figures are as the men. There are gardens and houris, or hunting-grounds and exhaustless deer, or crystal cities where white-robed pilgrims sing hymns forever,—(howbeit after Egypt no philosophic Howadji will hold that long white garments are of heaven.)

The flickering form waved a moment in the moonlight and resumed.

Heaven is a hint of Nature, and therein shall we feel how ever kind she is—opening the door of death into golden gloom, she points to the star that gilds it. She does this to all men, and in a thousand ways. But in all lands are seers who would monopolize the seeing—Bunyan pilots, sure you will ground in the gloom except you embark in their ship, and with their treatise of navigation. Meanwhile the earth has more years than are yet computed, and the Bunyan pilots are of the threescore and ten species.

Priests and physicians agree, that at last all men die bravely, and we are glad to listen. O Howadji, that bravery was ours. We should be as brave as the hundred of any chance crowd, and so indirectly we know how we should die, even if, at some time, Death has not looked closely at us over the shoulder, and said audibly what we knew—that he held the fee simple of our existence.

The Nubian moonlight waned along the wall. We praise our progress, said the white-haired shadow, yet know no more than these Egyptians knew. We say that we feel we are happier, and that the many are wiser and better, simply because we are alive, and they are mummies, and life is warmer than death. The seeds of the world were sown along these shores. There is none lovelier than Helen, nor wiser than Plato, nor better than Jesus. They were children of the sun, and of an antiquity that already fades and glimmers upon our eyes.

Venus is still the type of beauty—our philosophy is diluted Platonism—our religion is an imitation of Christ. The forms of our furniture are delicately designed upon the walls of Theban tombs. Thales after his return from Egypt determined the sun's orbit, and gave us our year. Severe study detects in Egyptian sculptures emblems of our knowledge and our skill. Have you, O Howadji, new ideas, or only different developments of the old ones? As the Ibis bears you southward, are you proud and compassionate of your elders and your masters—or do you feel simply that the earth is round, and that if in temperate regions the homely lark soars and sings, in the tropics the sumptuous plumage of silent birds is the glittering translation of that song?

Have you mastered the mystery of death—have you even guessed its meaning? Are Mount Auburn and Greenwood truer teachers than the Theban tombs? Nature adorns death. Even sets in smiles, the face that shall smile no more. But you group around it hideous associations, and of the pale phantom make an appalling apparition. Broken columns—inverted torches—weeping angels and willows are within the gates upon which you write, "Whoso believeth in me shall never die." Blackness and knolling bells, weepers and hopeless scraps of Scripture, these are the heavy stones that we roll against the sepulchers in which lie those whom you have baptized in his name, who came to abolish death.

Why should not you conspire with Nature to keep death beautiful, nor dare, when the soul has soared, to dishonor by the emblems of decay the temple it has consecrated and honored. Lay it reverently, and pleasantly accompanied, in the earth, and there leave it forever, nor know of skulls or cross-bones. Nor shall willows weep for a tree that is greener—nor a broken column symbolize a work completed—nor inverted flame a pure fire ascending. Better than all, burn it with incense at morning—so shall the mortal ending be not unworthy the soul, nor without significance of the soul's condition. Tears, like smiles, are of nature, and will not be repressed. They are sacred, and should fall with flowers upon the dead. But forgetting graveyards and cemeteries, how silent and solemn soever, treasure the dearest dust in sacred urns, so holding in your homes forever those who have not forfeited, by death, the rights of home.

The wan, white-haired shadow wasted in the yellow moonlight.

But all illness is not unto death. Much is rather like dark, stony caves of meditation by the wayside of life.

There is no carousing there, no Kushuk Arnem and Ghawazee dancing, but pains as of corded hermits and starving ascetics. Yet the hermit has dreams that the king envies. We come thousands of miles to see strange lands, wonderful cities, and haunts of fame. But in a week's illness in the blue cabin or elsewhere, cities of more shining towers and ponderous palace-ranges, lands of more wondrous growth and races than ever Cook or Columbus discovered, or the wildest dreamer dreamed, dawn and die along the brain. To those golden gates and shores sublime no palmy Nile conducts—not even the Euphrates or Tigris, nor any thousands of miles, would bring the traveler to that sight. Sick Sinbad, traveling only from one side of his bed to the other, could have told tales stranger and more fascinating than enchanted his gaping guests.

Ah! could we tame the fantastic genius that only visits us with fever for the entertainment of our health, we could well spare the descriptive poets, nor read Vathek and Hafiz any more. But he is untamable, until his brother of sleep, that good genius who gives us dreams, will consent to serve our waking—until stars shine at noonday—until palms wave along the Hudson shores.

XXX.

Southward.

The Nubians devote themselves to nudity and to smearing their hair with castor oil.

At least it seems so from the river. Nor have they much chance to do any thing else, for Nubia only exists by the grace of the desert or the persistence of the Nile in well-doing. It is a narrow strip of green between the mountains on both sides, and the river. Often it is only the mere slope of the bank which is green. You ascend through that, pushing aside the flowering lupin and beans, and stand at the top of the bank in the desert. Often the desert stretches to the stream, and defies it, shoring it with sheer sand. A few taxed palms, a few taxed Sakias, the ever neat little houses, the comely black race, and, walling all, the inexorable mountains, rocky, jagged, of volcanic outline and appearance—these are the few figures of the Nubian panorama.

Dates, baskets, mats, the gum and charcoal of the mimosa, a little senna, and farther south ebony, sandal-wood, rice, sugar, and slaves, are all the articles of commerce—lupins, beans, and dhourra, a kind of grain, the crops of consumption.

It is a lonely, solitary land. There are no flights of birds, as in Egypt; no wide valley reaches, greened with golden plenty. Scarce a sail whitens the yellow-blue of the river. A few solitary camels and donkeys pass, spectral, upon the shore. It seems stiller than Egypt, where the extent of the crops, the frequent villages and constant population, relieve the sense of death. In Nubia, it is the silence of intense suspense. The unyielding mountains range along so near the river, that the Howadji fears the final triumph of the desert.

Like a line of fortresses stretched against the foe, stand the Sakias, the allies of the river. But their ceaseless sigh, as in Egypt, only saddens the silence. Through the great gate of the cataract, you enter a new world, south of the Poet's "farthest south." A sad, solitary, sunny world—but bravery and the manly virtues are always the dower of poor races, who must roughly rough it to exist.

In appearance and character the Nubians are the superiors of the Egyptians. But they are subject to them by the inscrutable law that submits the darker races to the whiter, the world over. The sweetness and placidity and fidelity, the love of country and family, the simplicity of character and conduct which distinguish them, are not the imperial powers of a people. Like the Savoyards into Europe, the Nubians go down into Egypt and fill inferior offices of trust. They are the most valued of servants, but never lose their home—longing and return into the strange, sultry silence of Nubia, when they have been successful in Egypt.

Yet the antique Ethiopian valor survives. Divers districts are still warlike, and the most savage struggles are not unknown. The Ethiopians once resisted the Romans, and the fame of one-eyed Queen Candace, whose wisdom and valor gave the name to her successors, yet flourishes in the land, and the remains of grand temples attest that the great Ramses and the proud Ptolemies thought it worth while to own it. The Nubians bear arms, but all of the rudest kind—crooked knives, iron-shod clubs, and slings and a shield of hippopotamus hide—and in the battles the women mingle and assist.

Yet in the five hundred miles from Syene to Dongola, not more than one hundred thousand inhabitants are estimated. They reckon seven hundred Sakias for that distance, and that each is equal to one thousand five hundred bushels of grain.

These shores are the very confines of civilization. The hum of the world has died away into stillness. The sun shines brightly in Nubia. The sky is blue, but the sadness of the land rests like a shadow upon the Howadji. It is like civilization dying decently. The few huts and the few people smile and look contented. They come down to the shore, as the Ibis skims along, wonderingly and trustfully as the soft-souled Southern savages beheld with curiosity Columbus' fleet. They are naked and carry clubs, and beg powder and arms, but sit quietly by your side as you sketch or sit upon the shore, or run like hunting-dogs for the pigeons you have shot. If there be any impossible shot, the Howadji is called upon with perfect confidence to execute it—for a clothed Howadji with a gun is a denizen of a loftier sphere to the nude Nubians. Why does the sun so spoil its children and fondle their souls away? How neat are their homes, like houses set in order! For the mighty desert frowns behind, and the crushing government frowns below. Yet the placid Nubian looks from his taxed Sakia to his taxed palms, sees the sand and the tax-gatherer stealing upon his substance, and quietly smiles, as if his land were a lush-vineyarded Rhine-bank.

The Howadji had left the little, feline Reis at Syene, his home, for the indolent Nubian blood was mingled in his veins, and made him seem always this quiet land personified. The Ibis flew, piloted by a native Nubian, who knew the river through his country. For here the shores are stony, and there are two difficult passages, which the natives call half-cataracts.

Hassan was a bright-eyed, quiet personage, who discharged his functions very humbly, sitting with the Ancient Mariner at the helm, who seemed, grisly Egyptian, half jealous of his Nubian colleague, and contemptuously remarked, when we reached Philæ, returning, that no man need go twice to know the river. The men were uneasy at the absence of their head, nor liked to be directed by the Nubian, or the Ancient Mariner; but Hassan sang with them such scraps of Arabic song as he knew, and regaled them with pure Nubian melodies, which are sweeter than those of Egypt, for the Nubians are much more musical than their neighbors, and in a crew, they are the best and most exhilarating singers. He sat patiently on the prow for hours, watching the river, calling at times to Grisly to turn this way and that, and Hassan was uniformly genial and gentle, pulling an occasional oar, returning.

For the rest, he was clothed in coarse, white cotton, haunted the kitchen after dinner, and fared sumptuously every day. Then begged tobacco of the Howadji, and smoked it as serenely as if it were decently gotten.

At Kálabsheh we passed the Tropic of Cancer.

But are not the Tropics the synonym of Paradise? The tropics, mused the Howadji, and instantly imagination was entangled in an Indian jungle, and there struggled, fettered in glorious foliage, mistaking the stripes and eyes of a royal Bengal tiger, for the most gorgeous of tropical flowers. But escaping thence, imagination fluttered and fell, and a panorama of stony hills, a cloudless, luminous sky, but bare in brilliance, enlivened by no clouds, by no far-darting troops of birds—a narrow strip of green shore—silence, solitude and sadness revealed to the Howadji the dream-land of the tropics.

Yet there was a sunny spell in that land and scenery which held me then, and holds charmed my memory now. It was a sleep—we seemed to live it and breathe it, as the sun in Egypt. There was luminous languor in the air, as from opiate flowers, yet with only their slumber, and none of their fragrance. It seemed a failure of creation, or a creation not yet completed. Nature slept and dreamed over her work, and whoso saw her sleep, dreamed vaguely her dreams.

Puck-piloted and girdling the earth in an hour, would

not the Howadji feel that only a minute's journey of that hour was through the ripe maturity of creation—the rest, embryo—half conceived or hopeless? "The world" is only the fine focus of all the life of the world at any period; but, O Gunning in blue spectacles, picking gingerbread nuts off the Dôm palm, how small is that focus!

One Nubian day only was truly tropical. It was near Derr, the chief town, and the azure calm and brilliance of the atmosphere forced imagination to grow glorious gardens upon the shores, and to crown with forests, vine-waving, bloom-brilliant, the mountains, desert no longer, but divine as the vision-seen hill of prophets; and to lead triumphal trains of white elephants, bearing the forms and costumes of Eastern romance, and giraffes, and the priestly pomp of India, through the groves of many-natured palms that fringed the foreground of the picture. It was summer and sunshine—a very lotus day.

I felt the warm breath of the morning streaming over the Ibis, like radiance from opening eyes, even before the lids of the dawn were lifted. Then came the sun over the Arabian mountains, and the waves danced daintily in the rosy air, and the shores sloped serenely, and the river sang and gurgled against the prow, whereon sat the white-turbaned, happy Hassan, placidly smoking, and self-involved, as if he heard all the white Nile secrets, and those of the Mountains of the Moon. The Ibis spread her white wings to the warm wooing wind, and ran over the water. Was she not well called Ibis, with her long, sharp wings, loved of the breeze, that toys with them as she flies and fills them to fullness with speed?

The sky was cloudless and burningly rosy. To what devote the delicious day? What dream so dear, what book so choice, that it would satisfy the spell? Luxury of doubt and long delay! Such wonder itself was luxury—it rippled the mind with excitement, delicately as the wind kissed the stream into wavelets. Yet the Howadji looked along the shelves and the book was found, and in the hot heart of noon he had drifted far into the dreamy depths of Herman Melville's Mardi. Lost in the rich romance of Pacific reverie, he felt all around him the radiant rustling of Yillah's hair, but could not own that Polynesian peace was profounder than his own Nubian silence.

Mardi is unrhymed poetry, but rhythmical and measured. Of a low, lapping cadence is the swell of those sentences, like the dip of the sun-stilled, Pacific waves. In more serious moods, they have the grave music of Bacon's Essays. Yet who but an American could have written them? And essentially American are they, although not singing Niagara or the Indians.

Romance or reality, asked, dazed in doubt, bewildered Broadway and approving Pall Mall. Both, erudite metropolitans, and you, O ye of the warm slippers. The Howadji is no seaman, yet can he dream the possible dreams of the mariner in the main-top of the becalmed or trade-wind-wafted Pacific whaler. In those musings, mingles rare reality, though it be romantically edged, as those palms of Ibreem, seen through the glass, are framed in wondrous gold and purple—

On, on, deeper into the Pacific calm, farther into that Southern spell! The day was divine—the hush, the dazzle, the supremacy of light, were the atmosphere of the tropics, and if toward evening, and for days after, the anxious North blustered in after her children, she could never steal that day from their memories. The apple was bitten. The Howadji had tasted the Equator.

XXXI.

Ultima Thule.

We sought the South no longer. Far flown already into a silent land, the Ibis finally furled her wings at Aboo Simbel. But far and ever farther southward, over the still river-reaches, pressed piercing thought, nor paused at Khartoum where the Nile divides, nor lingered until lost, in the Mountains of the Moon. Are they sarcastically named, those mountains, or prophetically, that when they are explored, the real moon ranges shall be determined ?

Up through the ruins of the eldest land and the eldest race came two children of the youngest, and stood gazing southward into silence. Southward into the childishness of races forever in their dotage or never to grow—toward the Dinkas and the shores loved of the lotus, where they worship trees, and pull out the incisors for beauty, and where a three-legged stool is a King's throne.

The South! our synonym of love, beauty and a wide world unrealized. Lotus fragrance blows outward from that name, and steeps us in blissful dreams that bubble audibly in song from poets' lips. It is the realm of faery-fantasy and perfected passion. Dark, deep eyes gushing radiance in rapt summer noons, are the South, visible and bewildering to the imagination of the North. Whoso sails southward is a happy Mariner, and we fancy his ship gliding forever across tranced sapphire seas, reeking with rarest odors, steeped in sunshine and silence, wafted by winds that faint with sweet and balm against the silken sails, for the South has no wood for us but sandal and ebony and cedar, and no stuffs but silks and cloth of gold.

Sumptuous is the South—a Syren singing us ever forward to a bliss never reached; but with each mile won she makes the pursuit more passionate, brimming the cup that only feeds the thirst, with delicious draughts that taste divine. Then some love-drunken poet beholds her as a person, and bursts into song—

> "I muse, as in a trance, whene'er
> The languors of thy love-deep eyes
> Float on to me. I would I were
> So tranced, so rapt in ecstasies—
> To stand apart and to adore,
> Gazing on thee for evermore—
> Serene, imperial Eleanore."

The morning was bright when the Ibis stopped at Aboo Simbel. Nero presently arrived, and the blue pennant passed, flying forward to Wady Halfa and the second cataract. After a brief delay and a pleasant call, Nero stretched into the stream, and the Italian tricolor floated off southward, and disappeared. The Ibis was left alone at the shore. Over it rose abruptly a bold picturesque rock which, of all the two hundred miles between the cataracts, is the natural site for a rock temple.

A grand goal is Aboo Simbel for the long Nile voyage, and the more striking that it is approached from Cairo, through long ranges of white plaster mosques, and minarets, and square mud pigeon houses—the highest architectural attempt of modern Egyptian genius on the Nile. The Howadji is ushered by dwarfs into the presence of a God. The long four weeks' flight of the Ibis through such a race and works to this temple goal, is the sad, severe criticism of Time upon himself and his own changes. For although Time is wise, and buries, where he can, his past from his future, yet here is something mightier than he; and the azure of the sky which he can not tarnish, preserves the valorous deeds of his youth freshly and fair to his unwilling age. Vainly he strives to bury the proofs and works of his early genius—vainly in remote Nubia he calls upon the desert to hide them, that young England and young America may flatter their fond conceits, that now for the first time man fairly lives, and human genius plays. Some wandering Belzoni thwarts his plans—foils the desert, and on the first of August, 1817, with Mr. Beechy, and captains Irby and Mangles, pushes his way into "the finest and most extensive excavation in Nubia"—thinks it "very large" at first, and gradually his "astonishment increased," as he finds it to be "one of the most magnificent of temples, enriched with beautiful intaglios—painting—colossal figures, &c." which &c. is precisely the inexpressible grandeur of Aboo Simbel. For who has not flown up the Nile, must begin his travels again, if he would behold ruins. Standing at Aboo Simbel, and looking southward, Greece and Rome are toys of yesterday, and vapors wreathing away. When once the Egyptian temples are seen, they alone occupy the land, and suggest their own priests and people. The hovels of the present race are as ant-hills at their gates. Their prominency and importance can not be conceived from the value and interest of other ruins. Here at Aboo Simbel the Howadji, after potential potations and much meditation, is inclined to bless the desert—for he feels that in Egypt it is the ally of art, and the friend of modern times.

The Howadji entered now upon a course of temples. The Ibis pointed her prow northward, and sight-seeing commenced. Yet on these pages remains slight detail of what she saw as she threaded, homeward, that wonderful wilderness of ruin. Not a diary of details, but slightest sketches of impression, were found at Cairo under her wing.

This day at Aboo Simbel, while the first officer, Seyd, superintended the taking down of the masts and sails and the arrangement of the huge oars—for we were to float and row northward, when the wind would allow—and while the Hadji Hamed and his kitchen were removed to the extreme prow, to make room for the rowers on the middle deck, the Howadji climbed the steep sand-bank to the temples of Aboo Simbel.

The smaller one is nearest the river, and is an excavation in the solid rock, with six sculptured figures on the façade.

Two of these are Athor, the Egyptian Venus, to whom the temple was consecrate. She had beautiful names, and of delicate significance, as the Lady of the West, because she received the setting sun—the Night, not primeval darkness, but the mellow tropical night, breathing coolness and balm. Athor's emblems are so like those of Isis, that the two deities are often confounded. She was the later Aphrodite of the Greeks, to whom they built the Dendereh temple; and, like Isis, is cow-horned and mild-eyed, with a disk between the horns. Athor was a gracious and gentle Goddess, and properly was her temple encountered here, far in the gracious and gentle South, whose sweetness and languor were personified in the tender tranquillity of her mien.

But beyond and higher, is the great temple of Aboo Simbel, in front of which sit four Colossi, figures of Ramses the Great. Their grandeur and beauty are beyond expression, and the delight in their lofty character of beauty quite consumes the natural wonder at their uninjured duration for twenty or thirty centuries. Yet in Egypt, the mind gradually acquires a sense of permanence in the forms that meet the eye. Permanence is the spirit of the climate, and of the simplicity of the landscape, and of the supreme silence. What is built at the present time, is evidently so transitory in its construction and character, yet lasts so long, that the reasons of the fact of duration are clear to your mind before wonder is awakened. The dry warm air is the spell, and as it feeds your lungs and life, it breathes into your mind its most significant secrets.

In these faces of Ramses, seven feet long, is a Godlike grandeur and beauty, which the Greeks never reached. They are not only colossal blocks of stone, but the mind can not escape the feeling that they were conceived by colossal minds. Such only cherish the idea of repose so profound, for there is no type or standard in nature for works like these, except the comparative character of the real expression of real heroes, and more than heroes. If a poet should enter in dreams the sacred groves of the grandest mythology, these are the forms he would expect to see, breathing grandeur and godly grace. They sit facing the south-east, and as if necessarily expectant of the world's homage. There is a sweetness beyond smiling in the rounded, placid mouth. The nose is arched, the almond-eye voluptuously lidded as the lips are rounded, and the stillness of their beauty is steeped in a placid passion, that seems passionlessness, and which was necessarily inseparable from the works of Southern artists. It is a new type of beauty, not recalling or suggesting any other. It is alone in sculpture, serene and Godlike. Greek Jupiter is grand and terrible, but human. The Jupiter of any statue, even the Tonans or the Olympian, might have showered in gold upon Danaë, or folded Io in the embracing cloud, or have toyed with fond, foolish Semele till his fire consumed her. The Greek Gods are human. But these elder figures are above humanity—they dwell serenely in abstract perfection.

In their mystic beauty all this appears. And the American Howadji wonders to find this superhuman character projected into such expression. The face of one of these Aboo Simbel figures teaches more of elder Egypt than any hieroglyphed history which any Old Mortality may dig out, in the same way that the literature of Greece and the character of Greek art reveal the point of development reached by the Greek nature, which, standing as a world-student at Aboo Simbel, is the point of interest to the Howadji. Strangely they sit there, and have sat, the beautiful bloom of eternal youth and the beautiful balance of serene wisdom in their faces, with no trace there of the possibility of human emotion; and so they sit and benignly smile through the Howadji's mind forever, as the most triumphant realization in art of the abstract perfection of conscious being.

After which consolatory conclusion, that, with the resounding tongues of the figures, the Howadji would be glad to thunder chorally to the world, he descends the sand-slope into the interior of the temple, for the sand has so filled it, that although the entrance is some thirty feet high, he must stoop to enter. The day was waning, and the great hall was dark. The present Howadji was yet weak with the illness which the white-haired phantom watched, and remained with Congo upon the sand-slope, looking into the temple, as the light wood was kindled in a portable crate, to illuminate the interior. But the Pacha penetrated two hundred feet to the Adytum. He passed the Osiride columns, which are a grand feature of the early temples, being statues with placid features and arms folded upon their breast, cut upon the face of square pillars, and reached the four sitting figures in the Adytum—a separate interior niche and holy of holies, figures of the Gods to whom the temple was dedicate. Chiefly Aboo Simbel was dedicate to Ra, the sun, also to Kneph, Osiris, and Isis, by Ramses the Great. Upon all the walls are sculptures of his victories, his offerings to the Gods, and religious rites. These walls are blackened now by smoke, and each fresh party of Howadji, with its fresh portable crate of light wood, can not avoid smoking its share of the temple.

The sun was setting as the Howadji emerged, and looked their last upon the placid Gods, whose grace made the twilight tender. They slid slowly down the sand to the shore, and reached the poor, dismantled Ibis. Fleet, fair Ibis no longer—the masts were down and were stretched over the deck, like ridgepoles for an awning, and the smoke of Kara Kooseh ascended from the prow, and the sharp, lithe yards pierced the blue no more. The glory was gone, and the beauty. It was an Ibis no longer, but a "loggy old Junk, a lumpish Gundelow," said the sententious Pacha.

The golden-sleeved Commander received us, taking credit for all that had been done; and as the stars triumphed over the brief twilight, the crew, with a slow, mournful song, pushed away from the shore and we headed southward no longer. There was a sadness in that starlight beyond any other upon the Nile. The Howadji had reached their southest south, and the charm of exploration was over. Return is always sad, for return is unnatural

Ever forward, ever farther, is the law of life, and the outward seems not to keep pace with the inward, even if it does not seem to dwarf and defraud it, when we return to the same places and the old pursuits. As the South receded in the starlight, that silent evening, a duty and a right seemed to be slipping away—the Howadji were turning the farthest point of dreaming, their Cape of Good Hope, beyond which slept their Indian seas, and drifted again with the mystic stream slowly out of the Past toward the insatiable Future.

The moon rose and hung golden over Arabia, as the sad, monotonous song of the crew trembled and died away, and with the slow, measured throb of oars, the Howadji's hearts beat homeward.

XXXII.

Northward.

We floated and rowed slowly down the river. When the wind blew violently the crew did not row at all, and we took our chance at floating, spinning round upon the river, and drifting from shore to shore. When it swelled to a gale, we drew in under the bank and allowed its fury to pass. Once, for two days it held us fast, and the irate Howadji could do nothing but await the pleasure of a lull. But the gale outlasted their patience. They had explored all the neighboring shore, had seen the women with glass beads, and necklaces, and black woolen garments, and crisp woolly hair. They had sat upon the mud seats of the houses, and had been the idols of popular attention and admiration. But the wind would not blow away, and the too happy crew stretched upon the bank, and shielded by it, slept and chatted all day long. The third day, the gale still blew, though feebly, and orders for tracking were issued from the blue cabin. There was great reluctance, for it is hard work to pull a Junk or Gundelow against a wind. And as the supple-limbed, smooth-skinned Mohammad, one of the best workers of the crew, undertook, standing on the shore among the rest, who did not dare to speak, to expostulate and complain; the Pacha, in a royal rage, was about springing upon him for tremendous chastisement, when Mohammad, warned by his fellows, sprang up the bank and disappeared. The rest, appalled and abashed, seized the rope and went to work. We tracked but a few miles that day, however, for it was too heavy work.

The wind died at last, but it was never as peaceable as it should have been. For although the hopeful, ascending Howadji hears that with January or February the soft southern gales begin to blow, and will waft him as gently northward as the north winds blew him south, he finds that those southern gales blow only in poetry, or poetic memory.

In the calmer pauses, however, we tracked, and rowed, and drifted to Dekkar, and a yellow, vaporous moon led us to the temple. Seyd accompanied the Howadji with the portable crate, wherewith they were to do their share of smoking the remains. All Nubia was asleep in the yellow moonlight, and the inhabitants of Dekkar rushed forth from their huts as we passed along, the huge Seyd preceding, bearing the crate like a trophy, and snarling at all curs that shivered the hushed silence with their shrieks. Doubtless, as we approached the temple, and the glare of our torches flashed through its darkness, meditative jackals and other beasts of prey withdrew to the more friendly dark of distance. And then, if ever, standing in the bright moonlight among Egyptian ruins, the apostrophes and sentimentalities and extravagancies of Volney and his brood, flap duskily through the mind like birds of omen ill.

There is something essentially cheerful, however, in an Egyptian ruin. It stands so boldly bare in the sun and moon, its forms are so massive and precise, its sculptures so simply outlined, and of such serene objectivity of expression, and time deals so gently with the ruin's self, as if reluctant through love or fear to obliterate it, or even to hang it with flowery weepers and green mosses, that your feeling shares the freshness of the ruin, and you reserve for the Coliseum or the Parthenon that luxury of soft sentiment, of which Childe Harold's apostrophe to Rome is the excellent expression. We must add to this, too, the entire separation from our sympathy, of the people and principles that originated these structures. The Romans are our friends and neighbors in time, for they lived only yesterday. History sees clearly to the other side of Rome, and beholds the campagna and the mountains, before the wolf was whelped, that mothered a world. But along these shores history sees not much more than we can see. It can not look within the hundred gates of Thebes, and babbles very inarticulately about what it professes to know. We have a vague feeling that this was the eldest born of Time—certainly his most accomplished and wisest child, and that the best of our knowledge, is a flower off that trunk. But that is not enough to bring us near to it. The Colossi sit speechless, but do not look as if they would speak our language, even were their tongues loosed. Theirs is another beauty, another feeling than ours, and except to passionless study and universal cosmopolitan interest, Egypt has only the magnetism of mystery for us, until the later days of its decline.

Our human interest enters Egypt with Alexander the Great, and the Greeks, and becomes vivid and redly warm with the Romans and Cleopatra, with Cæsar and Marc Antony, with Hadrian and Antinous. The rest are phantoms and specters that haunt the shores. Therefore there are two interests and two kinds of remains in Egypt, the Pharaohnic and the Ptolemaic—the former represents the eldest, and the latter the youngest, history of the land. The elder is the genuine old Egyptian interest, the younger the Greco-Egyptian—after the conquest—after the glorious son had returned to engraft his own development upon the glorious sire. It was the tree in flower, transplanted. No Howadji denies that the seed was Egyptian, but poet Martineau perpetually reviles the Greeks for their audacity in coming to Egypt, can with difficulty contain her dissatisfaction at pausing to see the Ptolemaic remains, finds that word sufficient description and condemnation. But the Greeks, notwithstanding, rarely spoiled any thing they touched, and here in Egypt, they inoculated massiveness with grace, and grandeur with beauty. Of course there was always something lost. An Egyptian temple built by Greek-taught natives, or by Greeks who wished to compromise a thousand jealousies and prejudices, must, like all other architecture, be emblematical of the spirit of the time and of the people. Yet in gaining grace, the Howadji is not disposed to think that

Egyptian architecture lost much of its grandeur. The rock temples, or the eldest Egyptian remains, have all the imposing interest of the might and character of primitive races grandly developing in art. But as the art advances to separate structures and slowly casts away a crust of crudities, although it may lose in solid weight, it gains in every other way.

Then the perfection of any art is always unobtrusive. Yes, in a sense, unimpressive, as the most exquisite of summer days, so breathes balm into a vigorous and healthy body, that the individual exists without corporeal consciousness, yet is then most corporeally perfect. In the same way disproportion arrests the attention. Beautiful balance, which is the character of perfection in art or human character or nature, allows no prominent points. Washington is undoubtedly always underrated in our judgments, because he was so well proportioned ; and the finest musical performance has such natural ease and quiet, and the colors and treatment of a fine picture such propriety and harmony, that we do not at once know how fine it is. It is the cutting of a razor so sharply edged that we are not conscious of it. We have all seen the same thing in beautiful faces. The most permanent and profound beauty did not thrill us, but presently, like air to the lungs, it was a necessity of inner life, while the striking beauty is generally a disproportion, and so far, a monstrosity and fault. Men who feel beauty most profoundly, are often unable to recall the color of eyes and hair, unless, as with artists, there is an involuntary technical attention to those points.

For beauty is a radiance that can not be analyzed, and which is not described when you call it rosy. Wanting any word which shall express it, is not the highest beauty the synonym of balance, for the highest thought is God, and he is passionlessly balanced in our conception.

This is singularly true in architecture. The Greek nature was the most purely proportioned of any that we know—and this beautiful balance breathes its character through all Greek art. The Greeks were as much the masters of their world, physically, and infinitely more, intellectually, than the Romans were of theirs. And it is suspected that the Greek element blending with the Saxon, makes us the men we are. Yet the single Roman always appears in our imaginations as stronger, because more stalwart, than the Greek—and the elder Egyptian architecture seems grander, because heavier than the Grecian. It is a kind of material deception—the triumph of gross sense. It is the old story of Richard and Salah-ed-deen.

The grace of the Greek character, both humanly and artistically, was not a want of strength, but it was exquisite balance. Grace in character, as in movement, is the last delicate flower, the most bloomy bloom. The grandeur of mountain outlines—their poetic sentiment—the exquisite hues that flush along their sides, are not truly known until you have so related them to the whole landscape, by separating yourself from them, that this balance can appear. While you climb the mountain, and behold one detail swift swallowing another—though the abysses are grand, and the dead trunks titanic, and the single flower exquisite, yet the mass has no form and no hue, and only the details have character.

Beauty is reached in the same way in art. If parts are exaggerated, striking impressions may be produced, but the best beauty is lost. The early Egyptian architecture is exaggeratedly heavy. The whole art, in its feeling and form, seems to symbolize foundation—as if it were to bear all the finer and farther architectures of the world upon itself. It is massive and heavy and permanent, but not graceful. The beholder brings away this ponderous impression—nothing seems massive to him after Egypt, as nothing seems clean after a Shaker village, and if upon the shore something lighter and more graceful arrest his eye, he is sure that it is a decadence of art. For so impressively put is this massiveness of structure, that it seems the only rule, and he will hear of no others—as a man returning from a discourse of one idea, eloquently and fervidly set forth, believes in that, mainly, until he hears another fervid argument.

But the Greeks achieved something loftier. They harmonized strength into beauty, and therein secured the highest success of art—the beautifying of use. Nothing in nature is purely ornamental, and therefore nothing in art has a right to be. Greek architecture sacrifices none of the strength of the Egyptian, if we may trust the most careful and accurate engravings, but elevates it. It is the proper superstructure of that foundation. It is aerial and light and delicate. Probably, on the whole, a Greek temple charms the eye more than any other single object of art. It is serene and beautiful. The grace of the sky and of the landscape would seem to have been perpetually present in the artist's mind who designed it. This architecture has also the smiling simplicity, which is the characteristic of all youth—while the African has a kind of dumb, ante-living, ante-sunlight character, like that of an embryo Titan.

When the Greeks came to Egypt, they brought Greece with them, and the last living traces of antique Egypt began to disappear. They even changed the names of cities, and meddled with the theology, and in art the Greek genius was soon evident—yet as blending and beautifying, not destroying—and the Ptolemaic temples, while they have not lost the massive grandeur of the Pharaohnic, have gained a greater grace. A finer feeling is apparent in them—a lighter and more genial touch—a lyrical sentiment which does not appear in the dumb old epics of Aboo Simbel, and of Gerf Hoseyn. They have an air of flowers, and freshness, and human feeling. They are sculptured with the same angular heroes, and gods, and victims, but while these are not so well done as in the elder temples, and indicate that the Egyptians themselves were degenerate in the art, or that the Greeks who attained the same result of mural commemoration in a loftier manner at home, did it clumsily in Egypt—the general effect and character of the temples is much more beautiful to the eye. The curious details begin to yield to the complete whole—a gayer, more cultivated, farther advanced race has entered and occupied.

The Howadji will check himself here, as he stumbles over a fallen hieroglyphed column in the moonlight. But this temple of Dekkar was a proper place to say so much for the abused temples of Ptolemaic times; for this is a building of Ergamun, an Ethiopian prince, and a neighbor of Ptolemy Philadelphus, who had seen Greece and learned a little wisdom, and made a stand in a temple, probably on this very site, against the ignorant tyranny of priests, not supposing, as Sir Gardiner aptly remarks, "that belief in the priests signified belief in the Gods, whom he failed not to honor with due respect."

Sir Gardiner quotes the story from Diodorus, that "the most extraordinary thing is what relates to the death of their kings. The priests, who superintend the worship of the Gods and the ceremonies of religion, in Meroë, enjoy such unlimited power, that whenever they choose they send a messenger to the king, ordering him to die, for that the Gods had given this command, and no mortal could oppose their will, without being guilty of a crime. They also add other reasons, which would influence a man of weak mind, accustomed to give way to old custom and prejudice, and without sufficient sense to oppose such unreasonable commands. In former times, the kings had obeyed the priests, not by compulsion, but out of mere superstition, until Ergamenes, who ascended the throne of Ethiopia, in the time of the second Ptolemy, a man instructed in the sciences and philosophy of Greece, was bold enough to defy their orders. And having made a resolution worthy of a prince, he repaired with his troops to a fortress, or high place, where a golden temple of the Ethiopians stood, and there having slain all the priests, he abolished the ancient custom, and substituted other institutions, according to his own will."

We may thank Greece possibly for that. Yet that we may enjoy the satisfaction of making ourselves cotemporary with such histories, let us refer to Frederic Werne's White Nile, and discover that races, neighbors of our tree-worshiping friends, the Dinkas, if not sometimes our very friends themselves, continue this habit, and allow the priests to notify the kings to die. As yet has arisen no Dinka Ergamun. But such always do arise—some Ergamun or Luther or Strauss, and protest with blood or books against the priests, although tree-worshiping Dinkas, who unthrone their king on a three-legged stool, may plead the South, and so stand absolved from this duty.

Muse a moment longer in these moonlight ruins, and observing brave King Ergamun hieroglyphed (say the learned) "king of men, the hand of Amun, the living, chosen of Re, son of the sun, Ergamun ever-living, the beloved of Isis;" let the faint figures of those elders pass by and perceive that you honor them, though you do think the Greek architecture more beautiful. The glare of Seyd's torch reveals upon these walls figures and a faith that is not less dear to the Howadji, as history, than any other. But the forms fade in the misty moonlight, as their names are fading out of history. Perhaps, after all, Mohammad Alee was as good and glorious as Ramses the Great, whom the Greeks called Sesostris, or any of the Thothmes.

Who knows?—perhaps they were.

Harriet Martineau, indeed, and the other poetical Howadji, are inclined to doubt whether there were any wry necks or squint-eyes in those days of giants, and you can not say yea or nay, for the great darkness.

Who knows? perhaps there were not.

Great they clearly were, for they built these temples and graved the walls with their own glory. But they have the advantage of the dark, while Mohammad Alee and Julius Cæsar stand in the broad daylight with all their wrinkles. Besides, when men have been dead a few thousand years, if their names escape to us across the great gulf of Time, it is only decent to take them in and entertain them kindly; especially is it becoming to those Howadji who sail their river along the shores they so ponderously piled with grandeur.

But the Ptolemies, as well. Luxor, Dendereh, Edfoo, Kum Ombos, Philæ, and the temples at Karnak—these are part of Egypt. O poetic and antiquity-adoring Howadji, this jealousy of the Greeks is sadly unpoetic. Look at this little Dekkar temple and confess it. Remember Philæ and ask forgiveness. Why love the Ptolemies less, because you love the Pharaohs more? Spite of Volney and this Nubian moonlight, itself a rich reward of long voyaging, the Howadji will not be sad and solemn about the Egyptians, because they were a great people and are gone. The Greeks had a much finer architecture, and a much more graceful nature—they were not so old as these. But there were elder than the Egyptians, and wiser and fairer, even the sons of the morning, for heaven lies around the world in its infancy, as well as around us.

The Howadji left the little temple to the moonlight and the jackals. The village was startled from sleep again by our return, and the crew were sleeping upon the deck; but in a few moments there was no more noise, and the junk was floating down in the moonlight, while its choicer freight was clouded in the azure mist of Latakiá, and heard only the Sakias and the throbbing oars and at times the wild, satanic rowing-song of the men, which Satan Saleh led with his diabolical quaver and cry.

Yet when another day had burnt away, the same moonlight showed us Kalab-sheh, the largest Nubian ruin. It is directly upon the tropic, which makes it pleasant to the imagination, but is a mass of uninteresting rubbish of Roman days. For the Howadji will not plead for Roman remains in Egypt, which have no more character than Roman art elsewhere; and Roman art in Baalbec, in Egypt and in Italy, is only Grecian art thickened from poetry into prose. It is one vast imitation, and the essential character is forever lost. But close by is a small rock temple of the "golden prime" of Ramses the Great, and passing the animated sculptures, and entering, the Howadji stands between two Doric columns. They are fluted, and except that they are low, like foundation columns, have all the grace of the Greek Doric. These columns occur once more near Minyeh, in Egypt, at the caves or tombs of Beni Hassan, and are there quite as perfect as in any Grecian temple. In this moonlight, upon the very tropic, that fact looms very significantly upon the Howadji's mind. But how can he indulge speculation, or reach conclusions, while

Saleh who bears the torch crate is perpetually drawing his attention to the walls, on which are sculptured processions bearing offerings to great Ramses who built this temple, and who seems to have done every thing else in Egypt until the Ptolemies came? There are rings and bags of gold, leopard-skins, ostrich-eggs, huge fans, and beasts, lions, gazelles, oxen, then plants and skins. A historical sketch occupies another wall—the great Ramses, represented as three times the size of his foes, pursuing them into perdition. There is a little touch of a wounded man taken home by his comrades, while a little one runs to "announce the sad news to its mother," pathetically says Sir Gardiner, speaking of sculptures that, to the Howadji's eye, have no more human interest or tenderness, or variety of expression, than the chance forms of clouds or foliage.

But the Nubian days were ending, and the great gate of the cataract was already audible, roaring as it turned. Hassan piloted us safely through the half-cataracts, and the fantastic rock vistas about Philæ were already around us. Beautiful in the mild morning stood the holy island, full of fairy figures that came and went, and looked and lingered—Ariel-beauties among the Caliban grotesqueness of the pass. It was the vision of a moment only, scarcely more distinct than in memory, and the next we were pausing at Mahratta, where the Reis of the Cataract, by the terms of the Treaty, was bound to pilot the boat back again to Syene.

XXXIII.

By the Grace of God.

It was a bright, sparkling morning, and all the people of Mahratta seemed to be grouped upon the shore to receive with staring wonder the boat that had undergone in itself the Pythagorean Metempsychosis taught by the old teachers at neighboring Philæ—the boat that had flown southward a wide-winged Ibis, and floated slowly back again a cumbrous junk—a swift bird no longer, but a heavy bug rather, sprawling upon the water with the long clumsy oars for its legs. There were two or three slave boats at Mahratta—although we had passed scarce a sail in lonely Nubia. The brisk, busy shore was like awaking again after a long sleep—yet, believe me, it was only as one seems to awake, in dreams. For the spell was not dissolved at Mahratta—nor yet at Cairo—and if at Beyrout to the eye, yet it still thralls the mind and memory.

The Captain of the Cataract was absent, piloting an English Howadji through the rapids, but his lieutenant and substitute, one of the minor captains, and our former friend of the kurbash, were grinning gayly as we drove smoothly up to the bank—the latter touching up a dusky neighbor occasionally with his instrument, in the exuberance of his delighted expectation of incessant kurbashing for a brace of hours, on our way to Syene. The motley crowd tumbled aboard. As at Syene, our own crew became luxuriously superfluous—for a morning they were as indolent as the Howadji, and tasted for that brief space the delight which was perpetual in the blue cabin. For it is a sorrow and shame to do any thing upon the Nile or in Egypt but float, fascinated, and let the landscape be your mind and imagination, full of poetic forms. An Egyptian always works as if he were on the point of pausing, and regarded labor as an unlovely incident of the day. The only natural position of an Eastern is sitting or reclining. But these Nile sailors sit upon their haunches, or inelegantly squat like the vases that stand in the tombs, and with as much sense of life as they. The moment a man becomes inactive upon the shore, he is enchanted into a permanent figure of the landscape. The silence enchants him, and makes his repose so profound and lifeless, that it deepens the impression of silence. But the dusky denizens of Mahratta leaped and scrambled upon the boat, like impatient souls very dubious of safe ferryage—for returning to the Cataract confusion, we return to our old similitudes. Silence, too, shuddered, as they rushed yelping upon the junk, as if its very soul had gone out of it forever; and piling themselves upon the deck and the bulwarks, and seizing the huge, cumbrous oars, they commenced, under brisk kurbashing, to push from the shore, quarreling and shouting, and mad with glee and excitement, in entire insanity of the "savage faculty."

The Howadji stood at the blue cabin door, helpless—perhaps hopeless, in the grim chaos, and turning backward, as the boat slid from the shore upon the glassy stream, beheld Nubia and the farther South faint away upon the rosy bosom of the morning.

The day was beautiful and windless—the air clear and brilliant. No wind could have benefited us—so tortuous is the channel through these rapids; and once fairly into the midst of the river, its strong swift stream, eddying toward the cataract, swept us on to the frowning battlements of rock that rise along the rapid. The oars dipped slightly—but another power than theirs, an impetus from what bewitched fountain in the most glorious glen of the Mountains of the Moon, shoved us on—the speed, the nearing rapid, the exhilarating morning, making this the most exciting day of the Nile voyaging. The men tugging by threes and fours at the oars, laughed and looked at the Howadji—their backs turned to the rapid, and mainly intent upon the kurbash which was frenziedly fulfilling its functions. The pilot, whose eyes were fixed fast and firmly upon the rock points and the boat's prow, shouted them suddenly into silence at times—but only for a moment, then again like eager, fun-overflowing boys they prattled and played away.

In twenty minutes from Mahratta we were close upon the first and longest and swiftest rapid. The channel was partly cut away by Mohammad Alee, and although it conceals no rocks, it is so very narrow, and shows such ragged, jagged cliff sides to the stream, that with a large

Dahabieh like ours, driving through the gurgling, foaming and fateful dark waters—it is a bit of adventure and experience to have passed.

The instant that the strange speed with which we swept along, indicated that the junk was sliding down the horizontal cataract, and the Dahabieh and Howadji and crew felt as chips look, plunging over water-falls resistless, and entirely mastered, driving dreadfully forward like a tempest-tortured ship—that moment, the pilot thundered caution from the tiller, and a confused scrambling ensued upon deck to take in the oars, for it was not possible for us to pass with such wide-stretching arms through the narrow throat of the rapid. But there was no instant to lose. The river, like a live monster, plunged along with us upon his back. We too felt his eager motions under us—a swiftness of smooth undulation along which we rode; and so startling was the new sudden speed, when we were once on the currenty slope, that it seemed as if our monster were dashing on to plunge us wrecked against the bristling sides, before we could take in our arm-like oars, that, rigid with horrible expectation, reached stiffly out toward their destruction.

But vainly struggled and stumbled the "savage faculty." It was clear enough that the junk was Fate's and Fate's only. At the same instant the Howadji saw and felt that before one reluctant oar, which was tied and tangled inextricably, could be hauled in, its blade would strike a rocky reach that stretched forth for it into the stream—which foamed and fretted at the momentary obstruction, then madly eddied forward. But in striking the rock the oar would throw the boat with its broadside to the stream, capsize it, and send Howadji, crew, and Mahratta savages beyond kurbashing.

They saw this at the same instant, and the whole boat's company saw it too, and the pilot, who shouted like one mad, yet who was fixed fast to his post, for a single swerve of the rudder would be as fatal as the oar against the rock. The kurbash raged and fell and flourished, as if it foresaw the speedy end of its exercise and authority, and burned to use up all its vitality. But the mental chaos of the men of Mahratta was only more chaotic in this juncture, and while the oar still stretched to its fate, and like a mote upon a lightning flash, the frightfully steady boat darted through the rapid, the Pacha grasped one column of the cabin porch, and the other Howadji the other, awaiting the crisis which should throw them into the jaws of the monster, who would dash them high up upon the shore below, to consume at leisure.

All this was seen and transpired in less time than you occupy in reading the record. The pilot in vain endeavored to ease her from the side toward which she was tending, and on which still and hopelessly stretched the fatal oar. There was universal silence and expectation, and then crash! struck the oar against the rock, was completely shivered in striking, and the heavy junk, shuddering a moment, but scarce consciously, and not swerving from her desperate way, darted forward still, and drove high upon the sandy shore, at the sudden turning of the rapid, and the Howadji had safely passed the most appalling slope of the cataract.

Chaos came again immediately. The pilot descended from his post, and expressed his opinion that such accurate and able pilotage deserved an extraordinary bucksheesh, implying, with ethics not alone oriental, that having done his duty, he was entitled to more than praise. The men of Mahratta smiled significantly at the Howadji, as if such remarkable exertions as theirs were possibly hardly to be measured by merely infidel minds, and there was a general air of self-satisfaction pervading all faces, as if the savage faculty, and not the grace of God, had brought us through the cataract.

We tarried a little while upon the shore, and then glided again down the swift stream. It was only swift now, not startling, and the rockiness was farther withdrawn, and there were smooth reaches of water. We saw several Howadji loitering upon a sandy slope. The sun seemed not to sparkle, as before the descent, in the excitement of the morning, and there was the same old sunny tranquillity of Egypt breathing over the dying rages and up through the rocky ways of the cataract. It was the lull and repose that follow intense excitement, and of so suggestive a character, that the Howadji recalled with sympathy the aerial Aquarelle of Turner—the summit of the Gotthard Pass, looking toward Italy. It is a wonderful success of art, for in the warmth and depth and variety of the hue, which has the infinite rarity and delicacy of Italian air, and which seems rather a glow and rosy suffusion than a material medium—in that and through that, the bloom of Italy breathes warm beauty far into Switzerland, and steeps the spectator in the South. The eye clings to it and bathes in it as the soul and memory in Italian days. So in the tender tranquillity of that morning succeeding the rapids, all the golden greenness and sweet silence of Egypt below Syene, breathed beauty and balm over what was the Ibis. How few things are singly beautiful! Is there any single beauty? For all beauty seems to adorn itself with all other beauty, and while the lover's mistress is only herself, she has all the beauty of all beautiful women.

Thus with songs singing in their minds, came the Howadji swiftly to Syene. The current bore us graciously along, like the genii that serve gracefully when once their pride and rage is conquered. The struggle and crisis of the morning only bound us more nearly to the river. O blue-spectacled Gunning! the dream-languor of our river is not passionless sloth, but the profundity of passion. And I pray Athor, the Queen of the West, and the Lady of Lovers, that so may be charactered the many winding courses of your life.

But Verde Giovane and Gunning had flown northward toward Thebes, leaving only miraculous memories of a deieuner at Philæ, upon men's minds in Syene, and strange relics of bones and fruit-skins upon the temple ruins. Beaming elderly John Bull was also flown, and with him Mrs. Bull, doubtlessly still insisting that the Kaftan was a nightgown. And Wines and the Irish Doctor who plunged into the Nile mystery at Alexandria, were also gone. They were all off toward Thebes. But Nero was still deep in Nubia, solemnly cursing contrary winds, while Nera, quietly reposing in the sumptuous little cabin, shed the lovely light of a new thought of woman like a delicate dawn upon the dusky mental night of the "Kid's" crew. Far under Aboo Simbel, too, fluttered the blue pennant, still streaming backward to the south, whither it had pointed. The English consul's Dahabieh, a floating palace of delights, was at Syene, and the leisure barque of an artist, whose pencil, long dipped in the sunshine of the East, will one day magically evoke for us the great dream of the Nile. But we lingered long enough only to buy some bread, and as the full moon goldened the palm fringe of the river, the little feline Reis, happy to be in command once more, thrummed the long silent tarabuka, and with clapping hands and long, lingering, sonorous singing, the boat drifted slowly down the river.

XXXIV.

Flamingoes.

But while the Ibis flies no longer, but floats, a junk, and for the Howadji has forever furled her wings, they step ashore ast he boat glides idly along, and run up among the mud cabins and the palm-groves. They were always the same thing, like the lay-figure of an artist, which he drapes and disguises, and makes exhaustlessly beautiful with color and form. So the day, with varying lights and differing settings of the same relief, made endless picture of the old material. You are astonished that you do not find the Nile monotonous. Palms, shores and hills, hills, shores and palms, and ever the old picturesqueness of costume, yet fresh and beautiful every day as the moon every month, and the stars each evening. This is not to be explained by novelty, but by the essential beauty of the objects. Those objects are shapeless mud huts for instance, O Reverend Dr. Duck, voyaging upon the Nile with Mrs. Duck for the balm of the African breath, and finding the scenery sadly monotonous. But birds can not sing until the pie is opened, O Doctor, nor can eyes see, until all films are removed. Yet stretching your head a little upward, as we sit upon this grass clump on the high bank of the river, you shall see something that will make Egypt always memorable to you. For, as we sat there one morning, we saw a dark, undulating mass upon the edge of the fog bank that was slowly rolling northward away. I thought it a flight of pigeons, but the Pacha said that it did not move like pigeons.

The mass, now evidently a flight of birds, came sweeping southward toward us, high in the blue air and veering from side to side like a ship in tacking. With every sunward sweep, their snow-white bodies shone like a shower of most silver stars, or rather, to compare large things with small, if Bacchus will forgive, they floated suspended in the blue air like flakes of silver, as the gold flakes hang in a vessel of *eau de Dantzic.*

There was a graceful, careless order in their flying, and as they turned from side to side, the long lines undulated in musical motion. I have never seen movement so delicious to the eye as their turning sweep. The long line throbbed and palpitated as if an electric sympathy was emitted from the pure points of their wings. There was nothing tumbling or gay in their impression, but an intense feeling of languid life. Their curves and movements were voluptuous. The southern sun flashed not in vain along their snowiness, nor were they, without meaning, flying to the south. There was no sound but the whirring of innumerable wings, as they passed high over our heads, a living cloud between us and the sun. Now it was a streaming whiteness in the blue, now it was as mellowly dark, as they turned to or from the sun, and so advanced, the long lines giving and trembling sometimes, like a flapping sail in a falling breeze, then bellying roundly out again, as if the wind had risen. When they were directly above us, one only note was dropped from some thoughtful flamingo, to call attention to the presence of strangers below. But beyond musket-shot, even if not beyond fear, as they undoubtedly were, the fair company swept on unheeding—a beautiful boon for the south, and laden with what strange tidings from northern woods! The bodies were rosy white and the wings black, and the character of their flight imparted an air of delicacy and grace to all association with the birds, so that it is natural and pleasant to find that Roman Apicius, the Epicurean, is recorded to have discovered the exquisite relish of the flamingo's tongue, and a peculiar mode of dressing it. The Howadji had not been unwilling at dinner to have tasted the delicate tongue that shed the one note of warning. But long before dinner the whir of beautiful wings, and the rose-cloud of flamingoes had died away deep into the south.

The poor, unwinged Ibis claimed no kindred as the birds flew by, but clung quietly to the shore. The sun, too, in setting—well, is it not strange that in the radiant purple of sunset and dawn—the *Fellahs*, denizens of these melancholy mud cabins, behold the promise of the plague? What sympathy have we with those who see a plague-spot in the stately splendor of these sunsets?

Day by day, as we descended, we were enjoying the feast which we had but rehearsed in ascending. Edfoo,

Kum Ombos, El Kab—names of note and marks of memory. Men dwell in tombs still, and came out to offer us all kinds of trinkets and gay wares. Then upon dog-like donkeys we rode with feet dangling on the ground, across the green plain of the valley to the Arabian desert, whose line is as distinctly and straightly marked along the green, as the sea line along the shore. The cultivated plain does not gradually die away through deeper and more sandy barrenness into the desert, but it strikes it with a shock, and ends suddenly; and the wide-waving corn and yellow cotton grow on the edge of the sand, like a hedge. The Howadji, embarked in his little cockle-boat of a donkey, puts out to desert as little boats to sea, and scrambling up the steep sand-sides of the first hills, sees upon the grotto-walls of El Kab much of the cotemporary history of the life and manners of antique Egypt. The details of social customs and the habits of individual life are painted upon the walls, so that the peculiar profession of the occupant of the tomb can be easily determined. But let us cling to the sunshine as long as possible, for we shall explore tombs and darkness enough at Thebes.

XXXV.

Cleopatra.

"Ant. Most sweet Queen."

A voluptuous morning awakened the Howadji under the shore at Erment. Cloudless the sky as Cleopatra's eyes, when they looked on Cæsar. Warmly rosy the azure that domed the world, as if to-day it were a temple dedicate to beauty. And stepping ashore, to the altars of beauty we repaired. No sacrificial, snowy lambs, no garlands of gorgeous flowers, did the worship require. The day itself was flower and feast and triumphal song. The day itself lingered luminously along the far mountain ranges, paling in brilliance and over the golden green of the spacious plain, that was a flower-enameled pavement this morning, for our treading, as if unceasingly to remind us that we went as worshipers of beauty only, and the fame of beauty that fills the world.

The Howadji confesses that no Egyptian morning is more memorable to him than this, for nothing Egyptian is so cognate to our warm-blooded human sympathy as the rich romance of Cleopatra and her Roman lovers. After the austere impression of the elder Egyptian monuments, this simply human and lovely association was greatly fascinating. Ramses to-day was not great. He subdued Babylon, but Cleopatra conquered Julius Cæsar. Marc Antony called his Cleopatra-children, kings of kings. The conqueror of the conqueror was the divinity of the day.

I know not if it were the magic of the morning, but the world to-day was Cleopatra. Hers was the spirit of the air, the lines of the landscape. In any land the same day would have suggested her perpetually to the imagination—for there are Greek and Roman days, Italian and Sicilian, Syrian and African. And these days correspond in character with the suggestion they make. Many and many a day had the Howadji seen and loved the serpent of old Nile, before he beheld Africa, many a long June day had been tranced in Italy in the Fornarinà's spell, many a twilight had lingered along Galilean heights with him to whom the Syrens of the Syrian sky, Love and Pleasure and Ambition, sang in vain, and that long before he had trod the broad silent way of waters, that leads the Western to them, and which keeps them forever cool and consecrate in his imagination. These dreams, or realities of feeling, were not occasioned by pictures or poems, but were the sentiment of the day. The soul seems then sensuously to apprehend the intensity of emotion that is symbolized. And when you travel into the lands of which you read and dreamed, you will be touched with your want of surprise in their delights. But many an unheeded silent strain of sunshine, or night-appalling tempest, had sung and thundered their sacred secret to your mind. The day, therefore, was so much Cleopatra, that only the fairest fate could have drifted us upon that morning to the shore of Erment.

The forms and hues of old Egypt were vague and pale in the presence of this modern remembrance. I confess that the erudite Sir Gardiner, and the Poet Martineau, do not very lovingly linger around Erment. I confess their facts. The temple is of the very last genuine Egyptian days, the child of the dotage of Egyptian art, when it was diseased and corrupted by Roman prostitution. The antique grandeur is gone. It is the remains of an interregnum between the old and the new—the faint death-struggle of an expiring art, or if the insatiable poets demand, a galvanized quiver after death. All that, if the erudite and the antiquarian require. Here is no architectural, no theological or mystical—romantically historical and very dubiously moral (after the Bunyan standard) interest. This is the hieroglyph that might balk Champollion, yet which the merest American Howadji might read as he ran.

For what boots it? Is not Cleopatra a radiant, the only radiant image, in our Egyptian annals? Are we humanly related to Menmôphth, or any Amunoph? Are not the periods of history epically poetic that treat of her, while they grope and reel seeking Thothmes and Amun in the dark? Besides, Cleopatra sat glorious in beauty upon Ramses' throne, and the older thrones are, the more venerable are they. And if the great darling of Amun Re heroically held his heritage, grant that the child of Venus well lost it, melting the pearl of her inheritance in the glowing wine of her love.

Neocesar should have been a God's darling, and so have died young. And that he might have been, but for the whim of Nature, who will not give the fairest blossoms to the noblest trees. As if she were a housewife upon allowance, and had not illimitable capacity of mating beauty with power wherever they meet. But in this temple of Erment we will not reproach her. For Nature satisfied the Ideal in giving Cleopatra to Cæsar.

Such, I suppose to have been the ox-necked Abdallah's musings as he stumbled up the steep bank from the junk, bearing the torch crate, for all Egyptian temples require great light to be thrown upon the interior darkness of their Adyta or holy of holies, and skeptical Howadji suspect that the dog-faithful Abdallah did it more satisfactorily than the priests, who, ex-officio, were the intellectual lanterns of old Egypt.

Sundry shapeless heaps of dingy blanket strewn upon the wind-sheltered, sun-flooded bank were the crew. They had diligently rowed all night, and had crept ashore to sleep. They too had reason to bless the "most sweet Queen," and we left them, honoring the day and its divinity in their own way.

The picture of that morning is permanent. Like all Egyptian pictures composed of a few grand outlines, a few graceful details, but charged, brimming, transfigured with light, and brooding over all, the profound repose of the azure sky—which does not seem to be an arch so much as to rest rosily upon the very eye—and so transparent that the vision is not bluffed against a blue dome, but sinks and sinks into all degrees of distance, like Undine's in her native watery atmosphere. It would not surprise the happy eye, if forms, invisible in other qualities of atmosphere, should float and fade in the rosiness. Such delicate depths imply a creation as fair—and as the eye swims leisurely along, the Howadji feels that it is only the grossness of his seeing that hides the loveliness from his apprehension, and yet feeling the fascination, believes that somewhere under the palms upon these shores, flow the fountains whose water shall wash away all blindness. And if anywhere, why not here? Here, where she, the Queen of the South not less than her sister of Sheba, lived and loved. For the Persian poets sing well in the moonlight, that only the eyes of love see angels. Yet until that fountain is reached, this sky is the dream, the landscape its light-limned realm, and at Erment, near Esne, near Cleopatra, who but the gracious and graceful Ghawazee are the people of those dreams?

The Pacha with the cherished one-barrel went before, occasionally damaging the symmetry of family circles of pigeons upon the palms. Abdallah plunged like a mastiff after the fallen victims, and bore them grinningly in his hand—while I sedately closed the rear, dazed in the double radiance of the day and the Golden-sleeve. Our path lay across a prairie of young grain. The unwaving level stretched away to the Libyan mountains—that still ranged along the west, silver-pale in the intense sunlight. And still as we went, this glad morning, the world was flower-paven, and walled with sapphire. The plain seemed to shrink from the least unevenness, lest the nourishing Nile should not everywhere overspread it—or was it that it would lay a floor broad and beautiful enough to approach those ruined altars of beauty?

For they are ruins, and although it is a temple built by Cleopatra for the worship of Amun, upon its altars now no other homage is offered than to her. Gorgeous cactuses, and crimson-hearted roses, and glowing, abundant oleanders be your flower offerings when you bend before them at high, hot noon, and pour out no other libations there, than reddest and most delirious wine.

The great temple is quite destroyed, and the remains of the smaller one, like all the temples of Egypt, are quarries of materials for the building of the neighboring mud villages and chance factories, which Mohammad Alee commenced, and which will probably gradually fall into disuse and decay, now that he is gone. The temple is but a group of columns with the walls of a court, and two interior chambers upon which are sculptures representing Cleopatra and Neocesar with godly titles offering homage and gifts to the Gods. The few remaining columns rise handsomely from the sand and dust heaps that surround all temples here. They are evidently of the latest Ptolemaic days—but to the uninitiated in architectural accuracy—to those who can also enjoy what is not absolutely perfect in its kind but even very imperfect, these groups are yet graceful and pleasing. How can stately sculptures bearing forms so famous, be otherwise in a mud and sand wilderness? The sculptures themselves are poor and fast crumbling. Yet although fast crumbling, here is the only authentic portrait of Cleopatra. This is she—of whom Enotarbus said in words that shall outlive these sculptures and give her to a later age than any thing material may attain—

> "Age can not wither her—nor custom stale
> Her infinite variety. Other women
> Cloy the appetites they feed—but she makes hungry
> Where most she satisfies. For vilest things
> Become themselves in her; that the holy Priests
> Bless her when she is riggish."

The Persian poets sing farther when the moon is at the full, that only lovers' tongues speak truly.

You will not expect to find a perfect portrait upon these walls, and will see her sitting and holding Neocesar in her lap, as Isis holds Horus at Philæ—while she offers gifts to the bull Basis. And although this temple was covered all over with the rudely sculptured form and face of the fairest Queen of History, I could find but two which were tolerably perfect and individual.

The first is upon one of the columns of the transverse colonnade of the portico. The features are quite small. The nose, which seems strongly to mark the likeness, departs from all known laws of nasal perfection, and curves the wrong way. O Isis—and O Athor, Greek Aphrodite, if Cleopatra had a pug nose! Yet it is more pug than aquiline or Grecian,—a seemingly melancholy occurrence in a face so famously fair.

But I found that this peculiarity of feature, by its very discord with the canons of beauty, suggested the soul that must have so radiantly illuminated the face into its bewildering beauty. Greek statues are not the semblance of lovable women. The faces are fair, but far away from feeling. The features are exquisitely carved, and the graceful balance is musical to the eye. But they lack the play of passion—the heat-lightning of sentiment and soul that flushes along a thousand faces not so fair. The expression partakes of the quality of the material, and differs from life as that from flesh. Beautiful are the forms and faces, but they are carved in cold, colorless marble—not in rosy flesh. It is the outline of the Venus form, not her face, that is fascinating. Among Greek sculptures no face is so permanently beautiful as the head of Clytie—and that because it is so charged with the possibility of human experience. The others do not seem serenely superior to that experience like the Egyptian Colossi, but simply soulless. The beautiful story of Clytie is felt through her face. For when Apollo deserted her for Leucothoë, she revealed his love to the father of her rival. But Apollo only despised her the more, and the sad Clytie drooped and died into the heliotrope or sun-flower, still forever turning toward the sun. Nor less fair the fate of her rival, who was buried alive by her father; and love-lorn Apollo, unable to save her, sprinkled nectar and ambrosia upon her grave, which reached her body and changed it into a beautiful tree that bears the frankincense. How well sound these stories at Erment, while we remember Cleopatra and look upon her likeness!

The very departure from the ordinary laws of sculptured beauty only suggests that loftier and more alluring, where the soul suffuses the features. And this being ever the most intimate and profound beauty, the queenly charm spread from the face as we looked, and permeated the whole person. Cleopatra stands in imagination now, not a beautiful brunette merely, but a mysteriously fascinating woman. "My serpent of old Nile," was a truth of the lover's tongue.

Roman and man as Julius Cæsar was, he was too much a Roman and a man to have been thrall to prettiness merely. There must have been a glorious greed of passion in an Italian nature like his and Marc Antony's, which only the very soul of Southern voluptousness could have so satisfied and enchained. Nor allow any Western feeling to mar the magnificence of the picture which this place and day, set with those figures, offers to your delight. Let us please imagination with these stately figures of history. Granting all the immoralities and improprieties, if they seem such to you, let them go as not pertinent to the occasion. But the grace, and the beauty, and the power, the sun behind his spots, are the large inheritance of all time. Why should we insist upon having all the inconvenience of cotemporaries whose feet were pinched and sides squeezed by these so regal figures? Why should we encase ourselves triply and triply in a close ball of petty prejudices and enlightened ideas, and go tumbling, beetle-like, through the moonlighted halls of history, instead of floating upon butterfly wings and with the song and soaring of the lark? The Howadji will use his advantage of distance, and not see the snakes and sharp stones which he knows are upon the mountains, but only the graceful grandeur of the outline against the sky.

Education is apt to spoil the poetry of travel by so starting us in the dry ruts of prejudice, or even upon the turnpike of principle, that we can scarcely ever see the most alluring landscape except at right angles, and doubtfully and hurriedly over our shoulders. Yet if Cleopatra had done so, would the Howadji have tarried at Erment? The great persons and events that notch time in passing, do so because nature gave them such an excessive and exaggerated impulse, that wherever they touch they leave their mark; and that intense humanity secures human sympathy beyond the most beautiful balance, which indeed the angels love, and which we are learning to appreciate.

For what is the use of being a modern, with the privilege of tasting every new day as it ripens, if we can not leave in the vaults of antiquity what we choose? Was Alexander less the great because he had a wry neck? Leave the wry neck behind. You may bring forth all the botches of the stonecutters, if you will, but mine be the glorious booty of the Laocoon, of the Venus and the Apollo. I shall not therefore say that the artist who wrought works so fair, did not botch elsewhere. But I certainly shall not inquire.

In like manner Julius Cæsar and Queen Cleopatra being of no farther influence upon human affairs, imagination sucks from history all the sweet of their story and builds honey-hives nectarean. The Howadji fears that the clerical imagination at Erment might not do so—that all the reform and universal peace societies would miss the Cleopatra charm. But their vocation is not wandering around the world and being awakened by voluptuous mornings. Their honey is hived from May flowers of rhetoric in the tabernacle, to which the zealous and "panoplied in principle" must repair, passing Cleopatra by.

The village of Erment balances singularly this glowing Ghazeeyah fame by offsetting the undoubted temple of the doubtful Cleopatra with a vague claim of being the birthplace of Moses. We did not tarry long enough to resolve the question, although as he was found by Pharaoh's daughter among the bulrushes of the lower Nile, there is no glaring impossibility that he may have been born at Erment.

Disregarding Moses, we cordially cursed the shekh of the village, who has coolly put his mud hovel upon the roof of the adyta of the temple, and quite as coolly converting the adyta themselves into dungeons. The modern Egyptian has not the slightest curiosity or interest in the noble remains of his land. He crawls around them, and covers them with mud cells, in which he and his swarm like vermin. But speak them fair as you would water rats. Without ideas, how can they feel the presence of ideas? We passed through the mud-walled court below the shekh's dwelling to reach the adyta of the temple. The court was grouped with Arnout soldiers, crouching over a fire, smoking and chatting. These Albanians were the fiercest part of Grandfather Mohammad's army. They revolted when Belzoni was in Cairo, drove the Pacha into the citadel, ravaged the city at leisure, and were then quieted. But they became altogether too fierce—assassinating quiet and moral Mohammadans on the slightest provocation, and Christians as they would cockroaches—and Grandfather Mohammad was obliged to send the most of them to the destructive climate of upper Ethiopia, and so be gently rid of them.

They are light-complexioned, sharp-featured, smart-looking men, else had Mohammad Alee not used them so constantly, and are by far the most intelligent-looking class in Egypt, for they have dashes of Greek blood in their veins, and modern Greek blood is thick with knavery. But their faces are as bad as bright. Like fish, they seem to have cold blood, and you feel that they would rather shoot you than not, as boys prefer sticking flies to letting them be. Hence a certain interest with which the passing Howadji regards their silver-mounted pistols.

We paused a moment at the door of the Adytum, and a swarm of unclean women came clustering out. They were the relatives of the prisoners whom the government held in the dungeons. There was no light in the small chamber which we stooped to enter, except what curious daylight stole shrinkingly in at the low door. Abdallah lighted his torch, and we looked around upon the holy of holies of Queen Cleopatra. The Adytum was small, and reeked with filth and stench. Two or three prisoners lay miserably upon the damp floor, and we held our glaring torch over them, and looked at the sculptures on the walls. But without much heart. It was sorry work, and we made it brief—the indulgence of curiosity and sentiment in so sad a society.

There was a little inner room, upon the walls of which we found the other portrait of the queen. But I could not remain—imagination and the mere human stomach recoiled. For in this Adytum of Adyta in Cleopatra's temple,—the olive-browed,—the odorous,—was uncleanness such as scarcely the pilgrim to the Tarpeian rock has conceived.

We passed through the court unshot, and through the dusty village, whose myriad dogs, and of especial foul fame even in Egypt, barked frantically, and so emerged upon the corn stubble and the coarse hilfeh grass, upon the river bank. Then through a palm-grove we entered upon greener reaches, and sat down upon a high point over the river to await the boat, which was to float slowly down and meet us. The perfection of the day lacked only a vision of leisure, graceful life. And what other could the vision be upon that point in the calm air, high over the calm water, but that of the queen's barge, sumptuously sliding upon the golden gleam? Behold it, dreamer, where it comes:

> "The barge she sat in like a burnished throne,
> Burned on the water: the poop was beaten gold,

Purple the sails, and so perfumed, that
The winds were love-sick with them: the oars were silver,
Which to the tune of flutes kept stroke, and made
The water which they beat to follow faster,
As amorous of their strokes. For her own person,
It beggared all description: she did lie
In her pavilion (cloth of gold, of tissue)
O'erpicturing that Venus, where we see
The fancy outwork nature. On each side her
Stood pretty dimpled boys, like smiling Cupids,
With diverse-colored fans, whose wind did seem
To glow the delicate cheeks which they did cool—
And what they undid, did."

"O rare for Antony!"

"Her gentlewomen like the Nereides,
So many mermaids, tended her i' the eyes,
And made their bends adornings. At the helm
A seeming mermaid steers, the silken tackle
Swells with the touches of those flower-soft hands,
That yarely frame the office. From the barge
A strange, invisible perfume hits the sense
Of the adjacent wharves. The city cast
Her people out upon her, and Antony,
Enthroned in the market-place, did sit alone
Whistling to the air, which, but for vacancy,
Had gone to gaze on Cleopatra, too,
And made a gap in nature."

"Rare Egyptian."

"There's the junk," said the Pacha.

"She be float very quick," said Golden-sleeve, and sliding down the sand, we stepped on board and gave chase to Fancy's fair flotilla. Fair and fleet, it floated on, away, nor ever comes to shore. But still through the cloudless calm of sky and stream your dreaming sees it pass, with measured throb of languid oars, voluptuous music voicing the day's repose.

In the afternoon, we dropped leisurely down the river to Thebes. Before sunset we were moored to the shore of Luxor, on the eastern side of the stream, and almost in the shadow of the temple. A cluster of Howadji's boats clung to the shore with gay streamers and national flags, and all over the shore sat and stood groups of natives with trinkets and curiosities to sell, or donkeys to let. We strolled up to the temple of Luxor, and looked westward over the mountains of the "Libyan suburb," as Herodotus calls the part of the city upon the western shore. It was covered with temples and tombs then, but the great mass of the city was on the eastern bank, where Luxor now stands. The highlands were exquisitely hued in the sunset. But Patience was so belabored with an universal shriek of bucksheesh, that she fled to the junk again, and recovered in the cool calm of Theban starlight.

XXXVI.

Memnon.

"Heard melodies are sweet,—but those unheard are sweeter."

FROM earliest childhood Memnon was the central, commanding figure in my fancies of the East. Rising imagination struck first upon his form, and he answered in music—wondrous, wooing, winning, that must needs vibrate forever, although his voice is hushed. Whether this was from an instinctive feeling, that this statue and its story were a kind of completeness and perfection in art—the welcome recognition of art by nature—or more probably from the simple marvelousness and beauty of the tale, I shall inquire of the Sphinx. As we passed up the river, and I beheld in the solemn, sunless morning light, like a shadowed, thoughtful summer day, the majestic form sitting serenely upon the plain, the most prominent and noticeable object in the landscape, I knew that memories would linger around him as hopes had clustered, and that his calm grandeur would rule my East forever.

For throned upon ruined Thebes sits Memnon, himself a ruin, but regal still. Once seen he is aways seen, and sits as uncrumbling in memory as in the wide azure silence of his Libyan plain. Daily comes the sun as of old, and inspires him no longer. Son of the morning! why so silent? Yet not dumb utterly, sing still the Persians, when poets listen, kindred sons of the morning.

Yearly comes the Nile humbly to his feet, and laving them, pays homage. Then receeding slowly, leaves water plants wreathed around the throne, on which he is sculptured as a good genius harvesting the lotus, and brings a hundred travelers to perpetuate the homage.

The history of art says little of Memnon and his mate, and the more perfect colossi of Aboo Simbel. Yet it is in these forms that the Howadji most strongly feels the maturity of the Egyptian mind—more strongly than in the temples whose sculptures are childish. But here you feel that the artist recognized, as we do to-day, that serene repose is the attitude and character of godlike grandeur.

Nor are there any works of art so well set in the landscape, save the Pestum temples in their sea-shored, mountain-walled prairie of flowers. Standing between the columns of Neptune's temple at Pestum, let the lover of beauty look out over the bloom-brilliant plain to the blue sea, and meditate of Memnon. Then, if there be pictures or poems or melodies in his mind, they will be Minerva-born, and surprise himself. Yet he will have a secreter sympathy with these forms than with any temple, how grand or graceful soever. Yes, and more than with any statue that he recalls. And that sympathy will be greater in the degree that these are grander. Not the elastic grace of the Apollo will seem so cognate to him as the melancholy grandeur of Memnon. For these forms impress man with himself. These are our forms, and how wondrously fashioned! In them, we no longer succumb to the landscape, but sit individual and imperial, under the sky, by the mountains and the river. Man is magnified in Memnon.

These sublime sketches in stone are an artist's work. They are not mere masses of uninformed material. And could we know to-day the name of him who carved them in their places, not the greatest names of art should be haloed with more radiant renown. In those earlier days, art was not content with the grace of nature, but coped with its proportions. Vain attempt, but glorious! It was to show us as we are ideally in nature, not the greatest, but the grandest. And to a certain degree this success is achieved. The imitative Romans essayed the same thing. But their little men they only made larger little men by carving them fifty feet high. Out of Nero, Tiberius or Caligula to make an imposing work of art, although you raised the head to the clouds, was more than Roman or Greek, or any human genius could achieve. It was still littleness on a great scale. Size is their only merit, and the elaborate detail of treatment destroys, as much as possible, all the effect of size. But the Egyptian Colossi present kings, of kingliness so kingly that they became Gods in the imagination of men, and remain Gods in their memories.

Vain attempt, says truly the thoughtful artist. But glorious, responds the poet. Vain and glorious as the attempt of youth to sculpture in hard life its elastic hope. Failure fairer than general success. Like the unfinished statues of Michel Angelo—unfinished, as if an ideal ever too lofty and various haunted his imagination, whereto human tools were insufficient. Alone in sculpture, Michel Angelo's Night and Moses are peers of the realm of Memnon and the Aboo Simbel Colossi.

Looking into the morning mists of history and poetry, the Howadji finds that Homer mentions Memnon as a son of Aurora and Titho, King of Ethiopia, and brother of Priam, the most beautiful of warriors, who hastened with myriads of men to assist uncle Priam against the Greeks. Achilles slew Memnon under the walls of Troy, and the morning after his death, as Aurora put aside the darkness and looked vaguely and wan along the world, the first level look that touched the lips of the hitherto silent statue upon the plain, evoked mysterious music. There were birds, too, memnonides, who arose from out the funeral pyre of Memnon, and as he burned, fought fiercely in the air, so that more than half fell offerings to his manes. Every year they return to renew the combat, and every year with low wailings they dip their wings in the river water, and carefully cleanse the statue. Dew-diamonded cobwebs, fascinating fable, O history!

Emperors, historians, and poets heard this sound, or heard of it, nor is there any record of the phenomenon anterior to the Romans. Strabo is the first that speaks of it, and Strabo himself heard it. But the statue was then shattered, and he did not know if the sound proceeded from the Colossus or the crowd. Singularly enough, the sound is not mentioned before the statue was broken, nor after it was repaired, a space of about two hundred years. Yet during that time it uttered the seven mystic vowels, which are the very heart of mysteries to us. To Hadrian, the emperor, it sang thrice of a morning, yet to the Emperor Severus, who repaired it, it was always silent. But Severus came as a raging religionist, a pious Pagan, while Hadrian stood with Antinous, whom the morning loved and stole early away. For they die young whom the gods love, and Aurora is their friend. The Persian poets would like to be quoted here, but, O Persians, it was your King Cambyses who shattered our statue. You may yet read the words sculptured upon its sides, speaking sadly and strangely out of the dim depths of that antiquity, which yet waxed and waned under this same blue sky, with the same mountain outline upon which your eye, still wandering from Memnon, waves away into rosy reverie. "I write after having heard Memno. Cambyses hath wounded me, a stone cut into the image of the sun-king. I had once the sweet voice of Memno, but Cambyses has deprived me of the accents which express joy and grief."

> "You relate grievous things—your voice is now obscure,
> O wretched Statue ! I deplore your fate."

For these are ruins. Memnon is a mass of square blocks of sandstone, from the waist upward. His mate is less shattered. In Memnon, of course, the original idea is only hinted. But they were to be seen from a distance, and so seen, they have yet human grandeur. Memnon has still a distinct and mysterious interest, for no myth of the most graceful mythology is so significant as its story.

Science rushes in explanatory, with poetic theories of sounding stones in all countries. Humboldt, for Humboldt, as we saw, is a poet, is only too glad to find upon the banks of the South American Oronoko granite rocks hailing the morning with organ majesty of music. He ascribes the sound to the effect of difference of temperature between the subterranean and outer air. At Syene, too, unimaginative French Naturalists have heard a sonorous creaking in the granite quarries, and Napoleon's commission heard, rising from the granite ruins of Karnak, the same creak, at morning. Yet were it a vibration of expanding and contracting stone masses, why still and forever silent, O mystic Memnon!

Priests clambered over night into its lap, and struck a metallic stone at sunrise—exclaims erudition and Sir Gardiner, who climbed into the same lap at noonday, and striking the stone with a little hammer, produced a sound, which the listening peasants described in the same terms that Strabo uses. But were priests that struck thrice for Emperor Hadrian so unsycophantic grown, that even for Severus, the restorer of their statue and of their worship, they would not strike at all?

Back into romance, mystic Memnon! Neither the priests who cajoled with it—nor the Pharaoh who built it—nor the wise who deepen its mystery, can affect the artistic greatness of the work, or the poetic significance of its story.

The priests and Pharaohs died, and their names with them. But Memnon remains, not mute, though silent, and let the heirs of Amunoph III. claim it as his statue, from fame, poetry and thought, if they dare !

Memnon and his mate sat sixty feet into the air, before a temple of the said Amunoph—of which a few inarticulate stones lie among the grain behind. From them to the river, for about a mile's distance, went the Strada Regia, the street royal of Thebes. There was a street! upon which, probably, neither Grace church nor Trinity would have been imposing. Yet we are proud of the Neapolitan Toledo—of the Roman Corso—of the Berlin Unter den linden—of the Parisian Boulevards—of London Regent street, and we babble feebly of Broadway. But O, if Theban society was proportioned to Thebes, to have been a butterfly of that sunshine, a Theban sauntering of a sultry January morning along the Strada Regia, and to have paused in the shadow of Memnon and have taken a hand—any hand, for the mummy merchant here will select you a score from under his robe, shriveled, black, tough, smoked-beef sort of hands—and not her lover could distinguish the olive tapers of Thothmes III.'s darling, the princess Re-ni-no-fre, from the fingers of the meanest maid that did not dare look at her.

Here we stand in the shadow of Memnon on a sultry January morning, but the princess who should meet us here, lies dreamless and forever in these yellow hills. Sad moralists, these mummy merchants, yet they say not a word!

An earthquake and Cambyses divide the shame of the partial destruction of Memnon, but it can not be destroyed. This air will cheat Time of a prey so precious. Yearly the rising Nile heaps its grave around it. Gradually the earth will resume into its bosom, this mass which she bore—and there will hold it more undecaying than the mountains the embalmed bodies of its cotemporaries. Unworn in an antiquity in which our oldest fancies are young, it will endure to an unimagined future, then, Godlike, vanish unchanged.

Pause, poet, shoreward wending. Upon the level length of green young grain, smooth as the sea-calm, sits Memnon by his mate. If he greet the sun no longer in rising, feel in this serene sunset the song of his magnificent repose. The austere Arabian highlands are tender now. The lonely Libyan heights are sand no more, but sapphire. In ever delicater depths of blue and gold dissolve the landscape and the sky. It is the transfiguration of Nature, which each of these sunsets is—sweet and solemn and sad.

Pause, poet, and confess, that if day dies here so divinely, the sublimest human thought could not more fitly sing its nativity than with the voice of Memnon.

XXXVII.

Dead Kings.

A DAZZLING desert defile leads to the Kings' tombs at Thebes. The unsparing sun burned our little cavalcade as it wound along. The white, glaring waste was windless, for although its hill-walls are not lofty, the way is narrow and stony and devious. So dreary a way must have made death drearier to those death-doomed royalties. But we donkeyed pleasantly along, like young immortals with all eternity before, and to us, death and tombs and kings were myths only.

And what more are they, those old Egyptian monarchs for whom these tombs were built? Catch if you can these pallid phantoms that hover on the edge of history. King Apappus is more a brain-vapor than Hercules, and our fair, far princess Re-ni-no-fre than our ever sea-fresh Venus. We must believe in Apollo and the Muses, but Amun-m-gori III. is admitted into history solely by our grace. So much a living myth surpasses a dead man! Give me the Parthenon, and you shall have all the tombs of all the Theban kings.

They were separated from the rest of the world in the

tomb as in the palace. So regal was their royalty that no inferior was company select enough for their corpses. Unhappy hermits, they had to die for society, and then, unhappier, found only themselves. Fancy the mummied monarchs awaking immortal and, looking round, to find themselves and ancestors only! "Nothing but old Charlotte," said the third saint George of England. And the sameness of the old story must have infused most plebeian thoughts and desires of society, more spirited though less select, into the mighty monarchs' minds. For imagine the four English Georges buried together, and together awaking—would any celestial imagination fancy *that*, the choicest coterie of heaven?

Or young immortals donkeying of a bright, blue morning, under blue cotton umbrellas, and cheerfully chatting, can thus moralize upon monarchs at leisure, and snap our fingers at scurvy scepters, and crowns that make heads lie uneasy, and dribble Hamlet in the churchyard until we are sopped with self-complacent sentimentality. But cotemporary men, now adjacent mummies, looked on, I suppose, with more dazzled eyes when a dead king passing, made this defile alive.

Possibly men were blinded by the blaze of royalty in those days, as, spite of the complacent American Howadji, they are in some others. And a thoughtful Theban watching the progress of a royal funeral, over the Nile in barges, up the Strada Regia, wherein the mighty Memnon shielded the eyes of many from the setting sun, then winding with melancholy monotony of music and gusty wail, and all human pomp through the solitary, sandy, stony, treeless defile, possibly improvised sonnets on the glory of greatness, and mused upon the fate that so gilded a mortal life and death.

Seventy-two days the king lay dead in his palace. Then his body, filled with myrrh and cassia, and cinnamon and all sweet spices but frankincense, was swathed in gummed cloth, the cunning of life to cheat corruption, and was borne to the tomb which all his life he had been preparing and adorning. Yet life was not long enough to make the bed for his dreamless slumber, and usually the kings died before their tombs were ready.

Such is royal death, mused that Theban, a passage to the delights of heaven from the delights of earth—the exchange of the silver for the golden goblet. It is symbolized by this defile, dazzling if dreary—sunny, if stony and sandy. Ah! Osiris, royal death is the brief, brilliant desert between the temple palace and the temple tomb.

We saw several of these thoughtful Thebans, vapory shadows, musing upon the solitary rocks as we advanced. Presently we were embosomed in the hills. They were only barren and blazing, not at all awful or imposing, being too low and perpendicular. Besides, the rock of which they are composed is like a petrified sponge, and looks waterworn, which it is not, and unenduring. To-day the sun was especially genial, seeming to consider the visiting the tombs of kings a very cheerful business. So he shone ever more brilliant and burningly, and in the mazes of the spongy rock caught the Howadji and ogled them with the glaring fierceness of a lion's lust and hate.

"Ho, ho!" scoffed the sun. "These were kings of men and great Gods and Leviathans in the land. They must lie apart from others in the tomb, and be sweet and separate for eternity. And up this warm, winding way, a little after they had come hither dead, I saw Cambyses and his proud Persians rushing, broad alive, and after them, an endless host of kings, travelers, scholars, snobs, cockneys and all other beasts and birds of prey, and Cambyses to the latest shopman broke into the select society, shivered their porphyry sarcophagi, scattered and robbed and despoiled, sending away hands, feet, heads, and all cherished and sacred jewels and talismans, and now I can not distinguish the dust of Amun-neit-gori, or Osirei, or Thothmes from the sand of the hills."

"Kings!" scoffed the sun. "Here's a royal shin-bone—the shin of a real Theban king. You may buy it for a pound to-day, if it were not sold for a shilling yesterday, and for a farthing if you'll give no more. The ring in his slave's ear in the plebeian tombs is worth a hundred of it."

Vainly, a thoughtful Theban that lingered almost invisible in the intense light along the defile, suggested to the sun, that royalty was never held of the body—that monarchs and monarchies were only instruments and institutions—that the whole world was a convention, and virtue a draft upon heaven. The sun would gibe his gibe.

"Ho, ho! kings' shins, going, going! kings' hands and feet, who bids? Not a para from any of the crowd who sell their souls every day to kiss the hands and feet of some sort of royalty, the world over. Ho, ho, ho, kings!"

What a diabolical sun! He scoffed so fervently that the Howadji grew very silent, having previously thought it rather a good thing to show a mummy at home, that they had found in the kings' tombs at Thebes. But with that sun glaring out of the sky, who could dare? So they crept very humbly on, deftly defying him and warding off sun-strokes with huge, heavy umbrellas of two thicknesses of blue cotton, and consequently constantly on the point of melting and dripping down the donkeys' sides, while the spectral sponge-rock echoed the chirrups of the donkey boys mockingly. "Ah! my young gentlemen travel a long way to see tombs. But you will have enough of them one day, young gentlemen. What stands at the end of all your journeying?" The abashed Howadji crept still silently along, and reached at length the end of the tortuous, stony valley, in the heart of the Libyan hills.

Here was high society. If the field of the cloth of gold is famed because two live kings met there, what shall this assembly of numberless dead kings, and kings only, be? No squires here, no henchmen or courtiers. Nothing but the pure dust here. All around us, the low square doors sculptured in the hill bases, open into their presence-chambers. Nor any gold stick in waiting, nor lord high chamberlain to present us. What democracy so democratic as the congregation of dead kings? Let us descend. Even you and I, O Pacha, are as good as many dead kings. And is not Verde Giovane, himself, equal to *x*, or an unknown quantity of them? The runaway Mohammad who returned penitent at Syene, shall officiate as chamberlain with the torch crate.

Now down—but hold! The kings are not there. They are in the Vatican, in the Louvre, in London, at Berlin, at Vienna, in choice museums, and scattered undistinguished upon the rocks. The master of the house being out, of course you will not enter.

Leave them to museums and histories. What are they to us? Their tombs, not themselves, are our shrines to-day. Ramses' tomb is at this moment of greater moment to us than his whole life. Were he sitting now on Memnon's pedestal, would the Howadji sacrifice seeing his tomb to seeing him?

XXXIII.

Buried.

The Howadji descended into the tomb. It is the trump tomb of the kings' valley, and is named Belzoni, from the traveler. The peasants observed the ground sinking at this point of the hill, and suggested as much to Dr. Rüppell. But Germania, though sure, is slow, and while the Doctor whiffed meditative meerschaums over it, Belzoni opened it, thereby linking his name with one of the most perfect of Theban remains.

We went perpendicularly down a range of shattered stone steps, and entering the tomb, advanced through a passage still sloping downward. The walls were covered with hieroglyphs fresh as of yesterday. They are a most graceful ornament in their general impression, although the details are always graceless, excepting the figures of birds, which in all Egyptian sculptures are singularly life-like. In the wall and ceiling painting of these tomb-passages is the germ of the arabesques of the Roman epoch. Here is clearly the dawn of the exquisite delicacy of the ceilings of the baths of Titus, and the later loveliness of the Loggie. Looking at these rude lines, but multitudinous and fresh, I saw the beginnings of what Raphael perfected.

Still advancing, the Howadji descended steps and emerged in a hall. It is small, but the walls are all carefully painted. The Gods are there, and the heroes—some simple epic of heroic life, doubtless, which we do not quite understand, although we interpret it very fluently. Other chambers and one large hall succeed. In this latter are figures of four races upon the central columns, supposed to indicate the four colored races of the world. The walls and ceilings are all painted with figures of the King Osirei, father of Ramses, whose tomb it was, offering gifts to the Gods and receiving grace from them.

These subterranean halls are very solemn. The mind perpetually reverts to their host, to the embalmed body that was sealed in the sarcophagus as in a rock—surrounded in night and stillness with this sculptured society of earth and heaven. It is hard to realize that these so finely finished halls were to be closed forever. Nor were they so, for the kings, after three thousand years, were to come again upon the earth, and their eyes should first light upon the history and the faith of their former life. How much of this was pride, how much reverence of royalty, how much veneration for the human body?

Break a sarcophagus with Cambyses, and ask the tenant—or mayhap our thoughtful Theban has also meditated that theme. While you await the answer, we pass into a fourth room, and find that death, too enamored of a king, did not tarry for the tomb's completion, for here are unfinished drawings—completed outlines only and no color.

The effect is finer than that of the finished pictures. The boldness and vigor of the lines are full of power. There are boats and birds, simple lines only, which we should admire to-day upon any canvas. That old Egyptian artist was as sure of his hand and eye, as the French artist, who cut his pupil's paper with his thumb nail, to indicate that the line should run so, and not otherwise. The coloring is rude and inexpressive. The drawing of the human figure conventional, for the church or the priests ordained how the human form should be drawn. Later, the church and priests ordained how the human form should be governed. Yet, O sumptuous scarlet queen, sitting on seven hills, you were generous to art, while you were wronging nature.

There was going down dangerous steps afterward, and explorations of chambers dim, whose farther end had fallen in and shut out investigation. The same song was everywhere sung in different keys. Three hundred and twenty feet we advanced into the earth, and one hundred and twenty downward. In that space all the Gods were gathered, could we have known them, and wondrous histories told, could we have heard them. Fresh and fair the walls, but the passages and steps were broken, and the darkness was intolerably warm and stifling. Students of hieroglyphs, artists, the versed in Egyptian mythology, jackals and mummy merchants had longer tarried and increased their stores. But the Howadji did what the owner and builder of the tomb could not do. They crept out of it, and sat down upon the shattered steps of the entrance, to smoke peaceful chibouques.

At the door of this tomb, as of all others, were mummy merchants, who gathered round us and outspread their wares. Images, necklaces, rings, arms, heads, feet, hands, bits of the mummy case, and little jars of seed, charms, lamps, all the rich robbery of the tombs, placidly awaited inspection. The mummy merchants are the population of the Theban ruins. Grave ghouls, they live upon dead bodies. They come out spectrally from columns and walls, as if they were the paintings just peeled off, and sit at tomb doors like suspicious spirits, and accost you unintelligibly as you go gaping from wonder to wonder. But are grave always, the ghouls, and no shrieking pertinacious pedlers.

We descended a few doors off, into the Harpers' tomb, not that a harper is there buried, but there are two Homeric figures drawn upon the walls of a small room, singing hymns to the harp, and they give their name to the tomb. It belongs by right to Ramses III. But if that sneering sun could steal in, he would tell the Howadji that the harpers are more interesting, and that Time estimates Kings at their value.

This tomb is a cotemporary daguerreotype of old Egyptian life—the life of the field, of the river, of the house, of art, of religion. Fruits are here, birds, baskets, vases, couches, pottery, skins. It is a more vivid and accurate chronicle than Herodotus. These figures are drawn in small separate chambers, and each kind by itself, as if to symbolize the universality of the kings' kingdom and the arts in it. They do not seem pictures of separate scenes, as in the private tombs, but, as is proper in royal tombs, of the general forms and instruments of Egyptian life Yet what is the knowledge that our princess Re-ni-no-fre sat upon a chair like ours, if we know that she was beautiful and young?

For the name's sake we entered the tomb of Memnon, a title of Ramses V., and because it was the favorite of the Greeks. It was easy and pleasant to see why they preferred it, because of the symmetry of the arrangement and the extreme delicacy, finish and fineness of the paintings. In the farther chamber is a huge sarcophagus of Egyptian porphyry, broken by some invader, and over it and on all the ceilings are astronomical enigmas of fine color.

From all these royal tombs the occupants are long since departed. Not to heaven and hell but to choice cabinets of curiosity, and to the winds whither Cambyses and the other invaders incontinently sent them. The significance of their much painting is mostly a secret. The sacred symbols are too mystic for us moderns. That serpent with two men's heads at his tail looking backward—three snake heads in their proper places looking forward—two pairs of human legs walking different ways, and inexplicable sprouts upon his back, is more puzzling than the interior of Africa or the name of Charon's boat. Fancy, of course, figures magnificent meanings for the unintelligible, and the fair daughters of beamy John Bull, did they not explain at length those mysteries over the pleasant dinners at Shepherd's? Yet truth is a simple figure, though fond of dress.

In all the tombs was one God, a foxy-headed divinity, who greatly charmed us. He was in all societies, in all situations. Generally he was tapping a surprised figure upon the shoulder, and pricking the fox ears forward, saying, like an impertinent conscience, "Attend, if you please." Then he sits in the very council of heaven and hobnobs with Amun Re, and again farther on, taps another victim. Such sleepless pertness was never divine before. Yet he is always good-humored, always ready for pot-luck. Gods, kings, or Howadji, all is fish to the foxy. He seemed the only live thing in the tombs. Much more alive than sundry be-goggled and be-vailed male and female Howadji who explored with us these realms of royal death. We asked the foxy to join us in a sandwich and chibouque in the entrance of Memnon's tomb. But he was too busy with an individual who seemed not to heed him—and remained tapping him upon the walls.

In the late afternoon we crossed the mountains into the valley of priests' tombs. The landscape was lovely beyond words, and at sunset from the crumbling Sphinxes of El Kurneh we turned toward Memnon as the faithful turn to Mecca. The Howadji fleet, mostly English, lay at the opposite Luxor shore, gay with flags and streamers, and boats with mingled Frank and Muslim freight glided across the gleaming river. The huge pylon of Karnak towered, like the side of a pyramid, over the palms; and in a clumsy tub of a boat, and rowed by a brace of the common right angular oars, trimmed boughs of trees, we were forced through the rosy calm to our dismantled Ibis.

XXXIX.

Dead Queens.

For even Re-ni-no-fre must die and be buried suitably. Love and beauty were no more talismans then, than now. Death looked on Queens with the evil eye. What bowels of beauty and royalty have not the Libyan hills! What Sultan so splendid that he has a hareem so precious!

The ladies lie lonely and apart from their lords. The Kings are at one end of the old Libyan suburb—the Queens at the other. We approached the Queens' tombs through an ascending sand and stone defile. But, as becomes, it is not entirely sequestered from the green of the valley, and the door of a Queen's tomb framed as fair an Egyptian picture as I saw. These tombs are smaller and less important than those of the Kings. The kings, who, as at Dahr-el-Baree, inserted their cartouches or escütcheons over those of their predecessors, and so strove to cheat posterity, could not suffer their wives to be buried as nobly as themselves.

Yet after the elaboration and mystic figuring and toiling thought and depth and darkness and weariness of the kings' tombs, the smallness and openness of the queens' is refreshing. They are mere caves in the rock, usually of three or four chambers. The sculptures and paintings are gracious and simple. They are not graceful, but suggest the grace and repose which the ideal of female life requires.

Simple landscapes, gardens, fruit and flowers are the subjects of the paintings. No bewildering grandeurs of human-headed and footed serpents—of Gods inconceivable, bearing inexplicable symbols, all which, and the tangled mesh of other theological emblems, is merely human. But the largeness and simplicity of natural forms, as true and touching to us, as to those who painted them.

This simplicity, which was intended, doubtless, in the royal mind, to symbolize the lesser glory of the spouse, is now the surpassing beauty of the tombs. In the graceful largeness and simplicity of the character of the decorations, it seems as if the secret of reverence for womanly character and influence, which was to be later revealed, was instinctively suggested by those who knew them not. Eve was truly created long and long after Adam, and at rural Worcester, they doubt if she be quite completed yet. Those wise Egyptian priests knew many things, but knew not the best. And the profound difference of modern civilization from ancient, as the Western from the Eastern, what is it but the advent of Eve? In Cairo and Damascus, to-day, Adam sits alone with his chibouque and fingan of mocha; but his wives, like the dogs and horses of the Western, are excluded from the seats of equality and honor.

The cheerful yellow hues of the walls, and their exposure to the day, the warm silence of the hill seclusion, and the rich luminous landscape in the vista of the steep valley, made these tombs pleasant pavilions of memory. We wandered through them refreshed, as in gardens. They are all the same, and you will not explore many. But the mind digests them easily and at once—while those kings' tombs may yet give thought a dyspepsia.

While the Howadji loitered, *ecco mi qua*, stood our foxy friend upon the bright walls. "Well said, old mole! canst work i' the earth so fast?" "Yes," said he, "I thought I'd step over; their majesties might be lonely."

Foxy, Foxy! I elect thee to my Penates. To thee shall an altar be builded, and an arm-chair erected thereupon. Thereof shall punch-bowls be the vessels, and fragrant datakia the incense. A model God is Foxy, alive, active, busy,—looking in at the hareem, too, lest they be lonely!

XL.

Et Cetera.

The mere Theban subjects died, too, and they also had to be buried. Their tombs are in the broad face of the mountains toward the river, and between those of the kings and queens. They command a fairer earthly prospect than those of their royal masters, and, Osiris favoring, their occupants reached the heavenly meads as soon.

The great hillside is honey-combed with these tombs. There is no wonder so wonderful that it shall not be realized, and the Prophet's coffin shall be miraculous no longer, for here the dwellings of the dead overhang the temples and the houses. The romantic Theban could not look at the sunset, but he must needs see tombs and find the sunset too seriously symbolical. Clearly with the Thebans, death was the great end of life.

The patient little donkeys would have tugged us up the steep sand and rock-slope, from the plain of Thebes. But we toiled up on foot through a village of dust and barking dogs and filthy people inconceivable, and on and higher, through mummy swathings, cast off from rifled mummies and bleaching bones. If a civilized being lived in modern

Thebes, he would certainly inhabit a tomb for its greater cleanliness and comfort, and would find it, too, freshly frescoed.

In the kings' tombs, we encountered the unresolvable theological enigmas, with the stately society of Gods and heroes. The queens welcomed us in gardens and in barges of pleasure, while timbrels and harps rang, and the slaves danced along the walls, offering fruit and flowers,—or would have done so, had they not rejoined their spouses in choice cabinets.

But the plebeians receive us in the midst of their fields and families. The hints of the Harper's tomb are minutely developed in many of the private tombs. Every trade, and the detail of every process of household economy—of the chase and all other departments of Theban life, are there pictured. Much is gone. The plaster casing of the rock peels away. Many are caves only. But in some the whole circle of human labor seems to be pictorially completed.

The social scenes are most interesting. Very graceful is a line of guests smelling the lotus offered as a welcome; but times change and manners. Pleasant and graceful would it yet be to welcome friends with flowers. But all do not dwell upon rivers, neither are the shores of all rivers lithe with lilies. Haply for modern welcome, a cigar and glass of sherry suffice.

I say graceful, meaning the idea, for upon the walls you would see a very stiff row of stiff figures smelling at stiff flowers. With your merely modern notions, you would probably mistake the lotus for a goblet. Were you an artist, you would cherish the idea until you carved in a cup that graceful flower form. Figures of musicians, whose harps and guitars and tambourines would seem to you the germs of the tàr and the rabab, would awaken vague visions of Hecate and the old husband. But if you beheld the dancers, infallibly you would slide down three thousand years in a moment, and musily gazing from the door into the soft morning, your eyes would yearn toward Esne, and even your more severely regulated heart, memory, mind, or what you will, toward the gay Ghazeeyah and the modest dove.

These tombs like the rest are tenantless. At intervals come the scientific and open new ones. The mummy merchants and Howadji follow and seize the spoils. Time succeeds and preys, though tenderly, upon the labor of an antiquity that has eluded him—for he was busy in the plain below smoothing the green grave of Thebes. For the tomb of Thebes itself is the freshest and fairest of all. The stars come and go in the ceiling. The wheat waves and is harvested, flowers spring and fade upon the floor. The same processes of life are not repeated, but they are real there. Its tenant too has disappeared like the rest—but into no known cabinet.

We emerged from the tombs, and clomb down the hill. A house of unusual pretension, with a swept little court in front, attracted our notice. O traveler, heed not the clean little court—for the figure that sits therein, amply arrayed, sedately smoking as if life were the very vanity of vanities, is the monarch of mummy merchants, who exacts terrible tribute from the Howadji. A Greek ghoul is he, who lives by the living no less than the dead.

Fix your eye upon Memnon, and follow to the plain. Amble quietly in his sunset-shadow to the shore. The air will sway with ghosts you can not lay. Dead Thebans from the mountains will glide shadowy over dead Thebes in the plain.—Chapless, fallen, forgotten now, we too were young immortals—we too were of Arcady!

XLI.

The Memnonium.

THERE is a satisfaction in the entire desolation of Thebes. It is not a ruin, but a disappearance. The Libyan suburb, which seems to have been all tombs and temples, is now only a broad and deep green plain ending suddenly in the desert at the foot of the mountains. Thereon Memnon and his mate, the Memnonium and Medeenet Haboo, are alone conspicuous. Exploration reveals a few other temples and some mighty statues, which, as they lie broken at Titan length—their sharp outlines lost by the constant attrition of the sand, seem to be returning into rock.

This plain, making a green point in the river, is by far the most striking situation for a city. Yet we see it, deducting the few ruins, as men lost in the past saw it. Nor shall the American whose history is but born—stand upon this plain of Thebes which has outlived its history, without a new respect for our mother earth who can so deftly destroy, sand-grain by sand-grain, the most stupendous human works.

Step westward and behold a prairie. Consider the

beginnings of a world metropolis there—its culmination in monuments of art—its lingering decay and desolation until its billowy, tumultuous life is again smoothed into a flowery prairie. With what yearning wonder would the modern who saw it turn to us, lost in antiquity. Then step eastward and behold Thebes.

The Memnonium is not the remains of the temple before which Memnon sat. It was a temple-palace of Ramses the Great. It is a group of columns now with fallen and falling pylons, a few hundred rods from Memnon. You will find it one of the pleasantest ruins, for the rude, historical sculptures are well nigh erased. There are no dark chambers, no intricacy of elaborate construction to consider, and the lotus-capitaled columns are the most graceful I saw.

We must be tolerant of these Egyptian historical sculptures upon pylons and temple walls for the sake of history and science. But the devotee of art and beauty will confess a secret comfort in the Memnonium, where the details are fast crumbling, and the grandeur of the architecture stands unencumbered. Here is an architecture perfect in its grand style in any age. Yet on the truly rounded columns, palm-like below and opening in a lotus cup to bear the architrave, are sculptures of a ludicrous infancy of art. It is hard to feel that both were done by the same people. Had they then no feeling of symmetry and propriety? It is as if the Chinese had sculptured the walls of St. Peter's or the Vatican.

In the midst of the Memnonium, lies the shattered

Colossus of Ramses—a mass of granite equal to that of Memnon. How it was overthrown and how broken will never be known. It is comfortable to be certain of one thing in the bewildering wilderness of ruin and conjecture, even if it be only ignorance. Cambyses, the unlucky Persian, is here the scapegoat, as he is of Memnon's misfortune and of Theban ruin in general. "Cambyses or an earthquake," insists untiring antiquarian speculation, clearly wishing it may be Cambyses. An earthquake, then, and Oh! pax!

This Colossus sat at the temple gate. His hands lay upon his knees and his eyes looked eastward. And even the tumbled mass is yet serene and dignified. Is art so near to nature that the statue of greatness can no more lose its character than greatness itself?

Behind the statue was a court surrounded with Osiride columns, and a few shattered ones remain. I fancy the repose of that court in a Theban sunset, the windless stillness of the air and cloudlessness of the sky. The King enters, thoughtfully pacing by the calm-browed statue, that seems the sentinel of heaven. In the presence of the majestic columns humanly carved, their hands sedately folded upon their breasts—his weary soul is bathed with peace, as a weary body with living water.

Ramses' battles and victories are sculptured upon the walls—his offerings to the Gods and their reception of him. There is an amusing discrepancy between the decay and disappearance of these, and the descriptions in Sir Gardiner. Spirited word-paintings of battle-scenes, and scenes celestial, or even animated descriptions of them, are ludicrously criticized by their subjects. That, too, is pleasant to the Howadji, who discovers very rapidly what his work in the Memnonium is; and stretched in the shadow of the most graceful column, while Nero silently pencils its flower-formed capital in her sketch-book, he looks down the vistas and beyond them, to Memnon, who for three thousand years and more has sat almost near enough to throw his shadow upon this temple, yet has never turned to see it.

There sat the Howadji many still hours, looking now southward to Memnon, now eastward to gray Karnak over the distant palms. Perchance in that corridor of columns, Memnon and the setting sun their teachers, the moments were no more lost than by young Greek immortals in the porch of the philosophers. Yet here can be slight record of those hours. The flowers of sunset dreams are too frail for the Herbarium.

There dozed the donkeys, too, dreaming of pastures incredible, whither hectoring Howadji come no more. Donkeys! are there no wise asses among you, to bid you beware of dreaming? For we come down upon your backs, like stern realities upon young Poets, and urge you across the plain to Medeenet Haboo.

Ah! had you and the young poets but heeded the wise asses!

XLII.

Medeenet Haboo.

WONDERFUL are the sculptures of Medeenet Haboo—a palace-temple of Ramses III. They are cut three or four inches deep into the solid stone, and gazing at them, and in a little square tower called the pavilion, trying to find on the walls what Sir Gardiner and Poet Harriet say is there, you stumble on over sand heaps and ruin, and enter at length the great court.

The grave grandeur of this court is unsurpassed in architecture—open to the sky above, a double range of massive columns supported the massive pediment. The columns upon the court were Osiride—huge, square masses with the figures with the folded hands carved in bold relief upon their faces, and carved all over with hieroglyphs. The rear row was of circular columns, with papyrus or lotus capitals. The walls, dim seen behind the double colonnade, are all carved with history, and the figures upon them, with those of the architraves, variously colored.

It is solemn and sublime.—The mosaic, finical effect of so much carving and coloring is neutralized by the grandeur and mass of the columns. In its prime, when the tints were fresh, although the edges of the sculptures could never have been sharper than now, the priests of Medeenet Haboo were lodged as are no modern monarchs.

Time and Cambyses have been here too, and, alas! the Christians, the Coptic Christians, who have defiled many of the noblest Egyptian remains, plastering their paintings, building miserable mud cabins of churches in their courts, with no more feeling and veneration than the popes who surmount obelisks with the cross. I grant the ruined temples offered material too valuable to be left through regard to modern sentiment, and curiosity of Egyptian history and art. It is true, also, that the Christian plastering did preserve many of the pagan paintings. But you will grant that man, and especially the Howadji species, has a right to rail at all defiling and defilers of beauty and grandeur. Has not the name Goth passed into a proverb? Yet were the Goths a vigorous, manly race, with a whole modern world in their loins, who came and crushed an effete people.

But enough for the Copts.

They erected a church in the great court of Medeenet Haboo, piercing the architrave all round for their rafters, instead of roofing the court itself. Nor let the faithful complain of the presence of pagan symbols. For the Copts and early Egyptian Christians had often the pagan images and pictures over their altars. Nay, does not Catholic Christendom kiss to-day the great toe of Jupiter Olympans, with religious refreshment?

Now the Coptic columns of red sandstone encumber

this noble court and lie leveled, poor pigmies, amid the Titanic magnificence of the standing or fallen original columns. The Christian columns are about the size and appearance of those in the San Spirito, at Florence. Benign Brunellesco, forgive, but the architecture of modern Europe is sternly criticized by this antique African court.

The Howadji sat upon a fragment of ruin, and the graybeard guide, who happily could not speak ten words of English, lighted their chibouques. Then he withdrew himself behind a prostrate column, seeing that they wished to be still, and lay there motionless, like Time sleeping at his task. The donkey-boys spoke only in low whispers, curiously watching the Howadji, and the dozy donkeys with closing eyes, shook their significant ears, and shifted slowly from sun to shade. The musing, dreamy chibouque is, after all, the choicest companion for these ruins. Chibouques and dozy donkeys, a sleeping old man, and low whispering boys, scare not the spirits that haunt these courts. Time too, you will muse, smokes his chibouque as he lies at leisure length along the world. Puff, puff—he whiffs away creeds, races, histories, and the fairest fames flee like vapors from his pipe. India, Egypt, Greece, wreathing azurely away in the sunshine. Smoke, smoke, all

Pace with Sir Gardiner along the walls, if you will, and behold the triumphal processions, deifications, battles and glories, terrestrial and celestial, of the third Ramses. They are curious, and worth your while. It is well to see and know men's various ways in various ages of slaughtering each other, and glorifying themselves.

But in all this detail love it not too much. In these temple remains, in the nectar of Egyptian wisdom, as Plato and the old wise pour it to us in their vases of wondrous work, have we our heritage of that race. Spare us the inventory of their wardrobes and the bulletins of their battles. In history it is not men's features, but the grand effect and impression of the men that we want. Not how they did it, but what they did. Ramses marched to Babylon. Cambyses came to Thebes. Quits for them. Cambyses upset Memnon. That is the great thing, and if thereupon near-sighted wonder will see stars in a millstone, we will be thankful for astronomy's sake, and awaken old Time there to refill the chibouques.

For in this magnificent seclusion must we linger and linger. The setting sun warns us away, but in leaving, this evening, we leave the Libyan suburb forever, nor even the morrow with Karnak can paralyze the pang of parting.

It is only here, too—here in the warm dead heart of Egypt, that the traveler can see ruins as time has made and is making them. Thebes is not yet put in order for visitors. The rubbish of the ruined huts of the Christian settlement within and about this pile yet remains. The desert has drifted around it, so that many noble columns are buried in dust to their capitals. The chambers of the temple are entirely earthed. We climb a sand-hill from the court to the roof of the temple. Far down in fissures of rubbish are bits of sculptured wall, and upon the same dust-mountain we descend to view the historical sculptures of the outer wall.

This deepens the reality and solemnity of the impression. Were it all excavated, and the whole temple cleared and revealed, it were a glorious gain for art and science. But to the mere traveler—if one may be a mere traveler—the dust-buried chambers solemnize the court. If the head and unutterable neck of Isis are revealed, wonder for the rest is more worshipful than sight.

Besides, excavation implies Cicerones and swarms of romantic travelers in the way of each other's romance. You will remember, Xtopher, how fatal to sentiment was a simple English "good evening," in the moonlighted Roman forum. Imagination craved only salutations after the high Roman fashion, and when Lydia Languish did not find the Coliseum so "*funny*" as Naples, you regretted the facilities of steam, and yearned to pace that pavement alone with the ghosts of Cæsar and Marc Antony. Haste to Egypt, Xtopher, and that Roman wish shall be fulfilled, for you shall walk erect and alone with Persian Cambyses or mild-eyed Herodotus or inscrutable Ramses —for "there is every man his own fool, and the world's sign is taken down."

Excavation implies arrangement, and the sense of Time's work upon a temple or a statue, or even a human face, is lost or sadly blunted, when all the chips are swept away, and his dusty, rubbishy workshop is smoothed into a saloon of sentiment. Who ever entered for the first time the Coliseum, without a fall to zero in the mercury of enthusiasm, at the sight of the well-sanded area, the cross, shrines and sentinels? When it is not enough that Science and Romance carry away specimens of famous places to their museums, but Mammon undertakes the making of the famous place itself into a choice cabinet, they may be esteemed happy who flourished prior to that period.

And it is pleasant to see remains so surpassingly remarkable, without having them shown by a seedy-coated, bad-hatted fellow-creature at five francs a day. You climb alone to Aboo Simbel in that serene Southern silence, and half fear to enter the awful presence of the Osiride columns, or to penetrate into the Adyta, mysterious to you as to those of old, and you donkey quietly with a taciturn old Time over the plain of green young grain, where Thebes was, and feel as freshly as the first who saw it.

But these things will come. Egypt must soon be the favorite ground of the modern Nimrod, Travel—who so tirelessly hunts antiquity. After Egypt, other lands and ruins are young and scant and tame, save the Parthenon and Pestum. Every thing invites the world hither.

It will come, and Thebes will be cleaned up and fenced in. Steamers will leave for the cataract, where donkeys will be in readiness to convey parties to Philæ, at seven A. M. precisely, touching at Esne and Edfoo. Upon the Libyan suburb will arise the *Hôtel royal au Ramses le grand* for the selectest fashion. There will be the *Hôtel de Memnon* for the romantic, the *Hôtel aux Tombeaux* for the reverend clergy, and the *Pension Re-ni-no-fre* upon the waterside for the invalides and sentimental—only these names will then be English, for France is a star eclipsed in the East.

But before the world arrives, live awhile in the loneliness of the Theban temples and tombs with no other society than Memnon, and the taciturn old Time, and the chibouque. You will seem then, not to have traveled in vain, but to have arrived somewhere. Here you will realize what you have read and thought you believed, that the past was alive. The great vague phantom that goes ever before us will pause here, and turning, look at you with human features, and speak a language sweet and solemn and strange, though unintelligible.

You, too, will linger and linger, though the sunset warn you away. You, too, will tarry for the priests in the court of Medeenet Haboo, and listen for the voice of Memnon. You, too, will be glad that the temples are as time left them, and that man has only wondered, not worked, at them. You, too, will leave lingeringly the Libyan suburb, and own to Osiris in your heart, that if the young gods are glorious, the old gods were great.

XLIII.

Karnak.

KARNAK antedates coherent history, yet it was older the day we saw it than ever before. All thought and poetry inspired by its antiquity, had richer reason that day than when they were recorded, and so you, meditative reader, will have the advantage of this chapter, when you stand in Karnak. Older than history, yet fresh, as if just ruined for the romantic.

The stones of the fallen walls are as sharply-edged as the hammer left them. They lie in huge heaps or separately standing in the sand, and regarding the freshness, you would say that Cambyses and his Persians had marched upon Memphis only last week, while the adherents of the earthquake theory of Egyptian ruin, might fancy they yet felt the dying throes of the convulsion that had shattered these walls.

This freshness is startling. It is sublime. Embalming these temples in her amber air, has not Nature so hinted the preservation of their builders' bodies? Was the world so enamored of its eldest born, that it could not suffer even the forms of his races and their works to decay?

And, O mild-eyed Isis! how beautiful are the balances of nature! In climates where damp and frost crack and corrode, she cherishes with fair adorning the briefer decay. Italy had greenly graced Karnak with foliage. Vines had there clustered and clambered caressingly around these columns, in graceful tendrils wreathing away into the blue air its massive grace. Flowery grass had carpeted the courts, and close-clinging moss shed a bloom along the walls to the distant eye of hope or memory.

Haply it had been dearer so to the painter and the poet. But this death that does not decay is awful. On the edge of the desert, fronting the level green that spreads velvet before it to the river, Karnak scorns time, earthquakes, Cambyses, and Lathyrus, yes, and scorns also, romantic disappointment. For it is not the most interesting or pleasing of Egyptian remains. It is austere and terrible, and sure to disappoint the romance that seeks in ruins bowers of sentiment. Let the Misses Verde remember that, when they consider the propriety of visiting Karnak. Peradventure, also, they will there discover hieroglyphs more inexplicable than those of Theban tombs.

When Thebes was Thebes, an avenue of ram-headed sphinxes connected Karnak with Luxor. Imagination indulges visions of Ramses the Great, superb Sesostris, or the philosophical Ptolemies, going in state along this avenue, passing from glory to glory—possibly a statelier spectacle than the royal going to open parliament. Brightly that picture would have illuminated these pages. But reality, our coldest critic, requires cooler coloring from us.

It was a bright February morning that we donkeyed placidly from ruined Luxor to ruined Thebes. The Pacha bestrode a beast that did honor to the spirit of his species. But my brute, although large and comely, seemed only a stuffed specimen of a donkey. Stiffness and clumsiness were his points. A very gadfly of a donkey-boy, his head somewhere about my donkey's knees, piloted our way and filled our sails—namely, battered the animals' backs. But vainly with a sharpened stick he stung my insensible beast. Only a miserable, perpendicular motion ensued, a very little of which had rendered beneficent Halsted superfluous to a dyspeptic world.

Yet somehow we shambled up the sand from the boat, and passing through the bazaar of Luxor, entered upon the plain. A dusty, donkey path, through clumps of hilfeh grass and sand patches, is all that remains of that Sphinx avenue. We scented sphinxes all the way, a mile and a half, but unearthed no quarry until within a few rods of the Pylon. Nero told me afterward, that we had missed the Sphinx avenue, which I believed, for Nero was veracious and my friend. But, generally, the Howadji must reject all such stories. Not only in Egypt, but wherever you wander, if some owl has peered into a hole that you passed by, and he discovers the oversight, you are apprised that you had done better not to come at all, rather than miss the dark hole. But we passed along a range of headless, ruined sphinxes, that were ram-headed once, and reached the southern Pylon. It stands alone—a simple, sculptured gateway. Behind it, is a small temple of Ptolemaic days, partly, but yet a portion of the great temple, and we climb its roof to survey the waste of Karnak.

The vague disappointment was natural, it was inevitable. It was that of entering St. Peter's and finding that you can see the end. Things so famous pass into ideal proportions. "In heaven, another heaven," sings Schiller, of St. Peter's dome. But if Schiller had looked from Monte Mario upon Rome! It is a disappointment quite distinct from the real character of the object, whose greatness presently compels you to realize how great it is. It is simply the sudden contact of the real with the ideal.

For who ever saw the Coliseum or the Apollo? And when deep in the mountainous heart of Sicily, the Howadji saw, green and gentle, the vale of Enna—did he see the garden whence Pluto plucked his fairest flower? A Coliseum and an Apollo, enough have seen. But the impossible grandeur and grace of the anticipation are the glow of the ideal—the outline of angels alone. All the vagueness and vastness of Egyptian musing in our minds invest Karnak with their own illimitability, and gather around it as the type and complete embodiment of that idea. We go forth to behold the tower of Babel, and in ruins, it must yet pierce the heavens.

Ah! insatiable soul, Mont Blanc was not lofty enough, nor the Venus fair, yet you had hopes of Karnak! Try Baalbec now, and Dhawnlegiri, sky-scaling peak of the Himalaya.

Karnak was an aggregation of temples. Orsitasen's cartouche is found there, the first monarch that is distinctly visible in Egyptian history, and Cleopatra's—the last of the long, long line. Every monarch added a pylon, a court or a colonnade, ambitious each to link his name with the magnificence that must outlive them all, and so leave the Cartouche of Egypt forever in bold relief upon the earth.

The great temple fronted the river westward. We are at the south. The eye follows the line of the great central building, the nucleus of all the rest, backward to the desert. It is lost then in the masses of sand, buried foundations, and prostrate walls which surround it. Separate pylons fronting the four winds, stand shattered and submerged. Sharply two obelisks pierce the blue air. The northern gateway stands lofty and alone, its neighboring walls leveled and buried. The eastern gate toward the desert was never completed, it is only half covered with sculptures. The blank death of the desert lies gray beyond it. Karnak has grim delight in that neighboring grimness.

From each gate but that desert one, stretched an avenue of sphinxes—southward to Luxor, northward to a raised platform on the hills, westward to the river. The fragments yet remain. Yet here, too, is that strange discrepancy in taste and sense of grandeur, which strikes the eye in the temple sculptures compared in character with the architecture. These avenues are narrow lanes of crowded sphinxes, spoiling their own impression. The eye and mind demand a splendid spaciousness of approach. They are shocked at the meanness of the reality, and recognize the same inconstant and untrue instinct that built blank walls before noble colonnades. Perhaps they were matters of necessity. Let the artistic Howadji hope they were.

Immediately in front of the great pylon is the green Nile plain. But sand-drifts lie heaped around the court of the temple. Patches of coarse hilfeh grass are the only vegetation, and a lonely little lake of blue water sleeps cold in the sun, leafless and waveless as a mountain tarn.

Bare and imposing is this vast area of desolation. But the eye shrinks from its severity, and craves grace and picturesqueness. The heights command always the sad, wide prospects. Thither men climb and look wistfully at the dim horizon of humanity, even dreaming, sometimes, that they see beyond. But they are the melancholy men, who live high in watch-towers of any kind. Loftily are they lifted upon the architecture of thought, but love swoops upward on rainbow pinions, and is lost in the sun. The relevance, O testy Gunning? Simply that picturesqueness is more satisfactory than sublimity. So through the great western gateway, across a court with one solitary column erect over its fallen peers, which lie their length, shattered from their bases in regular rows, as if they had been piles of millstones carefully upset, we enter the great hall of Karnak. Shall I say, the grandest ruin of the world?

For this is truly Karnak. Here your heart will bow in reverence, and pay homage to the justice of this fame. A solemn Druidical forest shaped in stone and flowering with the colored sculptured forms of dead heroes, and a history complete. Not so graceful as the columned grove of the Memnonium, but grand and solemn, and majestic inconceivably.

Through the vast vistas the eye can not steal out to the horizon, or catch gladly the waving of green boughs. Only above, through the open spaces of the architrave, it sees the cloudless sky, and the ear hears the singing of unseen birds.

"Is it not strange, I never saw the sun?" So seems the song of birds never to have been heard until its sweetness was contrasted with the sublime, solemn silence of Karnak.

Here, could you choose of all men your companion, you would call Michel Angelo, and then step out and leave him alone. For it is easy to summon spirits, but hard to keep them company. And a man could better bear the imposing majesty of Karnak, than the searching sadness of the artist's eye. In the valley of the Nile, Michel Angelo would have felt that great artists unknown, saw with their eyes in their way, the form of the grandeur he sought. In Memnon, in the great hall of Karnak, distorted as through clouds and mists, yet not all unshaped, he would have seen that an ideal as grand was worshiped, nor have grieved that it was called by another name. His eye, too, would have wandered delighted over the mingled sweetness and severity of the Egyptian landscape, vast and silent, and sun-steeped as the inner realm in which he lived.

Failing Michel Angelo, there were other figures in the hall. Sundry vailed specters were sketching the unsketchable. Plaid pantaloons and turbaned wide-awakes flitted among the figures of gods and heroes. I saw a man with a callotype investing Karnak. Nimrod has mounted—tally-ho!

Nor fear a jest in Karnak, nor suppose a ringing laugh can destroy this silence. We speak, and the stillness ripples around the sound, and swallows it as tracelessly as mid ocean a stone. Nor because Karnak is solemn, suppose that we must be sentimental. The Howadji sat upon a sloping stone, and eat sardine sandwiches, desserting with dates and the chibouque, and the holy of holies was not less holy, nor the grandeur less grand.

In the afternoon we wandered over the whole wilderness of ruin, studying the sculptures, deciphering the cartouches, stumbling and sliding in the sand down to temples whose colored architraves showed level with the ground, so deeply were they buried. For travel and opportunity have their duties. But we returned to the great hall, as thought always will return to it, from grubbing in the wondrous waste of Egypt, and at sunset ascended the great pylon and looked across the river westward, to the Libyan suburb.

The Howadji returned the next day to Karnak, and the next. A golden sunset streamed through it as they were finally departing. In the tenderness of its serene beauty, Karnak became beautiful, too. The colors upon the architraves and columns shone more deeply, and a rainbow-radiance permeated the solemn hall. Nimrod was coursing through the Libyan suburb. Glowingly golden ranged the level grain, rank on rank, to the river. The birds gushed with their swift, sweet, sunset songs. How young, how shadowy were we, in that austere antiquity! Was it compassion that unbent its awful gravity?

No, gadfly! stinging my perpendicular trotting insensibility. Souls like ours conceived, hands like ours fashioned, this awful Karnak. Never succumb to Karnak, gadfly! Man shaped the desert into this divinity. Pygmalion carved the statue that smote his soul with love.

XLIV.

Pruning.

A SACRIFICIAL sheep stood in the starlight on the shore at Luxor. The golden-sleeved Commander was profoundly religious, and proposed to hold a sacred feast of sheep—"a swarry of biled mutton," as later poets have it—upon his return to Cairo. The victim was put below, the crew rose from squatting on the shore and came aboard, and with plaintive songs and beating oars we drifted down the river once more, and watched the dim Theban mountains melt slowly away into invisibility.

You fancy the Nile voyage is a luxury of languid repose—a tropical trance. There the warm winds lave groves forever green, of which, shivering in our wintry palaces, we dream. Stealing swiftly over the Mediterranean, you would, swallow-like, follow the summer, and shuffling off the coil of care at Cairo, would southward sail to the Equator, happiness, and Mountains of the Moon.

Well, single days are that delight, and to me, the whole voyage, but possibly not to you. A diamond-decked damsel is not a single jewel, although haply to the distant eye she brilliantly blaze like a star. Therefore to the distance of hope and memory will the Nile wear its best hue. Nor will we quarrel. To hope, all things are forgiven. Let us pardon memory that it remembers like a lover.

It is hard to believe in winds under a cloudless sky, or to feel chilly when the sun shines brightly. The mind can not readily separate the climate from the character of the land. We never fancy gales in churchyards, only sad twilight breaths, and Egypt being a tomb, to imagination, how should there be windy weather?

A tomb—but a temple. From the minareted mosques of Cairo you descend into it, and well believe that the back door opens into heaven. The river is its broad, winding avenue. The glaring mountains its walls, the serene sky its dome. On either hand as you advance is the way sculptured with green grain and palms of peace, as in those Theban tombs. And more splendid are the niches of the dead here, than the palaces of the living—Karnak, the Memnonium, Kum Ombos, Aboo Simbel. Ghosts are their tenants now—Champollion, Lepsius, and Sir Gardiner the tireless Old Mortalities that chisel their fading characters.

Here are enough buried to populate the world. The priests told Herodotus a succession of more than three hundred kings. The thought bores antiquity like an Artesian well. The Howadji looks upon Ramses as a modern, and grudges him that name of great. He appears everywhere. From the pyramids to Aboo Simbel, in all the best places of the best remains, his cartouche is carved. Why was he great? What do we know, who call him so, but the fact of his being a conqueror and a builder of temples with the captives he caught, to sculpture the walls with the story of their own defeat?

Tamerlane the Great, tickles the ear as well. Vain he clearly was, and enterprising. Let his greatness be proved. Ah! had we been Athenians, should we not have black-balled the bejusted Aristides?

When you descend into this tomb so stately, the Western world recedes, and you hear of it no more, and wonder only how easily you can accustom yourself to know nothing that happens in the world. The sleep of Egypt steals into your soul. Here, to apprise you of cotemporary affairs, roars no thunderous "*Times*," no eclectic "*Galignani*" reaches, speaking all sentiments and espousing none. No safe "*Débats*" is here. No rocket-sparkling "*Presse.*" No heavy-freighted "*Allgemeine Zeitung*" lumbers along this way, making a canal of the Nile. On this golden air float no yearling Italian leaves gracefully traced with dream-lines of liberty. How much less any "*Herald*" hot with special expresses from Crim Tartary, or thoughtful "*Tribune*," obviating the obliquity of the earth's axis.

You take your last draught of news at Cairo, and are the devotee of the old till your return. Knowing all this, how can the traveler, much more the anti-rolling-stone partisans, who read of sunshine in the glow of Liverpool or anthracite, imagine wind in Egypt? Wind! type of active life in that death silence! No, no, say you, hie to Egypt, and be still and warm.

Still? Why, the wild winds pace up and down the

valley of the Nile, like his mad hounds howling for Acteon, like all the ghosts of all the three hundred dynasties anterior to history, demanding to live again. Ally of the desert, the wind whirls the sand into columns and clouds that sweep athwart the eternal smile of the sky and sink, death-dealing, upon the plain. It smites the palms, and as they stretch straight their flexile limbs, utterly consumes their grace. It tortures the river into a foamy, billowy swell, and the soul of the be-vailed, begoggled traveller into rage and despair. Unless, indeed, it favor his course. Then all is forgiven. Even the loss of the calm, which the character of the land requires, is forgiven, for he fancies windless days returning, and dreamy drifting upon the stream.

So did we. Glad when the Ibis fled with full wings, we prophesied the peace of our return, and the gentle gliding before southerly winds. Yet the wind that blew us from Asyoot to Aboo Simbel, did not end its voyage with ours. As we returned, the northerly wind blew for a month, lulling a little now and then, even at times yielding to the south. But no sooner were we upon our way, than it was off with us. Sometimes it slept with us at night, but infallibly rose before we did at morning. "Dream-life," said Nero, at Thebes, deciphering a Greek inscription on Memnon's shin. "What with sketching, shooting, reading, writing, and all in this inexorable wind, a pretty dream-life I find it." There are the poets again, guilty of another count!

Warm? Why, the Howadji sat more voluminously

swathed in coats, cloaks, and shawls, than a mummy in his spiced bandages. They began bravely, with sitting in front of the cabin and warmly wrapped in winter clothes, and only a little chilly, played that it was summer, and conversed in a feeble, poetic way of the Egyptian climate. Gradually they retreated to the divans in the cabin, and cursed the cold. I was sure that a blue fleet of icebergs had undertaken the Nile voyage, and were coming up behind us. I knew that we should meet white bear for hippopotami, walruses for crocodiles, and the north pole for the equator. Why not push on and find Sir John Franklin!

So the wind and cold hovered, awful, upon the edges of dreaming. Southward, southward, no hope but the Tropic, and we entered the Tropic one chilly morning that would not let me think of Mungo Park, but only of Captain Parry.—

O cow-horned Isis, and thou, Western Athor, forgive, that so far this pen could go, so much treason trace, to the eternal warm repose of your land. Yet only by a force that compelled exaggeration could it be induced. The book is closed now, the daguerreotype of those days. Egypt is given to the past, and memory shows it windless as a picture. There it lies golden-shored in eternal summer. I confess it now; Egypt is that dream-land, that tropical trance. There lingers the fadeless green, of which, shivering in our white wintry palaces, we dream. The howling ghosts are laid; those wild winds have all blown themselves away; that fleet of icebergs has joined the Spanish armada. The Nile does not lead to the North West Passage, nor is Mungo Park a myth.

Memory is the magician. She cuts the fangs from the snakes that stung the past, and wreaths them, rainbow garlands, around its paling brows. The evil days are not remembered. Time, as a purging wind, blows them like dead leaves away, as winds winnow the woods in autumn

XLV.

Per Contra.

For the dream-days dawn, lotus-eating days of faith in the Poets as the only practical people, because all the world is poetry—of capitulation to Bishop Berkeley, and confession that only we exist, and the rest is sheer seeming—when thought is arduous, and reading wasteful, and the smoke of the chibouque scarcely aerial enough—days that dissolve the world in light. The azure air and azure water mingle. We float in rosy radiance through which waves the shore—a tremulous opacity.

In the Arabian Night days of life, come hauntingly vague desires to make the long India voyage. The pleasant hiatus in actual life—the musing monotony of the day—the freedom of the imagination on a calm sea, under a cloudless sky—the far floatings before trade-winds—the strange shores embowered with tropical luxuriance, and an exhaustless realm of new experience, are the forms and fascination of that longing.

But the Nile more fairly realizes that dream-voyage. The blank monotony of sea and sky, is relieved here by the tranquil, ever-varying, graceful shores, the constant panorama of a life new to the eye, oldest to the mind, and associations unique in history. The palms, the desert, the fair fertility of unfading fields, mosques, minarets, camels, the broad beauty of the tranced river,—these unsphere us, were there no Thebes, no Sphinx, no Memnon, Pyramids or Karnak, no simple traditions of Scripture, and wild Arabian romances—the sweetest stories of our reading.

In the early morning, flocks of water-birds are ranged along the river—herons, kingfishers, flamingoes, ducks, ibis—a motley multitude in the shadow of the high, clay banks, or on the low, sandy strips. They spread languid wings, and sail snowily away. The sun strikes them into splendor. They float and fade, and are lost in the brilliance of the sky. Under the sharp, high rocks, at the doors of their cliff-retreats, sit sagely the cormorants, and meditate the passing Howadji. Like larger birds reposing, shine the sharp sails of boats near or far. Their images strike deep into the water and tremble away.

Then come the girls and women to the water-side, bearing jars upon their heads. On the summit of the bank they walk erect and stately, profile-drawn against the sky Bending and plashing, and playing in the water, with little jets of laugh that would brightly flash, if we could see them, they fill their jars, and in a long file recede and disappear among the palms. Over the brown mud villages the pigeons coo and fly, and hang by hundreds upon the clumsy towers built for them, and a long pause of sun and silence follows.

Presently turbaned Abraham with flowing garment

and snowy beard, leaning upon his staff, passes with Sarah along the green path on the river's edge toward Memphis and King Pharaoh. On the opposite desert lingers Hagar with Ishmael, pausing, pausing, and looking back.

The day deepens, calmer is the calm. It is noon, and magnificent Dendereh stands inland on the desert edge of Libya, a temple of rare preservation, of Isis-headed columns, with the same portrait of Cleopatra upon the walls—a temple of silence, with dark chambers cool from the sun, and the sculptures in cabinet squares upon the wall. Let it float by, no more than a fleeting picture forever. It is St. Valentine's Day, but they are harvesting upon the shores, resting awhile now, till the sun is sloping. The shadeless Libyan and Arabian highlands glare upon the burning sun. The slow Sakias sing and sigh. The palms are moveless as in the backgrounds of old pictures. To our eyes it is perpetual picture slowly changing. The shore lines melt into new forms, other, yet the same. We know not if we wake or sleep, so dream-like exquisite is either sleeping or waking.

The afternoon declines as we drift slowly under Aboofayda with a soft south wind. Its cliffs are like masses of old masonry, and wheeling hawks swoop downward to its sharp, bold peaks. Ducks are diving in the dark water of its shadow. The white radiance of the roou is more rosily tinged. Every form is fairer in the westering light. We left Asyoot yesterday, at evening we saw its many minarets fade in the dark of the hills, like the strains of arabesqued Arabian songs dying in the twilight, and at dusk a solitary jackal prowled stealthily along the shore. Joseph's brethren pass with camels and asses, to buy corn in Egypt. Geese in arrowy flight pierce the profound repose of the sky. Golden gloom gathers in the palm-groves. Among the scaled trunks, like columns of a temple, passes a group of girls attending Pharaoh's daughter. Shall we reach the shore before her, and find the young Moses, Nile-nursed with the sweet sound of calmly flowing waters, and the sublime silence of the sky?

The sun sets far over Libya. He colors the death of the desert, as he tinges the live sea in his setting. Dark upon the molten west, in waving, rounding lines, the fading flights of birds are yet traced, seeking the rosy south, or following the sun. The day dies divinely as it lived. Primeval silence surrounded us all the time. What life and sound we saw and heard, no more jarred the silence, than the aurora lights the night. What a wild myth is wind! Wind—wind, what is wind?

The dazzling moon succeeds, and the night is only a day more delicate. A solitary phantom barque glides singing past—its sail as dark below as above, twin-winged in air and water. Whither, whither, ye ghostly mariners? Why so sad your singing? Why so languid-weary the slow plash of oars?

The moon in rising glows over Antinoë, under whose palms we float, and in the warm hush of the evening we see again, and now for the first time perfectly, the rounded ripeness of those lips, the divinely drooping lid, the matted curls clinging moist and close around the head and neck—

the very soul of southern Antinous breathed over the Nile. The moon, striking the water, paves so golden a path to the shore that imagination glides along the dream, fades in Arabia, and gaining the Tigris—for the last time, incensed reader!—pays court to the only caliph, and is entertained in that west-winded, rose-odored street, which the loves and lovers of the caliph know.

—Or only the stars shine. Strange that in a land where stars shine without the modesty of mist, women vail their faces. Clearly Mohammad received his inspired leaves in a star-screened cave, and not in the full face of heaven. But let him still suspended be, for dimly glancing among the palms, silverly haloed by the stars that loved his manger—behold the young child and his mother with Joseph leading the ass, flying into the land.

Tarry under the stars till morning, if you will, seeing the pictures that earliest fancy saw, dreaming the dreams that make life worth the living. The midnight will be only weirder than the noon, not more rapt. Come, Commander, spread that divan into a bed. Galleries of fairest fame are not all Raphaels, yet justly deserve their name, and so does our river life.

Good night, Pacha, the day was dreamier than your dreamiest dream.

XLVI.

Memphis.

> ———————" From the steep
> Of utmost Axumè, until he spreads
>   Like a calm flock of silver-fleeced sheep
> His waters on the plain; and crested heads
>   Of cities and proud temples gleam amid,
>   And many a vapor-belted pyramid."

"MEMPHIS," said the Commander, as he was rubbing a spoon one morning, pointing with his thumb over his shoulder.

The Howadji turned his eyes westward to behold magnificent Memphis—the last royal residence of genuine Egypt—the abode of Pharaohs and their queens—where Abraham left Sarah, when he went on to see the pyramids—a city built in the channel of the river, which was diverted by King Menes for that purpose.

The Howadji looked to see the sacred lake over which the dead were ferried, and on whose farther shore sat the forty-two judges who decreed or denied the rites of burial. The Acherusian lake near Memphis surrounded, as the old Diodorus said, by beautiful meadows and canals, fringed with lotus and flowering rushes. It was a boat called Baris that performed this office and a penny was paid to the boatman named by the Egyptians, Charon. He says that Orpheus carried to Greece the outlines of these stories, and Homer hearing, wrought them into the Greek mythology.

The Howadji looked to see the gorgeous temple of Isis and of Apis, the bull, who was kept in an inclosure, and treated as a god. He had a white mark on his forehead, and other small spots on his body, the rest being black. And when he died, another was selected, from having certain signs, to take his place.

He looked to see the ranges of palaces, which Strabo did not see until they were ruined and deserted, and all the pomp of royal and priestly and burial processions—the bearers of flowers, fruit and cakes that preceded—the friends in brilliant garments that followed—the strewers of palm-boughs that paved the way with smooth green, over which the funeral car slid more easily—barges of bouquets then, and groups of mourners—a high-priest burning incense over an altar and above, the images of serene Osiris and his cow-horned spouse. These were the pomps and shows he looked to see, and all the thousand glowing pictures of a realm without limit to the imagination,—luxuriant life developing in the most beautiful and brilliant display. And the Howadji turning, saw a few sand mounds and a group of pyramids upon the horizon.

Nothing remains of Memphis but a colossus of Ramses, with his head deeply buried in the earth—overflowed yearly by the Nile, yet full of the same fascinating character—another representation of the old Egyptian type of beauty, shattered and submerged near a palm-shored lake. Past the lake we went, and over the broad belt of green that separates the palms from the desert, and then up the steep sand slopes to the pyramids of Saccara.

Standing at the foot of the largest, and looking desertward, the Howadji beheld a landscape which is unlike all others. Upon the chaotic desert that tumbles eastward from an infinite horizon, jagged in sandy billows, that seem, in huge recoil, back falling upon themselves at the edge of the green, rose the multitude of pyramids—twelve or more in number—near and far—dumb, inexplicable forms—like remains of a former creation that had endured, through strength, all intervening changes. Dimmest, and farthest of all, the great pyramids of Ghizeh, looming in the faint haze of noon, like the relics of foreworld art, defying curiosity and speculation. The solid mass of these structures weighed palpably on the mind. A dead antediluvian silence settled around them, and seemed to benumb the faculties of the observer, unmooring him by its spell from the sentient sphere, to let him drift, aimless, and without guide, into black death and darkness. It was a basilisk fascination that held the eye to the sight. The pyramid-studded desert was the strange verge and mingling point of the dead and living worlds. Yet they stood there, telling no tales, and the eye at length released, slipped willingly far away over the palms and beheld the glittering minarets of Cairo.

The mummy merchants were here at Saccara, and offered endless treasure of amulet and idol and jewel, and from the great cat catacomb hard by, and the bird tombs, mummied cats and deified ibis done up in red pots, as the remains and memorials of mighty Memphis.

The Howadji returned over the same glad, green plain. They had prowled into a brace of dark, dismal tombs, and leaned against a pyramid—had seen the beautiful statue, with the body broken, and the face hidden—a sad symbol—and the pleasant palms and sunny green slopes under them. They returned through the most spacious and beautiful of palm-groves. Forgive their eyes and imaginations that they lingered long in those beautiful reaches, avenues, and vistas. It was as if the genius of palms knew that his lovers were passing, and he unrolled and revealed his most perfect beauty as an adieu. It was a forest of the finest palms, a tropic in itself—through whose foliage the blue sky streamed, and amid which bright birds flew. They are the last palms that shall be planted on these pages, and the last that shall fade from memory. The young ones seem not to expand from saplings into trees, but to spring, Minerva-like, fully formed and foliaged, through the earth, for they bear all their wide-waving crest of boughs when they first appear, and the trunk is so large that you fancy some gracious gnome, intent on adorning a world, is thrusting them by main force through the ground. As we reached the edge of this cheerful forest, we saw very plainly the white citadel of Cairo and its lofty minarets, high above the city.

We slipped down to Ghizeh, and the next morning donkeyed quietly to the pyramids. Except for the sake of the Sphinx, the Howadji would only advise the visit to the scientific and curious, and is the more willing to say so, because he knows that every traveler would not fail to go. But the pyramids were built for the distant eye, and their poetic grandeur and charm belong to distance. When your eye first strikes them, as you come up from Alexandria to Cairo, they stand vast, vague, rosy and distant, and are at once and entirely the Egypt of your dreams. The river winds and winds, and they seem to shift their places, to be now here, now there, now on the western shore, now on the eastern, until Egypt becomes to your only too glowing fancy, a bright day and a pyramid.

Walk out beyond the village of Ghizeh at twilight then, and see them, not nearer than the breadth of the plain. They will seem to gather up the whole world into silence, and you will feel a pathos in their dumbness, quite below your tears. They have outlived speech, and are no more intelligible. Yet the freshness of youth still flushes in the sunset along their sides, and even these severe and awful forms have a beautiful bloom as of Hesperidean fruit, in your memory and imagination. The Howadji may well learn with pleasure that the Cairo Bedlam is abolished, when he feels his memory putting the pyramids as flowers in her garden. For they are that. They are beautiful no less than awful, in remembrance.

But as you approach, they shrink and shrink; and when you stand at their bases and cast your eye to the apex, they are but vast mountains of masonry, sloping upward to the sky. Beastly Bedoueen, importunate for endless bucksheesh, will pull you, breathless and angry, to the summit, and promise to run up and over all possible pyramids, and for aught you know, throw you across to the peaks of the Saccara cousins. Only threats most terrible, and entirely impossible of performance, can restore the necessary silence. Express distinctly your determination to plunge every Bedoueen down the pyramid, when they have you dizzy and breathless and gasping on the sides as you go up from layer to layer, like stairs—swear horribly in your gasping and rage, that you will only begin by throwing them down, but conclude by annihilating the whole tribe who haunt the pyramids, and you work a miracle. For the Bedoueen become as placidly silent as if your threats were feasible, and only mutter mildly, "Bucksheesh, Howadji," like retiring and innocent thunder.

There are, also, who explore the pyramids: who, from poetic or other motives, go into an utterly dark, hot and noisome interior, see a broken sarcophagus, feel that they are encased in solid masonry of some rods from the air, hear the howls of Bedoueen, and smell their odors, and return faint, exhausted, smoke-blackened, with their pockets picked, and their nerves direfully disturbed. Poet Harriet advises none but firmly-nerved ladies to venture, and the Howadji may add the same advice to all but firmly-nerved men. To such, the exploration of the pyramids may be as it was to Nero—a grand and memorable epoch in life. For he said that he *felt* the greatness of old Egypt, more profoundly in the pyramids than anywhere else.

Yet you must seek the pyramids, else would you miss the Sphinx, and that memory of omission would more sadly haunt you afterward, than her riddle haunted the old victims of her spells.

The desert is too enamored of his grotesque darling, and gradually gathers around it, and draws it back again to his bosom. For it well seems the child of desert inspiration. Intense oriental imagination musing over the wonderful waste, would build its dreams in shapes as singular. It lies on the very edge of the desert, which recoils above the plain as at Saccara. The sand has covered it, and only head, neck and back are above its level. In vain Caviglia strove to stay the desert. More than half of the sand that he daily excavated, blew back again at night.

The Sphinx, with raised head, gazes expectantly toward the East, nor dropped its eyes when Cambyses or Napoleon came. The nose is gone, and the lips are gradually going. The constant attrition of sand grains wears them away. The back is a mass of rock, and the temple between the fore-paws is buried forever. Still unread is my riddle, it seems to say, and looks, untiring, for him who shall solve it. Its beauty is more Nubian than Egyptian, or is rather a blending of both. Its bland gaze is serious and sweet. Yet unwinking, unbending, in the yellow moonlight silence of those desert sands, will it breathe mysteries more magical and rarer romances of the Mountains of the Moon and the Nile sources, than ever Arabian imagination dreamed. Be glad that the Sphinx was your last wonder upon the Nile, for it seemed to contain and express the rest. And from its thinned and thinning lips, as you move back to the river with all Egypt behind you, trails a voice inaudible, like a serpent gorgeously folding about your memory —Egypt and mystery, O Sphinx!

XLVII.

Sunset.

"Tired with the pomp of their Osirean feast."

"With all Egypt behind you,"—so donkeyed the Howadji from the Sphinx and the silence of the desert. They reached the shore and stepped upon the boat while the sun was wreaking all his glory upon the west. It burned through the trees and over the little town of Ghizeh, and its people and filth, and as we moved into the stream, the pyramids occupied the west, unhurt for that seeing, large and eternal as ever, with the old mystery—the old charm.

The river was full of boats, in the vicinity of the city. The wind blew gently from the north, and fleets of sails were stretching whitely southward. Even some Howadji were just dotting down their first Nile notes, and we, mariners of two months, felt old and mature as we watched them. Had we not worshiped at Aboo Simbel and conquered the cataract, and heard Memnon, and stood on Memphis?

Back in that sunset came thronging the fairest images of the Nile; and may sweet Athor, lovely Lady of the West, enable you, retiring reader, to stand looking backward over these pages, like the figure with which the Howadji's artist friend has graced this book's beginning, and behold a palm-tree, or a rosy pyramid, or Memnon, or a gleam of sunshine brighter than our American wont, or the graceful Ghawazee beauty that the voyager so pleasantly remembers.

—And you, Italian Nera, who ask if the sherbet of roses was indeed poured in a fountained kiosk of Damascus, you know that Hafiz long since sang to us, how sad were the sunset, were we not sure of a morrow.

www.ingramcontent.com/pod-product-compliance
Lightning Source LLC
LaVergne TN
LVHW020229110826
845151LV00003B/868

* 9 7 8 1 4 2 5 5 3 1 2 2 5 *